Woman and
Chinese Modernity

Theory and History of Literature
Edited by Wlad Godzich and Jochen Schulte-Sasse

For other books in the series, see p. 198.

Woman and Chinese Modernity

The Politics of Reading between West and East

Rey Chow

Theory and History of Literature, Volume 75

University of Minnesota Press
Minnesota   London

Published by the University of Minnesota Press
111 Third Avenue South, Suite 290, Minneapolis, MN 55401-2520
Printed in the United States on acid-free paper

Second printing 1997

Library of Congress Cataloging-in-Publication Data

Chow, Rey.
    Woman and Chinese modernity : the politics of reading between West
and East / Rey Chow.
        p.   cm. — (Theory and history of literature ; v. 75)
    Based in part on the author's thesis (doctoral) — Stanford
University, 1986.
    Includes bibliographical references and index.
    ISBN 0-8166-1870-4. —
    ISBN 0-8166-1871-2 (pbk.)
        1. China—Civilization—20th century.   2. Women—China.
    3. Chinese literature—20th century—History and criticism.
    I. Title.   II. Series.
    DS775.2.C47   1990
    951.05—dc20   90-11080

A CIP catalog record for this book is available from the British Library

Cover design by Sheila Chin Morris

The University of Minnesota
is an equal-opportunity
educator and employer.

Ein Übermaaß der Historie dem Lebendigen schade.

[An excess of history is detrimental to life.]
—Friedrich Nietzsche

Die Tradition der Unterdrückten belehrt uns darüber, daß der
»Ausnahmezustand«, in dem wir leben, die Regel ist. Wir müssen
zu einem Begriff der Geschichte kommen, der dem entspricht.

[The tradition of the oppressed teaches us that the "state of
emergency" in which we live is not the exception but the rule. We
must attain to a conception of history that is in keeping with this
insight.]
—Walter Benjamin

Between patriarchy and imperialism, subject-constitution and object-
formation, the figure of the woman disappears, not into a pristine
nothingness, but into a violent shuttling which is the displaced
figuration of the "Third World woman" caught between tradition
and modernization.
—Gayatri Chakravorty Spivak

Contents

Acknowledgments

This book originated, in part, from the doctoral dissertation I completed at Stanford University in 1986. To the official readers of that dissertation – Russell Berman, David Halliburton, William Lyell, and William M. Todd III – I remain grateful for the intellectual space they gave me that allowed me to develop my own thinking on a difficult topic. Major portions of the book were conceived and drafted during 1988, when my mother was ill and I could not be with her. She directs my writing in the most demanding ways.

A number of people gave me useful comments on different parts of the book during different periods. They include my husband, Austin Meredith; my friends Bill Brown, Chris Cullens, Yao-chung Li, and Ming-Bao Yue; my colleagues Nancy Armstrong, Terry Cochran (who is also my editor), Wlad Godzich, and Leonard Tennenhouse. I thank all of them for their kindness and understanding.

I thank Brown University's Pembroke Center for Teaching and Research on Women for a generous fellowship during 1986-87 and a wonderful year of seminars, discussions, and friendships. In particular, I thank Elizabeth Weed for her support throughout that year, and the encouragement she has continued to give me since then.

The Office of International Education and the College of Liberal Arts McMillan Fund, both of the University of Minnesota, provided grants that enabled me to present portions of this book at various conferences during 1987 and 1988. Minnesota's McKnight-Land Grant Professorship, of which I am a recipient for 1988-91, enabled me to devote the summer of 1988 to writing. The completion of this book would have been much slower without these sources of financial assistance.

I must also acknowledge my copy editor, Mary Byers, and Sheila Chin Morris, whose graphic work gives the book an additional dimension that I appreciate, especially since I am incapable of it myself.

Finally, I want to thank my family—my parents, Chow Chak-hung and Tuet Wai-ching, who taught me the importance of knowing Chinese history and Chinese culture even when trends in Hong Kong, that brightest jewel in the British Crown, did not require them to do so; my sisters, Pearl Chow and Enn Chow Wahab, who remain to this day my loyal playmates; and Kaineung, who is always attentive.

Minneapolis
April 1990

Preface

We live in an era in which the critique of the West has become not only possible but mandatory. Where does this critique leave those ethnic peoples whose entry into culture is, precisely because of the history of Western imperialism, already "Westernized"? This is the primary question I raise in this book. As two critics put it: "Every time we speak or write in English, French, German, or one of the more marginalized European languages we pay homage to Western intellectual and political hegemony."[1] To this statement, we should add the crucial comment that these "European" languages have already become an ineradicable part of the lives of non-European peoples. The task facing us is not the advocacy of a return to pure ethnic origins. Rather, it is to articulate the specific ways in which ethnicity, as the site both of an inevitable cultural predicament and of possible formations of collective identities-in-resistance, functions.

This book is not a survey study of modern Chinese literature; it does not try to be comprehensive or complete. Instead, I offer discussions that thematize the problem of subjectivity in texts about modern China and that demonstrate, through my ways of reading, an instance of that subjectivity. The materiality of a Westernized Chinese subjectivity is thus not only the topic but also the mode of my discourse; it is what I "tell" and "show" at the same time. This double nature of my reading needs to be clarified from the outset as a way to emphasize the untenability of a "nativism" that would demand of non-Western critics dealing with non-Western topics an unanalytical rejection of everything "Western." Because the "ground" here is neither the Chinese nor the Western tradition that warrants affirmation, but the very instability upon which the dialectic between

"Chinese" and "Western" is played, the subjectivity of which and in which I write is not individual but an effect of historical forces that are beyond any in-dividuated "consciousness." The instability that constitutes subjectivity as such — an instability that escapes the personal subject — is what Wlad Godzich in a discussion of emergent literature calls "givenness." This givenness is some-thing "we must understand . . . not as a passive (or a resultative, in the linguis-tic sense of the term) but as an active principle. Givenness is agency. As such it never gives itself but is figured in that which is given, and it is knowable only through its figurations."[2]

Figurally, the chapters of this book are organized along four critical paths. These are the visual image, literary history, narrative structure, and emotional reception, which in turn allow four mutually implicated aspects of "Chinese" modernity to come to the fore — namely, the ethnic spectator, the fragmentation of tradition in popular literature, the problematic construction of a new "inner" reality through narration, and the relations between sexuality, sentimentalism, and reading. The physical actions around which the four chapters revolve are seeing, dispersing, detailing (cutting), and crying.

In reading modern Chinese writings in ways that were, to my knowledge, un-attempted before, I am setting myself a double task — that of criticizing both the hegemonic status of Western theoretical thinking and the entrenched ways of interpretation in the field of Chinese literature. These two types of criticism are inextricably related. In order to combat the restrictions that are imposed upon the reading of modern Chinese literature by specialist methodologies in sinology and China studies, it is necessary to show how such methodologies either refuse to engage with the materiality of modernity in modern Chinese texts or consign the irreversibility of modernity to the accidents in a "great" tradition. Because of such fundamental conceptual impasses, modern Chinese literature is almost al-ways read naturalistically, in ways that strip it of its constructedness and its ar-tifice. Reading modern Chinese stories *perversely* is thus a way of challenging the habits of tradition in the field, as well as a way of asking the nonspecialist: why have these stories been neglected *generally?* My criticism of Western hegemony is not conducted in the spirit of "Look, this, too, is a magnificent tradition!" Rather, it is conducted through discussions of textual problems whose formal complexities are bypassed *both* because of the West's indifference to literatures and languages outside hegemonic parameters and because of the tendency of China specialists to naturalize such complexities through positivistic methods of reading, often in the belief that the Chinese culture is completely different from its counterparts in the West. Substituting the word "Chinese" for "Japanese," I find this passage by Masao Miyoshi useful in illustrating my point:

> Exclusivism and essentialism are ethnocentric and fantastic, and as such both inappropriate and groundless. . . . Japanese literature, like any

other national or regional product, is definable only in its relation to temporal and spatial constraints. It might be particularly and conspicuously "Japanese"; but there is nothing ontologically sacred or absolute in its makeup. This aspect is important to keep in mind inasmuch as the need to de-universalize and particularize the Western norm remains foremost on our new critical agenda.[3]

It follows that several major points need to be made, the first being the primary role played by what can be loosely generalized as "fantasy" or "illusion" in my readings. One of the things I would like to problematize is the dichotomy between the "realpolitical" non-West and the "imaginative" West. Often, in an attempt to show "the ways things really are" in the non-West, our discourses produce a non-West that is deprived of fantasy, desires, and contradictory emotions. When it is not the site of warfare and bloodshed, when it is not what compels humanistic sympathies and charities, the non-West commands solemn, humorless reverence as the Other that we cannot hope to know. If it is true that fantasy structures, which are present in cultural forms as diverse as film, popular novels, and canonized texts, can tell us as much about politics as anything else, then a strictly corrective reading of the non-West by way of "factual," nonfantastical issues (such as demographic changes, wage systems, agricultural policies, and so on, which dominate the contents of conferences hosted by, say, the Association for Asian Studies) would only serve to perpetuate and rigidify the dichotomy in question further. Against the existence of this powerful dichotomy, which is currently supported by the unequal distribution of funding between the humanities and the social sciences, I find it necessary to read modern Chinese *literature* with a deliberate and "impractical" sense of complexity, even if my readings may not be immediately assimilable to the progressive rigor of critical enlightenment.

Another way of arguing the same point: since the West owns not only the components but also the codes of fantasy, the non-West is deprived not only of the control of industrial and commercial productions, but of imaginary productions as well. The stereotypical Asian student who is a genius in the "hard sciences" but who cannot express himself *verbally* in interesting ways is symptomatic of this division between "West" and "East" in terms of the former's hegemony in verbal, literary, and fantastic productions and the latter's often unwitting collaboration with that hegemony through an overinvestment in nonverbal, lucrative disciplines. I want to tip the balance of this systematically lopsided situation by foregrounding the mental dramas and struggles that are behind so-called Oriental inscrutability. Like many instruments of oppression, the "unconscious" is, yes, an export from Europe. But what happens to it in modern China? How is it used, circulated, and locally produced?

Second, my frequent use of psychoanalytic theories throughout the book is, in the light of what I just said, not an attempt to valorize psychoanalysis as the best means of analyzing femininity and subjectivity in modern Chinese texts. It is, quite simply, a reaction to the general lack of interest in psychoanalysis in the field, a lack that is often justified by reasons that may be paraphrased as follows: "Psychoanalysis is a Western practice that focuses on the private self, whereas the Chinese do not care that much about 'privacy.' They are more concerned with public life and the larger issues of history. Therefore, there is no need for psychoanalysis." While the historicity of the privileged institutionalized status enjoyed by psychoanalysis in the West cannot go unheeded, the exclusion of psychoanalytic understandings from a literature that is modern and "Western-ized" is itself highly challengeable. Reading the above paraphrase against the grain, we can say that perhaps it is precisely in a culture that has traditionally suppressed the "individual" under the State, be that State feudalist or Commu-nist, that modes of inquiry that center on "subjectivity" would force open hith-erto unasked questions. This does not necessarily mean that from now on Chi-nese fiction must be read in terms of "selves" that are preoccupied with "privacy," but it does mean that we are uncovering a methodological problem: What has been left out of the master narratives of the Chinese tradition? Why? If psychoanalysis can help explain certain issues in the "text" of modern China, why has it not been used more often? Doesn't the lack of interest in psychoanal-ysis constitute a significant lacuna in the more familiar approaches to modern Chinese literature, which have reduced it to drab, naturalistic "reflections of reality" only?

The tendency to disparage the relevance of psychoanalysis is disturbing espe-cially at a time when we need to deepen, as well as broaden, our understanding of the non-West. Such a tendency, itself historical, means that contemporary cultural studies are predicated on an opposed set of imperatives: let the "First World" critic continue to deal in speculative abstractions; let the "subaltern" speak of positivistic realities. In other words, the ideological division between "West" and "non-West" is duplicated in the very ways the two are institution-ally examined: the former, through painstakingly *refined* methodologies whose point is the absolute fragmentation of the human self (or the basic unit for social participation); the latter, through cathexes of *wholesomeness* that manifest them-selves in moralistically "correct" representations of "Third World" collective re-sistances and/or native traditions. (In the case of women, this often takes the form of an intellectual investment on the part of Western investigators in non-Western women's "purity" or "chastity," both sexual and nationalistic, as multiple research projects on "Chinese women" by American academics dem-onstrate.) Why should this ideological division, which is, strictly speaking, an in-house conflict between different strategies of interpretation in the West, dic-tate the way we approach non-Western cultures? In discussing psychoanalytic matters such as desires, fantasies, or neuroses in the context of modern China, my aim is not to applaud the hegemony of psychoanalysis per se, but to show how "protests," "resistance," "struggles," and so on, which belong to master thought systems such as Marxism and anti-imperialism, must also be recognized in the mundane affectivities that structure modern Chinese writings. To my mind, the exclusion of psychoanalysis as a method of reading the non-West reveals a no less hegemonic politics with its presuppositions of what the important messages from the non-West "really are." When progressive Western critics like Bertolt Brecht reject the psychologically oriented drama of the European tradition and turn, with fascination, to Chinese theater for its physical action and its conscious didacticism, what is left out is the fact that the nonpsychological, as a principal aspect of traditional Chinese aesthetics, is itself becoming incapable of dealing with the perceptual issues that newly surface among modern Chinese readers and audiences.

Third, apart from psychoanalysis, the analytical tools that are available to me, a "Westernized" Chinese woman who spent most of her formative years in a British colony and then in the United States, are varied and sophisticated. These include major theoretical apparatuses such as close textual reading or "practical criticism" (which I learned as early as age fourteen, when I began studying "Eng. Lit." at Form Four of the Anglo-Chinese Secondary School System in Hong Kong), structuralism, poststructuralism, feminist theory, popular culture theories, and theories of ethnicity. When I use such theories to explain modern Chinese culture, am I paying homage to the West? Undoubtedly. But if "the West" as such has become an ineradicable environment, it is not whether we "pay homage" to it but how we do it that matters. In sinology and China studies, where the emphases on "heritage" are clearly immovable, the homage to the West has long been paid in the form of what seems to be its opposite — in the idealist insistence on a separate, self-sufficient "Chinese tradition" that should be lined up against the Western one because it is as great if not greater. The "rejection" of the West in this instance is solemnly respectful; by upholding "China," it repeats the hegemonic overtones of that which is rejected.

How then does one begin to speak in a field that is densely populated by practitioners of what Friedrich Nietzsche calls "monumental" and "antiquarian" history? The third kind of history that Nietzsche mentions — the critical — is practiced by those who have a special need: "Only he who is oppressed by a present need, and who wants to throw off this burden at any cost, has need of critical history, that is to say a history that judges and condemns."[4] This category of the oppressed is where I put myself. In each of the following chapters, therefore, I try to show how essential it is to read against the metaphors of hierarchy, grandeur, purity, and patriotism, which belong to the language of imperialistic domination and which have been legitimated in various forms of literary criticism in the Chinese field. For my purposes, I borrow from "Western" theories that address issues of marginality, be they an attempt to explicate the female relationship to filmic images, literature's parodic function to ideology, the relationship of "details" to the narrative construction of a modernist national identity, or the "transparency" of sentimental readings. The point of my readings is to bracket, even as I repeat, the term "Chinese," and demonstrate the relevance of modern Chinese literature beyond its immediate "culturally specific" context, as part of a collective response to the worldwide effects of Western imperialism.

Fourth, what remains to be defined is the relation between "theory" and "ethnicity." What kinds of things can be said, with the help of "theory," that would undermine precisely the exclusiveness of Western models? What is the nature of that "exclusiveness"? The analytical tools I use become the means with which to restore the *elusive* realities of the Westernized ethnic subject. Such realities are elusive, not because they are mysterious or exotic, not because they are separated from the West by their linguistic and cultural arcaneness, but because they are, historically, the foundations on which the West constructs its patterns of domination and hegemony. The use of "Western theory," whose richness and sophistication is part and parcel an outcome of the uneven distribution of material well-being between the "First" and "Third" Worlds, is, from the perspective of the ethnic subject, a predicament. "Western theory" is there, beyond my control; yet in order to speak, I must come to terms with it.

For someone with my background, the awareness of the issues of ethnicity emerges as a "belated" consciousness, after I am thoroughly "educated" in other "neutral" issues. This belated consciousness, however, is ineluctable even while it must use the rarefied products of its own historical exploitation to reveal itself. The way we use "Western theory" to understand the non-West is, in this light, a reversal of what happens historically. For most ethnic peoples, the path by which they arrive at the consciousness of their prescribed "otherness" is not the convoluted one of theory, but the simple accident of birth. If theory has the power of elucidating the significances of ethnicity, it is only because theory must itself be regarded pathologically, as symptomatic of the mutual implications between modernity and imperialism, between the programmatic acts of fundamentally reconceptualizing the past on the one hand, and those of controlling and subjugating others, on the other.

For instance, the means of entry into the "Symbolic" that is our world with its well-defined territorial boundaries may have much to do with the Lacanian metaphysics of the Phallus, but the critical import of such a metaphysics, developed at a very late point in Western capitalist society, is symptomatic of the multifarious exclusions, performed at different types of national and cultural "borders" every day, of peoples who do not possess the right birth certificates, passports, and residence or work permits. Such exclusions provide the "ground" for the prospering of "theory" as we find it in Western Europe and North America today—a greatly diversified business whose many departments seldom agree with one another except on the conceptual indispensability of "exclusion" itself. For those who manage to enter by means of "naturalization," the process involved is inevitably one of abandoning their "origins" to the degree at which they can communicate with their oppressors-cum-benefactors with "native fluency," before those "origins," now permanently disassembled and dissembled, return with a repressed urgency. What looks like the latest hot issue in Western theory—the exploitation of peoples who are "ethnic"—is the condition that makes it possible for Western theory to achieve its profundities in the first place. These profundities now come face to face with their own historical origins.

My interest in modern Chinese culture and literature is, therefore, not nostalgic in nature. It is not that, having been sufficiently Europeanized and Americanized, I now yearn for "my" four-thousand-year-old Chinese heritage. It is rather an attempt to hold onto an experience whose marginality is embedded in the history of imperialism, a history that includes precisely the "opening up" of Chinese history and culture for "objective" and "neutral" academic research that thrives by suppressing its own conditions of possibility. Among American "China specialists," it is not unusual to hear this kind of authoritative disdain toward the Chinese: "Those from Taiwan know their Chinese but not their English; those from Hong Kong know English but not Chinese; those from the People's Republic are poor in both!" Even though so-called history is the predominant discipline—and disciplining instrument—in China studies, what is revealed in remarks like these is an utterly ahistorical conception of linguistic intactness, which is used as a means of discrimination against Chinese people. The oppressive nature of this experience of being despised precisely by those who take a missionary or intellectual interest in us is understood by everyone who lives through it. But the foundational significance of this "ethnic" experience for the development of Western thinking, including Western thinking's attempts at self-critique, can only be realized belatedly, through a reversal of the *already reversed* sequence in which major categories of inquiry appear in First World intellectual circles. The Spirit, Humanity, Tradition, the "otherness" of language, of identity, of Man, of the White Man, and so forth: this epistemological order must now be fundamentally re-turned.

Woman and
Chinese Modernity

Note on Romanization

All transcriptions of Chinese are in *pinyin*, except for cases in which a different system, usually the Wade-Giles, was used originally in a quoted text. Translations of Chinese titles that do not exist in English are given in square brackets.

Chapter 1
Seeing Modern China:
Toward a Theory of Ethnic Spectatorship

As contemporary critical discourses become increasingly sensitive to the wide-ranging implications of the term "other," one major problem that surfaces is finding ways to articulate subjectivities that are, in the course of their participation in the dominant culture, "othered" and marginalized. Metaphors and apparatuses of *seeing* become overwhelmingly important ways of talking, simply because "seeing" carries with it the connotation of a demarcation of ontological boundaries between "self" and "other," whether racial, social, or sexual. However, the most difficult questions surrounding the demarcation of boundaries implied by "seeing" have to do not with positivistic taxonomic juxtapositions of self-contained identities and traditions in the manner of "this is you" and "that is us," but rather, who is "seeing" whom, and how? What are the power relationships between the "subject" and "object" of the culturally overdetermined "eye"?

The primacy I accord "seeing" is an instance of the cultural predicament in which the ethnic subject finds herself. The institutionalized apparatuses of "seeing" on which I rely for my analyses—cinema, film theory, and the nexus of attitudes and fantasies that have developed around them—are part and parcel of a dominant "symbolic" whose potent accomplishments are inextricably bound up with its scopophilia. To this extent, the felicity with which my analyses *can* proceed owes itself to the reversal of history that informs the development of theory in the West. This reversal makes available to those who think and write in the West a spaciousness that is necessary for their conceptual mobility, experimentation, and advancement, and that is nonetheless possible only because

3

many others continue to be excluded from the same spaces. The following discussion should be read in this light.

1

During one of the press interviews inaugurating his film *The Last Emperor* in 1987, Bernardo Bertolucci recalls his experience of going to China:

> I went to China because I was looking for fresh air. . . . For me it was love at first sight. I loved it. I thought the Chinese were fascinating. They have an innocence. They have a mixture of a people *before* consumerism, *before* something that happened in the West. *Yet in the meantime* they are incredibly sophisticated, elegant and subtle, because they are 4,000 years old. For me the mixture was irresistible.[1]

The registers of time in which the European director organizes China's fascination are hardly innocent. His love for this "other" culture is inspired at once by the feeling that it exists "before" or outside his own world, the contemporary world of the consumerist West, and by the feeling that, within its own context, the Chinese culture is highly developed and refined—because, after all, it is "4,000 years old." In this rather casual and touristy response to China lies a paradoxical conceptual structure that is ethnocentric. By ethnocentric, I do not mean an arrogant dismissal of the other culture as inferior (Bertolucci's enthusiasm disputes this), but—in a way that is at once more complex and more disturbing—how positive, respectful, and admiring feelings for the "other" can themselves be rooted in un-self-reflexive, culturally coded perspectives.

The story of Pu Yi, as we know, is that of a boy who became China's last emperor at the age of three, who grew up pampered by a court of corrupt eunuchs at a time when China had already become a republic, who collaborated with Japan's invasion of China during the 1930s by agreeing to be emperor of the puppet state Manchukuo, and who, after nearly ten years of "reeducation" under the Chinese Communist regime in the 1950s, lived the rest of his life as an ordinary citizen in Beijing. For Bertolucci, Pu Yi's story is that of a journey that goes "from darkness to light." Pu Yi is a "great man who becomes little, but also, I think, free." The way in which positive values are assembled in these remarks is interesting. Situated in a culture that is thought to be "before" the West and sophisticated in its own way, the story of Pu Yi is also the story of a man's "liberation." This assemblage makes one ask: In relation to what is Pu Yi "free"? What is darkness and what is light? In the most rudimentary manner, the film's colors contradict this notion of a journey "from darkness to light." If "darkness" refers to Pu Yi's imprisonment in China's imperial past and "light" to his liberation under the Communist regime (those who read Chinese would notice that the wall against which the group activities at the Fushun Detention Center take place is painted with the characters *guangming*, meaning "light"), why is it that the "imperial" scenes were shot with such dazzling arrays of phantasmagoric golds and yellows, while the "Communist" scenes were done in a drab mixture of blues and grays?

Bertolucci's film is an excellent example of a response to modern China that is inscribed at a crossroads of discourses, all of which have to do with "seeing" China as the other. In demonstrating what some of these discourses are, my discussion necessarily leads into more general problems of Chinese modernity, particularly as these pertain to the formulation of a "Chinese" subject.

When he describes the differences among the Japanese and Chinese members of his film crew, Bertolucci makes a revealing comment:

> They are very different. The Chinese, of course, are more ancient. But also, the Japanese have this myth of virility. They are more macho. The Chinese are the opposite, more feminine. A bit passive. But passive, as I say, in the way of people when they are so intelligent and so sophisticated they don't need machismo.

He then goes on to describe how Pu Yi's passivity is a kind of "Oriental dignity" that the West may misunderstand, and so forth. Before we discuss how the equation of the Last Emperor with what is conventionally designated as the "feminine" quality of passivity is enunciated through the cinematic apparatus, let us consider for a moment what this kind of equation means, what its structural intentions are, and why, even if at a certain level it has a subversive potential, it is highly problematic.

A text that would assist us here, because it shares Bertolucci's idealization of China through the category of the feminine, is Julia Kristeva's *About Chinese Women*.[2] Written at a time when the post-Second World War disillusionment with the liberal West was at its peak in European and American intellectual circles, Kristeva's book should first of all be understood in terms of a *critique* of *Western* discourse, a critique that characterizes all of her works. *About Chinese Women* is primarily a book about the epistemological deficiencies of the West rather than about China. However, Kristeva's critique is complicated by the fact that it is sexualized: China is counterposed to the West not only because it is different, but also because it is, in a way that reminds us of Bertolucci's configuration of it, feminine. In the West, as Kristeva's recapitulation of the creation myth of Adam and Eve shows, woman is merely functional—"divided from man, made of that very thing which is missing in him" (p. 17). Even though woman has a body, her corporeality is already a sign of her exclusion from the relationship between man and God. Tracing this "conception" of Western woman through historical as well as mythical sources, Kristeva argues that female sexuality at its most irreducible, that is, physical, level is denied symbolic recognition, and that the sexual difference between man and woman is hence repressed for the more metaphysical fusion between man and God in a mono-theistic, patriarchal system. "China," on the other hand, organizes sexual difference differently, by a frank admission of genitality. One example of Kristeva's thesis can be found in the way she interprets the Chinese custom of foot binding. This example reveals in an economical way the problems inherent to the idealist preoccupation with another culture in terms of "femininity." I want therefore to elaborate on it.

Kristeva reminds us of Freud's observation (in the essay "Fetishism," 1927) that foot binding is a symbol of the "castration of woman," which, she adds, "Chinese civilization was unique in admitting" (p. 83). However, Kristeva's appraisal of the Chinese custom goes one step further than Freud's. While the latter sees foot binding as a *variety* of castration, which for him remains the fundamental organizational principle of human civilization, Kristeva emphasizes its specifically feminine significance. Comparing foot binding with circumcision, which she describes as a kind of symbolic castration, she offers the following analysis. Circumcision, which is the equivalent of a prohibitive mark, is made on the body of man. This means that symbolically in the West, it is man who is the recipient of the mark that signifies mutilation, subordination, and hence difference; Western man becomes thus at once man and woman, "a woman to the father" (p. 26), "his father's daughter" (p. 85), so to speak. Western woman, in spite of her physical difference, remains in this way uncounted and superfluous. In foot binding, on the other hand, Kristeva sees Chinese culture's understanding of woman's *equal claim* to the symbolic. The custom is a sign of the anxiety that accompanies that understanding, but more important, it is a sign that is conspicuously displayed on the body of woman, which becomes the conscious symbolic bearer of the permanent struggle between man and woman. The gist of Kristeva's reading of China is utopian. Reading *with* her, we would think that the Chinese practice of maiming women's bodies is Chinese society's recognition, rather than denial, of woman's fundamental claim to social power. Anthropologically, the logic that Kristeva follows may be termed "primitive," with all the ideological underpinnings of the term at work: the act of wounding another's body, instead of being given the derogative meanings attributed to them by a humanistic perspective, is invested with the kind of meaning that one associates with warfare, antagonism, or even cannibalism in tribal society; the "cruelty" involved becomes a sign of the way the opponent's worth is acknowledged and reciprocated — with awe.

Kristeva's insights into the Chinese symbolic belong to the same order that Bertolucci, in the remarks I quote at the beginning, marks with the word "Yet": "Yet in the meantime they are incredibly sophisticated, elegant and subtle, because they are 4,000 years old." These are the insights that situate another culture in an ideal time that is marked off taxonomically from "our" time and that is thus allowed to play with its own sophisticated rhythms. More important, this ideal time in which China is recognized for its "own" value is much in keeping with the way femininity has been defined in Kristeva's work. First of all, we remember that "Woman can never be defined."[3] To define woman as such is to identify with what Kristeva calls "the time of history"—"time as project, teleology, linear and projective unfolding, time as departure, progression, and arrival."[4] Instead, woman for Kristeva is a "space" that is linked to "repetition" and "eternity." Woman is thus *negative* to the time of history and cannot "be":[5]

> A woman cannot "be"; it is something which does not even belong in the order of *being*. It follows that a feminist practice can only be negative, at odds with what already exists so that we may say "that's not it" and "that's still not it." In "woman" I see something that cannot be represented, something that is not said, something above and beyond nomenclatures and ideologies.[6]

This belief in the "negative" relation occupied by women to the "time of history" helps us comprehend the subversive intent behind *About Chinese Women*. Because the existing symbolic order in the West precludes woman in an a priori manner, Kristeva's way of subverting it is by following its logic to the hilt, and by dramatizing woman as totally "outside," "negative," "unrepresentable." Her notion of the *chora*,[7] by which she designates the "semiotic," maternal substratum of subjectivity that can be located only negatively, in avant-garde or "poetic" language, or in the nonrational elements of speech such as rhythm, intonation, and gesture, receives here its further extension through her reading of another culture. The result of this reading is precisely to fantasize that other culture in terms of a timeless "before," as we have encountered in Bertolucci's laudatory description of the Chinese as "a people before consumerism, before something that happened in the West." Kristeva's rejoinder to Bertolucci can be found in statements like these: ". . . in China . . . The strangeness persists . . . through a highly developed civilization which enters *without complexes* into the modern world, and yet preserves a logic unique to itself that no exoticism can account for" (p. 12; my emphasis). The attributions of a reality that is "pre-Oedipal" and "pre-psychoanalytic" (p. 58) to China are what in part prompted Gayatri Spivak's criticism of Kristeva's project, which "has been, not to *deconstruct* the origin, but rather to *recuperate*, archeologically and formulaically, what she locates as the potential originary space *before* the sign."[8]

Even though Kristeva sees China in an interesting and, indeed, "sympathetic" way, there is nothing in her arguments as such that cannot be said without "China." What she proposes is not so much learning a lesson from a different culture as a different method of reading from within the West. For, what is claimed to be "unique" to China is simply understood as the "negative" or "repressed" side of Western discourse. In thus othering and feminizing China, is Kristeva not repeating the metaphysics she wants to challenge? Especially since she has so carefully explicated the *superfluous* relation that Western woman has to the symbolic, might we not repeat after her, and say that the triangle Kristeva-the West-China in fact operates the same way as the triangle Man-God-Woman, with the last member in each set of relationships occupying the "excluded" position? Isn't the Western critic writing negatively from within her symbolic like Western Man in the "homosexual economy," being reduced to "a woman to the father," "his father's daughter," while China, being "essentially" different, can only be the "woman" whose materiality/corporeality becomes the sign of her repression?

One way out of this metaphysical impasse is, I think, by going against Kristeva's reading of China as an absolute "other." Much as this act of "othering" China is accompanied with modesty and self-deprecation, which Kristeva underscores by emphasizing the speculative, culture-bound nature of her project, perhaps it is precisely these deeply cultivated gestures of humility that are the heart of the matter here. We should ask instead whether the notion that China is absolutely "other" and unknowable is not itself problematic. I will cite three examples of Kristeva's unnecessary attribution of "otherness" to China to illustrate my point.

1. The suggestion that the Chinese language, because it is tonal, preserves an archaic "psychic stratum" that is "pre-Oedipal," "pre-syntactic," "pre-Symbolic" and hence dependent on the "maternal" (pp. 55-57). To look at Chinese, and for that matter any language, in this manner is to overlook the uses by its speakers, which are precisely what cannot be written off in such terms as "pre-syntactic" and "pre-Symbolic." To put this criticism differently, what is the meaning of an "archaic" "psychic stratum" in a culture that Kristeva has herself shown to be "pre-psychoanalytic"? If "archaic" and "pre" are the same, what can China's relevance be other than that of "primitivism"? And, if a *contemporary* culture is valued for its primitivism, doesn't this mean it is "outside" our time, confined to its own immobility?

2. Kristeva's idealization of the "maternal" order in China in terms of an "empty and peaceful center" (p. 159) — in other words, of what she identifies as *chora*. Kaja Silverman's comments in another context apply equally to Kristeva's treatment of Chinese women as they do to her treatment of "China": "By relegating the mother to the interior of the *chora*/womb, Kristeva reduces her to silence."[9] As my analysis of her reading of foot binding shows, her structural understanding of the "primitive" logic behind Chinese society's practice of maiming women's bodies leaves the problem of Chinese women's suffering intact. Instead of seeing women in an active discursive role expressing discontent with this practice, her reading says, "In your suffering, you are the bearers of an archaic truth." Thus negated, women are refused their place as subjects in the symbolic.[10]

3. Ironically, this refusal goes smoothly with Kristeva's affirmation of another strand of "otherness" about China: Taoism. In glorifying the "subversive" and "liberating" impact Taoism has on Chinese society, Kristeva, like many Westerners who turn to the "East" for spiritual guidance, must leave aside the consideration that perhaps it is exactly Taoism's equation of the female principle with "silence" and "negativity" that traditionally allows its coexistence and collaboration with Confucianism's misogyny. In a culture constructed upon the complicity between these master systems, Chinese women not only are oppressed but also would support their own oppression through the feelings of spiritual resignation that are dispersed throughout Chinese society on a mundane basis. Kristeva is told this bitter truth by a Chinese woman whom she interviews, but, intent on her own "materialist" reading of China, she does not want to believe it:

> The mother of three children, of whom the eldest is ten, she studied history for four years at the University and has been working at the museum for the past five years. I ask her:
> Wang Chong, for you, is a materialist. What is your definition of a materialist? Wasn't it he who fought against the treatises on the body, and certain Taoist rituals as well? Doesn't the Taoist tradition represent — albeit in mystical form — certain materialist demands against Confucianism?
> But my question will remain unanswered, except for her affirmation of "the complicity between Taoism and Confucianism, two aspects of idealism, both of which are surpassed by Wang Chong". Surpassed? Or suppressed? (p. 177)

So, as Chinese "woman" acquires the meanings of the Kristevian materialism that is said to exist in a timeless manner, from ancient to Communist China, *About Chinese Women* repeats, in spite of itself, the historical tradition in which China has been thought of in terms of an "eternal standstill" since the eighteenth century.[11] By giving that tradition a new reading, Kristeva espouses it again, this time from a feminized, negativized perspective. The seductiveness of this metaphysics of feminizing the other (culture) cannot be overstated. Bertolucci's film gives us a text whose beauty and power depend precisely on such a metaphysics.

2

In one of the early scenes in *The Last Emperor*, after the three-year-old Pu Yi has been installed on the throne, we are shown some of the intimate details of his daily life. The little boy, surrounded by a group of eunuchs who are eager to please him, is seen perching over a miniature model of the Forbidden City. His playmate, one of the eunuchs, takes pains to match the model with "reality," emphasizing where His Majesty was crowned, where he lives, where he now is, and so forth. The model therefore functions as an instrument that gives the little boy his "bearings." To use the language of contemporary psychoanalytic criticism, we witness in this scene a kind of "mirror stage" in which a child learns his "identity" through a representational structure that coheres the present moment of looking with the chaotic, tumultuous events that take place around him. While this profound lesson of self-recognition triggers rings of giggles in little Pu Yi, our attention to it is displaced by another event—the completion of Pu Yi's defecation. Swiftly, one eunuch puts a woven lid over the imperial chamber pot, and the camera, following his movements, shows him delivering this precious item to the imperial doctor, who removes the lid, looks at the feces, smells it, and gives advice on the emperor's diet. Meanwhile Pu Yi is taking his bath, again surrounded by eunuchs who are at once servants, entertainers, respondents to questions, and bearers of the little boy's anal-sadistic tantrums. This series of scenes culminates in the moment when Pu Yi's wet nurse appears at the door. At the sight of her, Pu Yi abandons his play and runs toward her, crying, "I want to go home, I want to go home." A eunuch hastens from behind to cover his small naked body with a cloth. This kind of caring, protective gesture from a servant would be repeated a few times during the course of the film, always at a moment when Pu Yi feels utterly deserted.

This series of scenes epitomizes one of the several orders of visualism[12] that are crucial to the film's organization. As emperor, Pu Yi *commands* attention no matter where he is. He is thus the "center" of a universe that "belongs" to him. In this respect, "attention" is one of the many embellishments that accompany the emperor's presence. Be they in the form of colors, objects, or human attendants, embellishments as such have no separate existence of their own, but are always part of the emperor's possessions. This "attention" is meanwhile a slanted, not direct, gaze: in the scenes where the emperor is about to approach, people stand aside, turn their heads away, or avert their gaze; the eunuchs dare not contradict what the emperor says; people want to kowtow to him even in 1950, when he is no longer emperor. The emperor's position is thus one of dominance, with all the "phallic" meanings of exclusivity that such a position connotes. As we recall the words of the dying Empress Cixi: no men except the emperor are allowed to stay in the Forbidden City after dark, and "these other men—they are not real men. They are eunuchs." However, intersecting this first order of visualism, in which Pu Yi is seen with imperial power, is another, in which Pu Yi is seen as totally passive. "Commanding" attention becomes indistinguishable from the experience of being watched and followed everywhere. The complexities of this second order of visualism are, as I argue in the following, what constitute the film's "gaze."

As Pu Yi cries "I want to go home, I want to go home," the fascination of the ubiquitous attention he receives as emperor is transformed and superseded by another meaning—one that reveals "from within" Pu Yi's lonely condition as a human being. A doubled gaze, then, is at work; the task that Bertolucci sets his camera is that of portraying the absolutely forlorn *inner* existence of a man whose outer environment bespeaks the most extraordinary visual splendor. How can the camera do this?

In her discussion of Laura Mulvey's classic essay, "Visual Pleasure and Narrative Cinema," Kaja Silverman recalls two representational strategies proposed by Mulvey for neutralizing the anxiety caused by female lack in classical narrative cinema. The first of these strategies "involves an interrogation calculated to establish either the female subject's guilt or her illness, while the second negotiates her erotic over-investment."[13] If we substitute the words "female subject" with "Pu Yi," this statement becomes a good description of how the space occupied by Pu Yi vis-à-vis the camera is, in fact, a feminized one. What enables this is the portrayal of him primarily as a child who never grew up, and who is aligned metonymically with the ancient and inarticulate (i.e., temporally and linguistically "other") world of his mothers.

Instead of being the straightforward inscription of his imperial power, then, the first order of visualism that shows Pu Yi to be the recipient of ubiquitous attention already belongs to what Silverman calls "erotic over-investment." Of all the components to this "over-investment," the most obvious are, of course, the visible elements of a re-created imperial China: the exotic architecture, the abundance of art objects, the clothes worn by members of the late Manchu court, their peculiar mannerisms, the camel or two resting on the outskirts of the Forbidden City, and the thousands of servants at the service of the emperor. The endowment of museum quality on the filmic images feeds the craving of the eyes. The cinema audience become vicarious tourists in front of whom "China" is served on a screen. And yet what is interesting about the erotic overinvestment is perhaps not the sheer visible display of ethnic imperial plenitude, but the amorous attitude the camera adopts toward such a display. To give one example, in the scene when Pu Yi is practicing calligraphy with his brother Pu Jie, he notices that the latter is wearing yellow. This greatly displeases him, because "only the emperor can wear yellow." A verbal confrontation between the two boys follows, which soon becomes a debate over the question of Pu Yi's status as emperor. Pu Jie puts down his trump card: "You are not the emperor any more." Our attention to a detail of the sensuous kind—the color yellow—gives way to an awareness of ritual proprieties, but the information pertaining to the ethnic class hierarchy is quickly transformed into the pronouncement of a historical and political *fait accompli*. This transformation, this movement from one kind of attention to another, indicates that the erotic overinvestment of Pu Yi is negotiated by a kind of sympathetic understanding, the understanding that he is the victim of a lavish, elaborate world that is, itself, a historical lie.

Although Pu Yi's perception of the coded meaning of yellow is correct, the environment in which that perception would be of significance has already vanished. At this point, "erotic over-investment" intersects with the other representational strategy, the "interrogation calculated to establish either the female subject's guilt or her illness." The "sympathetic understanding" that I am speaking about can thus be rewritten as a historical interrogation that shows Pu Yi to be "ill" or "deluded"; hence, it follows, we have many suggestions of his entrapment in his dream of being emperor, and of the guilt that he eventually feels. At the same time, however—and this is what makes the film's "message" highly ambiguous—it is as if the camera refuses to abandon a certain erotic interest in Pu Yi in spite of such historical knowledge. Precisely in its "sympathetic" attitude toward him, the camera takes over the attention bestowed upon the Last Emperor by other filmic characters and makes it part of *its own trajectory in courting him*. In the scene where Pu Jie is introduced, which precedes the one we are discussing, this courting is orchestrated through a combination of memorable image and memorable sound. We first see a pair of human legs walking toward the prison cell in which Pu Yi is waiting alone, while faintly but audibly, the beat from the film's theme, which we heard once already with the opening credits, prepares us for something important. As Pu Jie enters and the two men's eyes meet, the moment of recognition between brothers is amplified by the music, which now comes to the fore and takes us back to the day when they met each other for the first time as young boys. The forlorn inner condition of a man whose heart is warmed by the renewed closeness of a kinsman is thus not merely "displayed," but constructed, interpreted, and interwoven with richly suggestive "subjective" memory. It is this kind of careful, attentive "courting" that establishes the second order of visualism and that ultimately accounts for the film's eroticism.

However, having located the eroticism between Pu Yi the feminine, feminized object and the aroused, caressing strokes of Bertolucci's camera, we must add that the latter are figural: they can be felt and heard, but cannot be seen. If Bertolucci's humanistic sympathy for Pu Yi's predicament belongs to a certain historical "interrogation," that interrogation must remain *invisible* in the film precisely because it functions as the structuring "gaze." As if by a stroke of fate, this gaze finds in Chinese history a "stand-in" behind which it can hide—the interrogation of Pu Yi by the Chinese Communists.

This other, visible interrogation is in fact what introduces the story of the film, which begins with Pu Yi returning as a prisoner of war from the Soviet Union to China in 1950. The harshness of this interrogation is made apparent from the very beginning, when some fellow prisoners of war, on recognizing Pu Yi, come forward and kowtow to him and are quickly hustled away by others who are wary of the danger involved in such gestures of loyalty to a national traitor. Pu Yi's (fictional) attempt to commit suicide fails. As he wakes up at the slapping of the Fushun jail governor, he asks, "Where am I?", a question that reminds us of the instruction he received over the miniature model of the Forbidden City decades before. This time his recognition of "himself" must begin with the loud and cold words, "The People's Republic of China!" The insensitive and impersonal nature of the interrogation awaiting Pu Yi is obvious. The contrasting lack of sensuality in the scenes in the Fushun Detention Center goes hand in hand with the interrogators who are eager for their famous prisoner's confession. The irony of Bertolucci's direction is subtle: Pu Yi's chief interrogator is played by an actor who reminds one of the young Mao Zedong. There is also the suggestion that the Chinese Communists, apart from coercive terrorizing, understand little about their own history. At the beginning stage of Pu Yi's confession, we are shown a scene in which the jail governor, wanting to find out more about his prisoner's life, turns to the pages of *Twilight in the Forbidden City*, the book written by Pu Yi's Scottish tutor, Reginald Johnston (one-time magistrate of the British Leased Territory of Weihaiwei in Shandong Province), after he returned to England. This scene is remarkable because it shows the elderly Chinese man opening the book in an attempt to know more about recent Chinese history; what he reads, however, becomes the voice of Johnston narrating events that take us back to the time when he first arrived in Beijing. It is Johnston's voice, then, that the camera follows, and Johnston's account that shapes the elderly Chinese man's understanding of Pu Yi. As Johnston's entry into Pu Yi's life is placed at the point when Pu Yi loses his wet nurse, he is the symbol of the boy's embarkment on a phase of educational "enlightenment" and his departure from the hallucinatory, decadent, maternal world of breast sucking. In this way, the Chinese Communist interrogation of Pu Yi falls in line with the "Western" education represented by Johnston. During the interrogation, Johnston's name is invoked at the strategic moment when the jail governor wants Pu Yi to confess to having voluntarily submitted to the Japanese plot to make him emperor of Manchukuo.

The appearance of the Japanese at this point in the film's narrative serves to amplify the utterly passive nature of Pu Yi's political existence. Here, his life as a prisoner—first under the waning Manchu Dynasty, then in the political turmoil of the Chinese Republic, then in Manchukuo, and finally in Communist China—comes together in its multiple layers of "castration," to use once again the language of contemporary psychoanalytic criticism. It is here, therefore, that he appears his most handsome and plays his assigned role as "lack"/the "castrated" to the full. With his eyes staring dreamily into the distance and the flicker of a smile appearing on his face, he responds to the moralistic charge of his pro-foreignness with an abandoned, easeful matter-of-factness: "Of course, everything foreign was good . . . especially Wrigley's chewing gum, Bayer aspirin, and cars." But while Pu Yi's defiance does not go unnoticed, it serves only to fuel the eroticism that has determined the way we look at him all along. These statements from Silverman's description of the film *Gilda* apply equally well to Pu Yi: "Confession and fetishism do not here work to deflect attention away from female lack to male potency, but to inspire in the viewer (fictional and actual) the desire to have it fully revealed—to have it revealed, moreover, not as a repellent but as a pleasurable sight" (Silverman, p. 231). Hence, Pu Yi's defiance only leads the interrogators to pressure him for more in what increasingly amounts to their sadistic desire to "have it all" in the name of reform and rehabilitation.

This process of interrogation is conducted over a series of filmic signifiers onto which are displaced the motifs of enlightenment, nationalism, and political progressiveness. As we can see, the interrogative process, like the sensual display of Pu Yi's imperial past, is also directed by a voyeuristic gaze. But with a difference: while the "imperial" display amounts to a museum aesthetics, the "interrogation" comes across with a great sense of domination and oppression. As I have already suggested, the most disturbing question is how the Chinese Communist interrogation has been used as a stand-in for the camera's, so that the harshness and cruelty of the act of interrogating can be safely displaced onto the Chinese authorities, while the camera's gaze retains its freedom to roam about the body of the "other" with its "sympathetic" humanism. Silverman's observation that "a gaze within the fiction serves to conceal the controlling gaze outside the fiction" (Silverman, p. 204) is poignantly relevant in the cross-cultural context of Bertolucci's film. While the Chinese Communist interrogation is shown in an ambivalent light (at best historically necessary, at worst inhumane), the camera is able to sustain its amorous relationship with Pu Yi as a dignified human individual whose truth needs to be protected from the devastation of the interrogators' thirst for facts, thus aesthetically demonstrating what Bertolucci means when he says, "There is a kind of universal meaning in this figure." If my reading of Pu Yi as a figure for China-as-woman is at all tenable, then this interested, protective gesture on the part of the European director can be read as an allegory of what Spivak in a different context refers to as "white men saving brown women from brown men."[14]

The eroticized relationship between the camera's gaze and the last emperor also means that we cannot confront the issue of femininity in terms of the film's women characters. In the private conversations I had with a couple of female American sinologists, I gathered a favorable response to the women characters, especially the empress, who they thought represents a kind of wisdom and courage that they associate with "Chinese" women. I think this kind of reading misses the complexities of the cinematic apparatus because it is content with a straightforward correspondence between "images of women" and "femininity." As a result, femininity as the "space" and "spectacle" that functions in relation to the camera's gaze into another culture, and the politics that are inscribed therewith, are comfortably bypassed. In actuality, because it is Pu Yi and "China" who occupy the feminized space in this cinematic structure of eroticism, the women characters are pushed to what I'd call an astructural outside, the "other" of the other, as it were, that wavers between the ontological statuses of "nature" and "hysteria." The wet nurse, the high consorts of the court, the empress, the Second Consort, and "Eastern Jewel" all appear as either objects of pleasure or addicts to pleasure, strung together through a narrative that remembers them as gratifying female breasts, partners in sex games, perverse lesbians, and opium smokers. Meanwhile, whenever these women characters think and act with "courage" and "wisdom," their thoughts and acts become indistinguishable from excessiveness if not downright insanity. The empress's contempt for Pu Yi's collaboration with the Japanese in Manchukuo is represented through her "crazy" behavior at the inaugurating banquet. The film thus corroborates the commonsense feeling that for a woman to make a sensible point, she must first become a spectacle and show herself to be "out of her mind." As the bearer of truthful political understanding, the empress survives only as an invalid.

That *The Last Emperor* is a perfect example of how another culture can be "produced" as a feminized spectacle is confirmed by its reception in Hollywood. The film was nominated for nine Oscars at the sixtieth Academy Awards ceremony and won all nine. A look at the list reveals more specifically what exactly is rewarded: the *making* of the film. The categories included best motion picture, best director, best screenplay adopted from another medium, best cinematography, best art direction, best film editing, best costume, best sound, and best original score. In spite of his excellent performance, John Lone, who plays Pu Yi, was not even nominated for best actor. The question that arises is of course not whether an Oscar is "genuinely" valuable, but how it is that in a production that seems to be recognized for its excellence in so many respects, the same kind of recognition is not granted its "players." The repeated emphases on the "international" nature of the film's production[15] can hardly disguise the fact that what appear on the screen are mostly what would be identified as "Chinese" faces enacting a "Chinese" story/history. My point is not that Hollywood's neglect of the Chinese actors and actresses is a sign of racial discrimination *tout court*; rather, that in this failure to give equal recognition to the film's acting lies perhaps a confusion of the players with what they play. After all, one of the interesting problems about film acting is that the actor/actress straddles the roles of film *maker* and film *image*. Categorically, therefore, acting contains an ambivalence that distinguishes it from other aspects of film production. In the case of a saga like *The Last Emperor*, this ambivalence can only be more pronounced. In turn, we can say that when an actor/actress is given an award for acting, it is an indication that he/she, the actual individual *outside* the film, has done a good job playing a fictional role. An award for acting can thus be looked upon as the film industry's way of distinguishing an actor/actress from a role and of putting him/her on the side of the film "makers."

On the other hand, I hope my analysis of Pu Yi and *The Last Emperor* as a feminized space in the structure of Bertolucci's commercialized aesthetics has made it clear by now why it is indeed not surprising that the "acting" of this film cannot be recognized as "creative" talent. After all, if this feminized spectacle has grown out of Bertolucci's need for "fresh air" in the first place, it must remain and can only be rewarded as *his* creation, *his* story. (Bertolucci: "I am a storyteller, I am not a historian. . . . To history I prefer mythology. Because history starts with the truth and goes toward lies. While mythology starts from lies and fantasy and goes toward truth.") What at first sight looks like a sensational advertisement announcing the availability of the film on video cassette and laser videodisc offers an accurate summary of Bertolucci's story: "Emperor. Playboy. Prisoner. Man."[16]

3

So far, my reading strategy with regard to *The Last Emperor* has been more or less congruent with the method of dissecting "narrative cinema and visual pleasure" given to us by Laura Mulvey in her essay of the same title. Mulvey argues that, on the basis of vision, there is a fundamental difference in the classical film between the roles it assigns to men and women. The camera's gaze, associated with scopophilia, is "masculine," while images on the screen, in the state of being looked at and thus eroticized, are "feminine." Silverman comments: "This opposition is entirely in keeping with the dominant cultural roles assigned to men and women, since voyeurism is the active or 'masculine' form of the scopophilic drive, while exhibitionism is the passive or 'feminine' form of the same drive" (Silverman, p. 223). Accordingly, as they look at cinematic images, the spectators identify with the camera's gaze; identification is thus a "masculinizing" identification that perpetuates the reduction of women to an eroticized image. Although visual pleasure is "threatening in content" (Mulvey, p. 309) (since, to retrace the logic of Freud's castration complex, it implies male fear and anxiety), it is primarily its function in constructing women as passive and inferior that concerns Mulvey as a feminist.[17]

Mulvey's essay has been controversial since its first publication. Criticisms of her argument converge on what most consider to be its ahistorical theoretical determinism. Fairly recently, Mulvey revised and critiqued her own position, notably in an essay called "Changes: Thoughts on Myth, Narrative and Historical Experience."[18] Her self-critique alerts us to the historicity of the *form* in which her original thesis was constructed. Looking at it retrospectively, Mulvey describes the polarization of male and female positions ("active" versus "passive," "spectator" versus "spectacle," and so on) as a conceptual typology that, despite its relevance to a particular moment in time, may obstruct further the-oretical developments:

> It is as though the very invisibility of abstract ideas attracts a material, metaphoric form. The interest lies in whether the forms of this "conceptual typology", as I have called it, might affect the formula-tion of the ideas themselves and their ultimate destiny. Is it possible that the way in which ideas are visualised can, at a certain point, block the process that brings thought into a dialectical relationship with history? . . .
>
> A negative aesthetic can produce an inversion of the meanings and pleasures it confronts, but it risks remaining locked in a dialogue with its adversary. . . .
>
> Apart from inversion, shifts in position are hard to envisage.
> (Mulvey 2, pp. 163, 164, 168)

While I agree with the historical impetus behind Mulvey's self-critique, I find the metaphors that accompany her efforts to decenter her own original argument disturbing. Two examples: "I feel now that its [her classic essay's] 'conceptual typology' contributed in some way to blocking *advance*"; "negative aesthetics can act as a motor force in the *early phases* of a movement, initiating and ex-pressing the desire for change" (Mulvey 2, pp. 163, 164; my emphases). These metaphors are metaphors of a teleological construction of history, which as a rule emphasizes the immaturity, the rashness even, of "early" concepts. The rhe-torical return to this conventional, almost chronological sense of history is par-adoxical in an essay that otherwise offers a very different kind of argument about the historical through the notion of the "pre-Oedipal." Citing as an example the way the image of Our Lady of Guadalupe was used as an emblem for political revolt against Spanish rule in Mexico in the early nineteenth century, Mulvey argues for an understanding of the "pre-Oedipal" that is not in teleological terms: the "pre-Oedipal" is "in *transition* to articulated language" (Mulvey 2, p. 167; emphasis in the original); it is not dominant, yet meaningful. Although I would disagree with Mulvey's subscription to the Freudian notion for the same reasons I would with Kristeva's, what is valuable in this part of her argument is not so much the "pre-Oedipal" per se as *where* she tries to locate it. This is not some exotic past or ancient culture, but "the rhetoric of the oppressed"—"a rhetoric that takes on the low side of the polar opposition, in order to turn the world upside down, and stake out *the right to imagine* another" (Mulvey 2, p. 167; emphasis in the original).

To turn the world upside down, to stake out the right to imagine another: these are the tasks we are still faced with. I think Mulvey's original argument should be read in the light of these statements rather than simply against her later attempt to "historicize" that argument in a more conventional way. What

is most productive about her polarization of male and female positions is a radicalness that is often the only means of effecting change. Only when things are
put in the bold, so to speak, can a thorough dismantling of the habits of seeing be
achieved. The perception of the need to be uncompromisingly thorough is itself
historical. It is *this* kind of historical perceptiveness that is behind Mulvey's extremely direct, and only thus effective, statement of her original project: "It is
said that analysing pleasure, or beauty, destroys it. That is the intention of this
article" (Mulvey, p. 306).

It follows that the most useful aspect of Mulvey's essay lies not so much in the
division between masculinity and femininity as "gaze" and "image," as in the
conceptual possibilities that inevitably emerge once such a division is so bluntly
and crudely crafted. As Mulvey puts it, "A negation or inversion of dominant
codes and conventions can fossilise into a dualistic opposition *or* it can provide
a spring-board, a means of testing out the terms of a dialect, an unformed language that can then develop in its own signifying space" (Mulvey 2, pp. 168-69;
my emphasis). This "unformed language" is the language of the oppressed.

In Mulvey's original argument, this language of the oppressed is conceived in
visual terms, as part of the state of being-looked-at. This state of being-looked-at
is built into the cinematic spectacle itself: "Going far beyond highlighting a
woman's to-be-looked-at-ness, cinema builds the way she is to be looked at into
the spectacle itself" (Mulvey, p. 314). What this enables is an understanding of
the cinematic image not simply as some pure "thing" to be perceived, but as
what already contains the gaze (the act of gazing) that cannot be seen itself.

We have seen how, in *The Last Emperor*, it is precisely this invisible gaze that
directs our paths of identification and nonidentification. It does so by hiding
behind other filmic signifiers such as the Chinese imperial order, which bestows
attention on the emperor to the finest detail, and the Chinese Communist *interrogation* of Pu Yi. What we see on the screen, then, is already something that has
been profoundly worked on. For the camera's gaze does not simply "hide," but
negotiates, mediates, and manipulates; it builds on the "gazes" that are visibly
available on the screen, turning them into occasions for eroticism or humanistic
sympathy and in this way "suturing" the spectators' response.[19]

My use of Mulvey's mode of critique therefore complicates it in two ways.
First, I extend the interpretation of image-as-woman to image-as-feminized
space, which can be occupied by a man character, Pu Yi, as much as by a
woman. Once this is done, "femininity" as a category is freed up to include fictional constructs that may not be "women" but that occupy a passive position in
regard to the controlling symbolic. At the same time, this use of "femininity"
does not abandon the politics of "to-be-looked-at-ness," which, as Mulvey's argument shows, is most readily clarified through women's assigned role in culture.

The second complication is my use of the elements of this cinematic analysis
for a polemics of cross-cultural inquiry. The image-as-feminized space raises dis-

turbing questions as to what is involved in the representation of another culture, especially when that representation is seen by members of that culture. Does it call for the "destruction of visual pleasure" that is the point of Mulvey's critique? Who should destroy it, and how? If not, why not? What are the problems that watching a film like *The Last Emperor* produces—for a Chinese audience? If it is a matter of criticizing Bertolucci for using "good drama" to "falsify" Chinese history, one can simply recite historical facts and rechronicle the reality that was not the one of the film.[20] But that precisely is not what matters. What matters is rather how "history" should be reintroduced materially, as a specific way of reading—not reading "reality" as such but cultural artifacts such as film and narratives. The task involves not only the formalist analysis of the *producing* apparatus. It also involves rematerializing such formalist analysis with a pregazing— the "givenness" of subjectivity I indicated in the Preface—that has always already begun.

To rematerialize this pregazing, we need to shift our attention away from the moment of production to the moment of reception. In retrospect, it is the lack of this shift that constitutes the vulnerability in Mulvey's original argument. Given that "visual pleasure" is indeed the "evil" of the scopophilic cinematic apparatus, does it mean that the spectator is affected by it in a uniform way? Indeed, the logic of "Visual Pleasure and Narrative Cinema" would indicate that all spectators are "masculinized" in reception, since they would be identifying with the camera's gaze. The woman whose ontological status is supposedly that of the image on the screen and who nonetheless also sits in the audience hence poses a very special problem. With what does she really identify? Must she simply become schizophrenic?

In her book *Alice Doesn't: Feminism, Semiotics, Cinema,*[21] Teresa de Lauretis takes up this important question of the female spectator that is left largely unexplored. She does this by supplementing the filmic position of woman as "visual object" with something else—"narrative." De Lauretis argues that the position occupied by "woman" on the screen is not simply a visible "image" but a "narrative image," a term she borrows from Stephen Heath. The "narrative image" of woman refers to "the join of image and story, the interlocking of visual and narrative registers effected by the cinematic of the look" (de Lauretis, p. 140). In cinema as much as in conventional narrative, the female position, "produced as the end result of narrativization, is the figure of narrative closure, the narrative image in which the film . . . 'comes together'" (de Lauretis, p. 140). By introducing narrative into the understanding of filmic images, de Lauretis is thus able to distinguish *two* sets of identifying relations for the female spectator. The first, well known to classical film theory, consists of "the masculine, active, identification with the gaze (the looks of the camera and of the male characters) and the passive, feminine identification with the image (body, landscape)" (de Lauretis, p. 144). The second set of identifying relations is *fig-*

ural in nature. It does not consist so much of gazes and looks as it does "the double identification with the figure of narrative movement, the mythical subject, and with the figure of narrative closure, the narrative image" (de Lauretis, p. 144). Moreover,

> Were it not for the possibility of this second, figural identification, the woman spectator would be stranded between two incommensurable entities, the gaze and the image. Identification, that is, would be either impossible, split beyond any act of suture, or entirely masculine. The figural narrative identification, on the contrary, is double; both figures can and in fact must be identified with at once, for they are inherent in narrativity itself. It is this narrative identification that assures "the hold of the image," the anchoring of the subject in the flow of the film's movement. (de Lauretis, p. 144)

In thus supplementing the understanding of filmic images with terms other than those of the visual order alone, de Lauretis accomplishes several things at once. First, by reintroducing the processes of narrative, she revises the film theory that relies heavily on the sexual division based on vision, since that division, as all criticisms of Mulvey's original argument indicate, leads to a rigid polarization between man-as-gaze and woman-as-image. Second, in doing so, she enables a critique of the kind of technical analysis involved in a reading strategy such as Mulvey's while at the same time salvaging and reaffirming the valid political import of Mulvey's project, namely, that women, as the oppressed side of the polarization, must also be understood as *subjects*, not objects, in social discourse. Third, this is possible because the political question of female subjectivity is now posed in different terms: not simply that "woman is reduced to the image," but "woman" is a locus of double identification. It is through a careful discussion of what this "doubleness" signifies that the "female spectator" offers the potential of a new means of sociocultural inquiry.

Put in more mundane terms, the paradigm of gaze-as-male and image-as-female breaks down once we think of women who willingly buy tickets to go to the cinema and derive pleasure from the experience. The rejection of the relevance of this experience would result in the kind of denunciation of mass culture that we associate with Adorno and Horkheimer in their classic piece, "The Culture Industry: Enlightenment as Mass Deception."[22] It is a rejection because, in spite of often attentive analyses of how the mass culture industry works by subjugating the masses, the experience of the masses is not itself considered a problem except insofar as it is assumed to signify, uniformly, "stupefaction." However, if we are to theorize precisely from the perspective of the receiving masses, then the problem is infinitely complicated. As recent studies of popular culture such as Tania Modleski's *Loving with a Vengeance*, Janice Radway's *Reading the Romance*, and Ien Ang's *Watching Dallas* repeatedly indicate, the female viewing/

reading subject is elusive, ambivalent, always divided between "conventional" values and expectations on the one hand, and socially disruptive or destructive tendencies on the other. Central to such conflicts in the processes of reception is the issue of identification, and with it, the problem of pleasure.

Because theoretically the female spectator's position offers an example of a division that is "irreparable" and "unsuturable" (de Lauretis, p. 143), film theorists tend to disregard the problem of sexual differentiation in the spectators altogether. This leads to the facile thinking of reception purely in terms of a transcendental or ideal subject, presupposed to be male. Feminist readings such as Mulvey's, also following this thinking but revolting against it, therefore seek to destroy it totally. De Lauretis summarizes this state of affairs with a thoughtful comment about women and pleasure:

> Within the context of the argument, a radical film practice can only constitute itself against the specifications of that cinema, in counterpoint to it, and must set out to destroy the "satisfaction, pleasure and privilege" it affords. The alternative is brutal, especially for women to whom pleasure and satisfaction, in the cinema and elsewhere, are not easily available. (de Lauretis, p. 60)

Since the need to destroy visual pleasure stems from the belief that what gives pleasure is pure illusion, de Lauretis goes on to suggest that the word "illusion" be "dislodged from the particular discursive framework of Mulvey's argument" and be interpreted along the associations given to it by E. H. Gombrich, for whom illusion is a process "operating not only in representation, visual and otherwise, but in all sensory perception, and a process in fact crucial to any organism's chances of survival" (de Lauretis, p. 61). Readers must turn to de Lauretis's book to realize for themselves the vast implications of this argument based on perception theories. For now, I will limit my discussion to an amplification of "the particular discursive framework of Mulvey's argument" and of how the notion of "illusion" may be mobilized and generalized for a *departure* from that framework.

Briefly, I think the discursive framework of Mulvey's essay takes us back to the formulation of "ideology" advanced by Louis Althusser in his work.[23] Althusser defines ideology in terms of two types of "apparatuses," the "Repressive State Apparatuses" and the "Ideological State Apparatuses." While the former work by brute, militant force, the latter, under which Althusser lists churches, public and private schools, the family, the law, the political system, the trade union, the media, and "cultural" activities such as literature, the arts, and sports (Althusser, p. 143), work by what we might call "civility." It is such "civil" apparatuses that help reproduce the conditions of capitalist production by "interpellating" individuals into the existing system even as these individuals imagine their actions to be spontaneous and voluntary. Mulvey's essay, I think, draws on this general notion of ideology and localizes it in a specific apparatus, cinema. In this respect, her analysis of the classical narrative film contains two mutually implied equations: first, that between ideology and the masculine gaze; second, that between ideology and falsehood. The critique of cinema as dominated by the masculine gaze is therefore also a critique of ideology as falsehood. And it is, I think, this approach to ideology that de Lauretis means by the "particular discursive framework of Mulvey's argument." The notion of "falsehood" is analogous to that of "illusion" as defined by *The American Heritage Dictionary*: "something, as a fantastic plan or desire, that causes an erroneous belief or perception." Defined this way, "illusion" calls for its own destruction and, by implication, for the restoration of what is nonillusory. For very understandable reasons, much of the work undertaken in feminism partakes of this anti-illusion tendency, resulting in some extreme cases where a profound lack of interest in or a total disregard of anything related to men is heartily applauded.

Althusser's theory, however, indicates another direction in which feminism and the awareness of "ideology" can join forces. For this, we need to ponder anew his way of formulating ideology, as "the *reproduction* of the conditions of production" (Althusser, p. 127; my emphasis). Or, restating it to the same effect, he says:

> Every social formation must reproduce the conditions of its production at the same time as it produces, and in order to be able to produce. It must therefore reproduce:
> 1. the productive forces,
> 2. the *existing relations* of production (Althusser, p. 128; my emphasis)

What else could be the "existing relations" of production but the mental attitudes, wishes, sufferings, and fantasies of the individuals involved in the processes of active production? When he discusses the "reproduction of labor-power," Althusser includes not only quantifiable value (wages) but also a "historically variable minimum"—"needs." He adds in parentheses that "Marx noted that English workers need beer while French proletarians need wine" (Althusser, p. 131). Ideology is thus understood by Althusser not really as "something" that "causes" a falsified perception, but more as the experience of consumption and reception, as that store of elusive elements that, *apart from* "wages" and "surplus value," enable people to buy, accept, and enjoy what is available in their culture. This understanding of ideology, then, includes the understanding that any reception of culture—however "passive" and thus "ideological"—always contains a responsive, performative aspect. However neglected by cultural theorists busy with the criticism of ideology-as-falsehood, this aspect of reception is crucial to the notion of "illusion" that de Lauretis would like to dislodge from a deeply ingrained, Platonic tradition of criticism and reinvest with the meaning of social survival. As she puts it succinctly:

The present task of theoretical feminism and of feminist film practice is to articulate the relations of the female subject to representation, meaning, and vision, and is so doing to construct the terms of another frame of reference, another measure of desire. *This cannot be done* by destroying all representational coherence, by denying "the hold" of the image in order to prevent identification and subject reflection, by voiding perception of any given or preconstructed meanings. (de Lauretis, p. 68; my emphasis)

In a way that echoes de Lauretis, Silverman points out in her discussion of "suture" the intimate link between suture and "interpellation" (Silverman, p. 219). Her explanation of suture reminds us of Althusser's analysis of the individual's response to the "interpellating" call: "The operation of suture is successful at the moment that the viewing subject says, 'Yes, that's me,' or 'That's what I see' (Silverman, p. 205). She mentions also that, as viewing subjects, "we want suture so badly that we'll take it at any price, even with the fullest knowledge of what it entails—passive insertions into pre-existing discursive positions (both mythically potent and mythically impotent); threatened losses and false recoveries; and subordination to the castrating gaze of a symbolic Other" (Silverman, p. 213). These statements serve to emphasize that the task of critiquing processes of ideology, illusion, and suture cannot be performed at the level of pitting reality against falsehood, because in what we think of as "falsehood" often lies the chance of continued survival, sometimes the only way to come to terms with an existing oppressive condition. This is especially true in the case of the female spectator, as de Lauretis is at pains to demonstrate.

Instead of seeking to "free" the filmic illusion, de Lauretis restores and redefines its value. She does this by avoiding the tendency in avant-garde film practices to reinscribe materiality *exclusively* in the process of filmmaking. For these practices, by "roughening" and "defamiliarizing" the workings of the apparatus (to borrow terms from the Russian Formalists), often demand of the spectator a cool-headed "detachment" from what they see. Instead, de Lauretis moves toward reinscribing materiality in film watching. Through the writings of Pasolini, she draws attention to the "translinguistic" function of cinema, showing that cinema "exceeds the moment of the inscription, the technical apparatus, to become 'a dynamics of feelings, affects, passions, ideas' in the moment of reception" (de Lauretis, p. 51). These words, adds de Lauretis, should not be construed as an emphasis on the purely existential or personal, for they point to "spectatorship as a site of productive relations" (de Lauretis, p. 51).

It is by rearguing the relationship between image and spectator and by foregrounding the cultural components that are specific to an *imaged spectatorship* that a film like *The Last Emperor* can be instrumental in an analysis of modern Chinese subjectivity. Here, once again, I would like to extend the feminist basis of de Lauretis's arguments to a cross-cultural context, by asking how the insights she develops around the female spectator could fruitfully become a way of articulating the ethnic—in this case, Chinese—spectator.

Take this statement: "Spectators are not, as it were, either in the film text *or* simply outside the film text; rather, we might say, they intersect the film as they are intersected by cinema" (de Lauretis, p. 44). What happens when a Chinese person sees *The Last Emperor?* Is the process comparable to the one described by de Lauretis with regard to the female spectator, who is caught between the feminine (Chinese) image on the screen and the masculine (non-Chinese) gaze of the camera? How does the double, figural identification—with both narrative movement and narrative closure—work?

I cite my mother's response to the film: "It is remarkable that a foreign devil should be able to make a film like this about China. I'd say, he did a good job!" Instead of being stranded schizophrenically between an identification with Bertolucci's "gaze" and the projection of herself ("Chinese") as image on the screen, my mother's reaction indicates a successful "suturing" in the sense of a cohering of disjointed experiences through "illusion." As an ethnic spectator, she identifies at once with the narrative movement, the invisible subject that "tells" the story about modern China, *and* with the narrative image centering on Pu Yi, signifying "Chinese" history. Even as she highlights the film's non-Chinese making in the phrase "foreign devil," the process of identification appears uninterrupted. In fact, one can say that her identification with the narrative image is most successful when she compliments Bertolucci for doing a good job in spite of being a "foreign devil." For, although "foreign devil" is a mark of the awareness of difference, the "in spite of" attitude points rather to the process in which a seamless interpellative exchange can take place between the spectator and the filmic image. Instead of doubting Bertolucci's version of modern Chinese history, my mother's reaction says, "Still, that's me, that's us, that's our history. I see it in spite of the hand of the foreign devil." This response, coming from someone who, while a young girl, was brutalized and abducted by Japanese soldiers in southwest China during the Second World War, is much more complex and more unsettling than the one suggested to me by some of my academic friends who, not surprisingly, criticize the film as an instance of what Edward Said calls "Orientalism" and thus miss its appeal to many Chinese spectators in Hong Kong, Taiwan, and the People's Republic. I am not applauding the "Orientalism" that is obviously crucial to the film's structure. However, it seems to me equally important to point out how, much like the female spectator, the ethnic spectator occupies an impossible space that almost predetermines its dismissal from a theoretical reading that is intent on exposing the "ideologically suspect" technicalities of production only. In such a reading, my mother's response could only be written off as "unsophisticated," "simplistic," or "manipulated."

If, on the other hand, we are to take de Lauretis's discussion of "illusion" seriously, refusing, that is, to reduce "illusion" to the polarized opposition between "truth" and "illusion," then the position occupied by the ethnic spectator must be reaffirmed in the inquiry of cultural intercourse. To this position belongs, first, "historical" awareness: the knowledge of China's imperialized status vis-à-vis the West for the past century or so, and the memories, more recent and more overwhelming, of the millions of rapes and murders, the massacres, and the "biological experimentations" perpetrated by the Japanese on Chinese soil, in which Pu Yi was undoubtedly chief collaborator in the Northeast. Chinese idioms such as "foreign devil," as part of this historical awareness, emphasize — sentimentally and defensively — Chinese people's "holding their own," implying by that logic an intuitive distrust of any "foreigner's" story of Chinese history. But overlapping with the pain of historical awareness is another, equally intense feeling, describable only partly by phrases like "mesmerization," "nostalgia," and "a desire to be there, in the film." All these phrases belong to "illusion" as de Lauretis would understand it, that is, perceptive operations that are, regardless of their so-called falsity, vital to a continual engagement with what is culturally available.

The identification with an ethnic or "national" history, and the pain and pleasure that this involves, cannot be understood simply in terms of "nativism." The spectator is not simply ethnic but ethnicized: the recognition of her "Chineseness" is already part of the process of cross-cultural interpellation that is at work in the larger realm of modern history. To use the words of C. T. Hsia with regard to modern Chinese literature, there is, among many Chinese people, an "obsession with China."[24] Why? An answer to this question cannot be given unless we reinsert into the overtones of a collective identity the subjective processes — the desires, fantasies, and sentimentalisms — that are part of a response to the solicitous calls, dispersed internationally in multiple ways, to such an identity. In this light, the phrase "imagined communities" in the title of Benedict Anderson's book is especially thought-provoking.[25] In spite of being a specialist in Southeast Asia, however, Anderson's analysis is surprisingly indifferent to the rise of imagined communities in the non-West as a response to European colonialism. His insights into the origins of imagined communities in Europe — origins that encompass capitalism, technology, and the development of languages — are accompanied by a lack of interest in crucial differences in, say, postcolonial Asia. Take, for instance, this matter-of-fact observation: "So, as European imperialism smashed its insouciant way around the globe, other civilizations found themselves traumatically confronted by pluralisms which annihilated their sacred genealogies. The Middle Kingdom's marginalization to the Far East is emblematic of this process."[26] What, we should ask, is the nature of this traumatization and marginalization? The potency of Anderson's two-word phrase — a potency that remains unrealized in his book — lies, I think, not so much in its rapport with the urge in contemporary critical theory to deconstruct centrisms such as "communities" with their rings of monolithic closure, as in the word "imagined" as an index to the involved conceptual movements that may or may not coincide with their imagined content.

The word "imagined" is immensely rich in its suggestions of the process in which the subject is constituted by recognizing, in external objects, that part of herself that has been "dismembered" for cultural and historical reasons. Within contemporary psychoanalytic theories, Lacan's term *"objet petit a"* (object a), generally interpreted to mean the objects in the life of a subject that are neither fully distinguishable from the self nor clearly apprehensible as other, and which receive their value from the subject's representation of them as missing, would be one way of formulating this process.[27] A more concrete, because visually specific, formulation lies with Freud's theory of fetishism.[28] Central to Freud's theory is that a fetish is a substitute for something that is imagined to be lost or losable; in Freud, that something is the penis. But if we should disengage Freud's theory from its masculinist emphasis on the penis as the paradigm signifier, we would see that what is most interesting about fetishism is the process of loss, substitution, and identification that is at play in the formation of a subject. The fetishist is someone who translates the importance of that part of himself which he fears to be lost/losable into "its" lack outside himself, a "lack" that is, moreover, relocalized in another body in multiple ways (e.g., in female hair, feet, breasts, etc.), endowed with a magical power, and thus "fetishized." What should be emphasized is that this "translation" is, in Freud's texts, an imagining process that involves the mutual play between an emotion and a "sight," but more precisely a sight-in-recollection. What is seen (the female body) in a first instance (when no neurosis occurs) is remembered in a second instance amid feelings of fear (when the little boy is caught masturbating and threatened to be reported to his father); his "translation" of these feelings into the female body-as-lack is thus the result of a mental sequence. As such, fetishism is the process of a belated consciousness, a consciousness that comes into itself through memory substitution, and representation. Meanwhile, the "original" belief in the mother's "penis" (that is, her complete identification with and indistinguishability from oneself, thus her omnipotence and plenitude) undergoes a twofold change: (1) the knowledge that she does not "have a penis" is disavowed, and (2) the "lack" she signifies is repressed and represented in other forms, forms we call "fetishes." The original belief, in other words, does not disappear but reappears repeatedly as a wish, which is attached to "fetishes" in the form of emotions—the emotions of pleasure and of identification.

Removing these formulations of subjectivity from an exclusively psychoanalytic and metaphysical framework, and placing them in modern Chinese history, we see how the experience of "dismemberment" (or "castration") can be used to describe what we commonly refer to as "Westernization" or "modernization."

Typically, as the history of the non-West is divided into the classical/primitive and the "modern" stages, modern non-Western subjects can be said to be constituted primarily through a sense of loss—the loss of an attributed "ancient" history with which one "identifies" but to which one can never return except in the form of fetishism. The "object" with which Chinese people are obsessed— "China" or "Chineseness"—cannot therefore be seen as an emotional simplism, but must rather be seen as the sign of a belated consciousness and a representation, involving mental processes that are not, as Kristeva would have it, "prepsychoanalytic." We might say that a response such as "Yes, that's me, that's Chinese" is a fetishizing imagining of a "China" that never is, but in that response also lies the wish that is the last residue of a protest against that inevitable "dismemberment" brought about by the imperialistic violence of Westernization.

The point must be emphasized, especially from the position of those that are feminized and ethnicized: these identificatory acts are the sites of productive relations that should be reread with the appropriate degree of complexity. This complexity lies not only in the identification with the ethnic culture, but also in the strong sense of complicity with the "dismembering" processes that structure those imaginings in the first place. For instance, the Chinese person obsessed with China emotionally is not necessarily one that would dress and live in a "Chinese" manner, as any superficial acquaintance with "Westernized" Chinese would reveal. Unlike what Oriental things still are to many Europeans and Americans, "Western things" to a Chinese person are never merely dispensable embellishments; their presence has for the past century represented the necessity of fundamental adaptation and acceptance. It is the permanence of imprints left by the contact with the West that should be remembered even in an ethnic culture's obsession with "itself."

4

In the preceding analysis, I demonstrate the problems pertaining to the ethnic spectator through a specific cultural instance, a film about modern China. I argue that the film, as a technical apparatus, provides the means of redistributing that "primitive" history to the ethnic subject as "her own," but it is the ethnic subject's contradictory response—a historical awareness combined with a pleasurable identification with the film's narrative-imagistic effects—that reveals the full complicity of the cross-cultural exchange. The difficulty of the ethnic, and ethnicized, spectator's position can be shown another way, through the currently prevalent academic attitudes revolving around the study of "China."

A few years ago, while attending an Association for Asian Studies meeting, I found myself face-to-face with an American-trained China historian who was lamenting the fact that China was becoming more and more like the West.

Among the things that disturbed him the most were the diminishing differences in terms of the technical, cultural, and even linguistic aspects of Chinese life. China's recent development, in other words, makes it more and more impossible to disprove the "convergence" theory advanced by some social scientists about world modernization. Over the years, many versions of the same concern reveal themselves to me in sinological methodology, usually in the form of an eager emphasis on the uniqueness of Chinese history and a defense of "China" studies against the "West." Depending on the interest of the person, "sinocentrism" can either take the theoretical position that China's tradition is adequate to itself, or perform, in practice, elaborate reinscriptions and hermeneutical readings of Chinese history/texts. Often, the sinocentric approach to "China" boils down to an assertion of this kind in the field of literature: if one is studying Chinese texts, one should use "Chinese" methodologies, not "Western" ones. To read "Chinese" texts in terms of "Western" methodologies is to let the latter distort the former.

These encounters, personal or textual, have been instructive for me in that they make me ask myself: Why is it that these China scholars, who argue for the integrity of China studies, have not struck one chord of enthusiasm in me, a Chinese? What is missing in the dialogue between them and me, when in all likelihood I should feel grateful toward them for defending "my" culture? It becomes necessary for me to reflect on the nature of their defense of "Chinese culture," which I would describe as an idealist preoccupation with "authentic" originariness. This kind of preoccupation is, of course, not unique to China studies. But in China studies, it runs into specific difficulties. How to strive for authentic originariness, when the history of China in the nineteenth and twentieth centuries is inundated with disruptive contacts with the West? Where could authentic origins possibly come from? In other words, what is "Chinese"? The concentration on China as "tradition" is an understandable way out, for as an idea, tradition offers the comfort precisely of adequacy, self-sufficiency, and continuity. It is supported, outside academia, by antique collecting, museums, restaurants, tourism, and the pastime of *chinoiserie*, all of which confirm the existence of a Chinese tradition. What is missing from the preoccupation with tradition and authentic originariness as such is the experience of modern Chinese people who have had to live their lives with the knowledge that it is precisely the notion of a still-intact tradition to which they cannot cling—the experience precisely of being impure, "Westernized" Chinese and the bearing of *that* experience on their ways of "seeing" China. Instead of recognizing the reality of this "ethnic spectator," much of China studies prefers, methodologically, taxonomic divisions of China into "premodern" and "modern," "traditional" and "Westernized" periods, and so forth, even as the fragmented, dispersed, ironic developments of Chinese modernity make the clarity of these conceptual divisions useless. Thus, as is often felt though never directly stated, Chinese from the mainland are more "authentic" than those who are from, say, Taiwan or Hong Kong, because the latter have been "Westernized." A preference for the purity of the original ethnic specimen perhaps? But if so, one would have to follow this kind of logic to its extreme, and ask why sinologists should "study" China at all, since studying already implies "othering" and "alienating" it; and to that effect, how even the most sinocentric of sinologists could possibly justify writing about China in any language other than classical Chinese. Doesn't this state of affairs reenact exactly the problematically bifurcated nature of that nineteenth-century Chinese dictum vis-à-vis the West—zhongxue wei ti, xixue wei yong (Chinese learning for fundamental structure, Western learning for practical use)? China historians may criticize the conservatism of this dictum for retarding China's progress into the modern world, but aren't those who opt for a "sinocentric" approach to China repeating this conservatism themselves?

This problem becomes especially acute as students of Chinese culture attempt to articulate issues in their field by using the tools of "Western" concepts and theory they have learned. Consider the example of twentieth-century Chinese literature. In his book Chinese Theories of Literature, James J. Y. Liu explicitly refrains from discussing this period because it is Westernized:

> I shall not deal with twentieth-century Chinese theories, except those held by purely traditionalist critics, since these have been dominated by one sort of Western influence or another, be it Romanticist, Symbolist, or Marxist, and do not possess the same kind of value and interest as do traditional Chinese theories, which constitute a largely independent source of critical ideas.[29]

The message is loud and clear: twentieth-century Chinese literature is too polluted by the West to merit discussion. On the other hand, however, should one attempt to read modern Chinese literature by means of "Western" theories, one is, to this day, likely to be slapped in the face with a moralistic and nationalistic disapproval of this kind: "Why use Western theory on Chinese literature?"

To this extent, de Lauretis's notion of "imaging" — "the articulation of meaning to image, language, and sound, and the viewer's subjective engagement in that process" (de Lauretis, p. 46)—is crucial to an understanding of Chinese modernity from the point of view of the Westernized Chinese subject/reader, who is caught between the sinologist's "gaze" and the "images" of China that are sewn on the screen of international culture. Between the gaze and the image, the Chinese experience of being "spectators" to representations of "their" history by various apparatuses is easily erased. China scholars who defend with earnest intent Chinese history's claim to the status of world history help to further the erasure of this spectatorship precisely by their argument for the "adequacy" of the Chinese tradition, for this argument disregards the quotidian truth with which every Chinese person grows up in the twentieth century, the truth that this "adequacy" is not so, for "the world" does not think so. When one has been taught, as a way of survival, the practical necessity of accepting "the West" and of having good French or English, only to be confronted with the charge, from those who are specialists of one's "own" culture, that one's methodology of thinking and reading is "too Westernized," the politics implied in ethnic spectatorship cannot be more stark and bitter. Such a charge demolishes the only premises on which the ethnic spectator can see and speak — premises that are, by necessity, impure and complicitous. The notion that "China" is beautiful and adequate to itself, which arises from an act of sentimental fetishizing on the part of the Chinese, becomes for those who are professionally invested a way to justify fencing off disciplinary territories. For a "Westernized" Chinese spectator/reader, it is impossible to assume an unmediated access to Chinese culture. To use a notion proposed by Yao-chung Li, this spectator/reader is "in exile";[30] to use a notion proposed by Biddy Martin and Chandra Talpade Mohanty, this spectator/reader is "not being home." Exile and homelessness do not mean disappearance. As Martin and Mohanty specify, " 'Not being home' is a matter of realizing that home was an illusion of coherence and safety based on the exclusion of specific histories of oppression and resistance, the repression of differences even within oneself."[31] If an ethnicized reader does not simply read by affirming Chinese tradition's continuity and adequacy to itself, how might she read? How might the "Westernized" Chinese spectator be recognized?

In his illuminating study, *Time and the Other: How Anthropology Makes Its Objects*, Johannes Fabian offers many insights that are germane to our discussion. Earlier, I refer to one of them, visualism. Fabian's analysis of "visualism" is situated in a larger analysis of the uses of time in anthropology, which, as he points out, often denies "coevalness" or cotemporality between the subjects and objects of an inquiry. This denial occurs at the moment of writing, when anthropologists are away from the field, where they share an immediate present with their objects. The discrepancy between "field" time and "writing" time is, once again, encapsulated in Bertolucci's remarks that I quote at the beginning, a discrepancy that is between Bertolucci's "Yet in the meantime" and "before." While a coeval engagement with their objects "in the field" may reveal their sophistications, anthropologists slip into what Fabian calls "allochronism" in the process of writing, when shared time is replaced by a more linear, progressive use of time that enables the distinctions between "primitive" and "developed" cultures. Allochronism, the casting of the other in another time, goes hand in hand with "cultural relativism," a process in which other cultures are territorialized in the name of their central values and vital characteristics:

> Once other cultures are fenced off as culture gardens or, in the
> terminology of sociological jargon, as boundary-maintaining systems
> based on shared values; once each culture is perceived as living its

Time, it becomes possible and indeed necessary to elevate the
interstices between cultures to a methodological status. (Fabian, p. 47)

Sinology and China studies, which have significantly structured the ways we
"see" China in the West, partake of "cultural relativism" in obvious ways. Typically, "cultural relativism" works by fostering the distinction between "classical" and "modern" China. This is a distinction that shapes the structuring of
Kristeva's *About Chinese Women*, in which, "reflecting a broader Western cultural practice, the 'classical' East is studied with primitivistic reverence, even as
the 'contemporary' East is treated with realpolitical contempt."[32] The same distinction exists in Bertolucci's "making" of China; in his film the contrast between the sensuous colors of the "imperial" scenes and the drabness of the
"Communist" scenes is too sharp not to become emblematic. In different but
comparable ways, sinologists who are so much in love with the China of the
classical Chinese texts that they refrain from visiting China; who only read the
Chinese language silently as pictures but do not speak it; or who, lamenting China's "convergence" with the rest of the world, emphasize the methodological
self-sufficiency of Chinese studies in an attempt to preclude readings of Chinese
texts with non-Chinese strategies—these sinologists are also reinforcing and per-
petuating the "allochronism" to which China has been reduced among world
cultures.

Furthermore, in universities where the study of China is often part of "area
studies" programs that are made up of political scientists, linguists, anthropologists, geographers, historians, musicologists, as well as literary critics, scholastic
territorialization corroborates the bureaucratic. For, once "China" is fenced off
in this way, its "fate" is left to the grossly uneven distribution of interests and
funding between the humanities and the social sciences. While classical Chinese literature can hold on to a well-established, though isolated, tradition of
refined textual study, modern Chinese literature, marginalized against classical
hermeneutics but also against the data-yielding "China" of the social scientists,
is inevitably deprived of the necessary institutional support that would enable its
researchers to experiment with radical theoretical approaches in such a way as to
make it accessible and interesting to nonspecialists.

My somewhat personal emphasis on the necessity to change the state of affairs
in modern Chinese culture and literature has to do with my feeling that it is in
this vastly neglected area that a theory of the ethnic spectator can be most urgently grounded, as Westernized Chinese students come to terms with themselves both as objects and subjects of "seeing" China. Fabian states:

Tradition and modernity are not "opposed" . . . nor are they in
"conflict." All this is (bad) metaphorical talk. What are opposed, in
conflict, in fact, locked in antagonistic struggle, are not the same

societies at different stages of development, but different societies facing each other at the same Time. (Fabian, p. 155)

Supplementing the terms of Fabian's analysis with those of our ongoing arguments, we can say that the position of the ethnic spectator is the position of "different societies facing each other at the same Time," that is, the position of coevalness.

5

In this chapter I have introduced the problematic of "seeing" modern China from the point of view of the Westernized Chinese spectator. China exists as an "other," feminized space to the West, a space where utopianism and eroticism come into play for various purposes of "critique." Kristeva's book about Chinese women shows us how the alluring tactic of "feminizing" another culture in the attempt to criticize Western discourse actually repeats the mechanisms of that discourse and hence cannot be an alternative to it. "China" becomes the "woman" that is superfluous to the relationship between Kristeva the critic and the metaphysical entity of "the West." Bertolucci's *Last Emperor* seems a timely instance illustrating how the feminizing of another culture can be explained cogently in terms of film theory, which casts the problems in a clear light because of cinema's use of visual images. The writings of Mulvey, Silverman, and de Lauretis make it possible for us to see the initially necessary cooperation between feminism and the critique of ideology as falsehood, while indicating what that combination leaves out—the position of the female spectator, whose interpellation by as well as rejection of the screen images is crucial for an understanding of reception as a mode of performative, not merely passive, practice.

Extending the notion of the female spectator, I ask whether we cannot also begin to theorize the position of the ethnic spectator, who is caught, in a cross-cultural context, between the gaze that represents her and the image that is supposed to be her. I argue that it is by acknowledging the contradictory, complicitous reaction to a film like *The Last Emperor* on the part of some Chinese spectators—a reaction that consists in fascination as well as painful historical awareness—that we can reintroduce the elusive space of the ethnic spectator. In the realm of sinology and China studies, I propose, it is the experience of this space that is often dismissed. Instead, the study of China remains caught in the opposition between "modernity" and "tradition." While Westernization is acknowledged as an idea and a fact in history, its materiality as an indelible, subjective part of modern Chinese people's response to their own "ethnic" identity is consistently disregarded. In thus excluding from its methods of inquiry the position of the ethnic spectator who has never been and will never be purely "Chinese," sinology and China studies partake of what Fabian calls "allochronism," which is central to "a nation-centered theory of culture" (Fabian, p. 48). It is only through thinking of the "other" as sharing our time and speaking to us at the moment of writing that we can find an alternative to allochronism. The position of the feminized, ethnicized spectator, as image as well as gaze, object of ethnography as well as subject in cultural transformations, is a position for which "coevalness" is inevitable. How might the argument of coevalness affect our reading of China's modernity? What would it mean to include the "other," the object of inquiry, in a cotemporal, dialogic confrontation with the critical gaze? How might we read modern Chinese literature other than as a kind of bastardized appendix to classical Chinese and a mediocre apprentice to Western literature? The following chapters offer a set of responses to these questions.

Chapter 2
Mandarin Ducks and Butterflies:
An Exercise in Popular Readings

1. What Is "Mandarin Ducks and Butterflies"?

Modern Chinese literary history, as it is presented in the West, has, until fairly recently, been dominated by the May Fourth movement and the cultural revolution that clusters around its memory.[1] "May Fourth" is now generally understood not only as the day in 1919 when students in Beijing protested against the Chinese government's self-compromising policies toward Japan and triggered a series of uprisings throughout the country, but as the entire period in early twentieth-century China in which Chinese people of different social classes, all inspired by patriotic sentiments, were eager to reevaluate tradition in the light of science and democracy and to build a "new" nation.[2] In literature, the term "May Fourth" signifies the call for a reformed practice of writing that was to be based on *baihua*, the vernacular.[3] Following the debates among May Fourth intellectuals such as Hu Shi, Chen Duxiu, Zheng Zhenduo, and Mao Dun on the need to create an "improved" people's language and literature,[4] writers of the period experimented with a myriad of "novel" forms that took their inspiration from Western romanticism, naturalism, realism, and pragmatism. Hence the process of cultural purification, which was ostensibly iconoclastic, was instigated with the "West" as "theory" and "technology." Chinese culture itself, meanwhile, increasingly turned into some kind of primitive raw material that, being "decadent" and "cannibalistic," was urgently awaiting enlightenment.[5] There was not a better indication of this cultural ferment than the frequency with which the word "new" (*xin*) appeared as a sign of change: "new youth," "new

34

fiction," "new literature," "new woman," "new times," "new China," and so on. This desire for the new quickly acquired the force of an ideological impera- tive that successfully rationalized China's contact with the West. In one of his discussions of the May Fourth movement as a Chinese cultural revolution, Hu Shi concludes: "Without the benefit of an intimate contact with the civilization of the West, there could not be the Chinese Renaissance."[6] In the word "ben- efit," the Chinese predicament of the twentieth century is concisely summed up. According to the arguments of cultural revolutionaries like Hu Shi, the new or the "modern" is not only absolutely necessary but also good. And, it is good because it comes from the West.

The breakdown of traditional Chinese culture is thus self-imposed as much as it is coerced through China's relations with the outside world. We must now view the eagerness of May Fourth leaders like Hu Shi as the sign of desperation among a particular class that was traditionally appointed the guardian of its so- ciety, and which conceded perhaps too naively to seeing China's problems in terms of its *inferiority* to the West. The open and willing espousal that resulted, the espousal of the Western as the "new" and the "modern," and thus the "civ- ilized" (*wenming*), meant the beginning of a long process of cultural imperialism that was to last beyond China's subsequent retrieval of its leased territories and official concessions.

But if the modernization of Chinese culture has been part and parcel of im- perialism, the condemnation of which has become an ethical platitude in the late twentieth century, the subtle ramifications of imperialism are most actively with us today in the form of established cultural history, where residual,[7] mate- rial specificities are smoothed over for the sake of "major" landmarks that are upheld as "epochal" and thus representative. The May Fourth movement, how- ever contradictory and complex its developments might have been, now stands in modern Chinese literary history as a primary event, a historic watershed be- tween the old and the new Chinas. As a topic that is amply researched within modern Chinese studies, the periodization "May Fourth" thus exists as the syn- onym for "modern Chinese literature": its problems function as signs of Chinese literature's "modernity"; its theories and experiments testify to a Chinese literary "modernism." What such a periodization emphasizes is the alignment of Chi- nese literature to a "world" status through "modernity," while "premodern" Chinese literature continues to remain in the esoteric realm of "sinology."

The issues of "modernity" and "modernism" in Chinese literature, however, have to be rethought precisely because they are bound up with imperialism. Could "modern" here be strictly the "new"? Progress from Oriental primitivism to the enlightenment of Western science and democracy? Cultural renaissance? Or could it be the process whereby all such concepts are parochialized as they are confronted with a culture that seems persistently subversive of their recognized rhythms of development? Could "modernity" in China be in fact a depletion of the usefulness of forms both "old" and "new," because the old have lost their relevance and the new have been applied from without? As an approach to these problems, the culturally monumental status of May Fourth literature as representative of "modern" Chinese literature must be resituated in a historical context of multiple forms of writings, which in turn gave rise to distinct modes of reception.

During the first three decades of the century, both before and after the May Fourth movement and its related progressive motifs became popularized and, as it were, nationalized, a large number of "old school" novelists produced an extremely popular body of fiction by adhering to more traditional styles. These writers are known collectively in history as the "Mandarin Duck and Butterfly School" (yuanyang hudie pai), and their writings, "Mandarin Duck and Butterfly literature" (yuanyang hudie pai wenxue, abbreviated to "Butterfly literature" in the following discussions). This hilarious name was first used to refer to Xü Zhenya's Yü li hun [Jade pear spirit], a bestseller published in 1912. Written skillfully in classical parallel prose, which consists of rigidly stylized parallel sentences made up of either six or four characters, Xü's novel is strewn with sentimental poems in which lovers are compared to mandarin ducks and butterflies. A related series of jokes and rumors among some writers of the period resulted in the use of "Mandarin Duck and Butterfly" as a pejorative label for the authors of this type of sentimental love story.[8] These writers included Xü, Li Dingyi, Wu Shangre, and a few others.[9]

During the twenties, as the May Fourth movement gathered momentum, the label "Mandarin Duck and Butterfly" was used generally to attack all types of old-style fiction that continued to enjoy popularity. "Butterfly" fiction henceforth included not only the love stories but also "social" novels, "detective" novels, "knight-errant" novels, "scandal" novels, "ideal" or "fantasy" novels, "comic" novels, "legendary" novels, and others. This broader definition of the label remains the one adopted by Chinese Communist critics today, while non-Communist writings tend to adhere to its narrower definition as "love stories" only. My discussions will concentrate on the narrower definition, but in such a way as to show that the predominant structures of the love story reveal meanings that are, on close reading, not simply romantic.

In his study of Butterfly literature, E. Perry Link analyzes the development of Butterfly literature according to "waves." Each wave indicates "a sudden increase in both number of stories and number of readers,"[10] but we should also remember that "waves were only matters of degree, . . . as every kind of story was circulating almost all the time" (Link, p. 22). Accordingly, the first major wave was the love stories (aiqing xiaoshuo) of the early teens, which thematized the freedom of marriage; an example of this would be Xü Zhenya's Yü li hun. The second wave, arising in the later teens from a general disillusionment with the Revolution and with the monarchist dictatorship of Yuan Shikai, consisted of satirical "social" novels (*shehui xiaoshuo*) such as Li Hanqiu's *Guangling chao* [Tides of Yangzhou], Western-style detective stories such as Cheng Xiaoqing's *Huosang tanan* [Cases of the Chinese Sherlock Holmes, Huosang], and "scandal" fiction (*heimu xiaoshuo*), which exposed corruption in all walks of life and which appeared most frequently in the "mosquito" papers or single-sheet tabloids such as Shanghai's *Jing bao*. The third wave, touched off by Xiang Kairan's "knight-errant" novel *Jianghu qixia zhuan* [Chronicle of the strange roving knights], consisted of novels that were generally anti-warlord in sentiment; it was most popular from 1927 to 1930.[11]

The flourishing of Butterfly fiction was part and parcel of the new cultural conditions that had sprung up in Shanghai, one of the first Chinese cities to be opened to the West in the mid-nineteenth century.[12] By the early twentieth century, Shanghai had developed into the leading attraction for Western traders. To many historians, Shanghai's entire existence was an inauthentic one. Being the largest of the treaty ports, Shanghai was distinguished not just as a modern city but also as a city of coexisting native and alien cultures: side by side with the Chinese, rural landmarks were "French cafés, British and American banks, white Russian prostitutes and massage parlors, mass dance halls, a city orchestra composed mainly of foreigners, numerous Peking opera and K'un-ch'ü theaters, gambling houses, opium dens."[13] The city's growth, which began as a result of foreign money, was accelerated particularly during the period in which foreign investments in China rapidly increased. The extent of those increases can be briefly glimpsed through the following figures: the amount of foreign capital, which was 787 million gold dollars in 1896, had reached 1,610 million gold dollars by 1914, while the number of foreign businesses on Chinese soil had soared from 499 in 1890 to 6,865 by 1923.[14] But even though the Chinese economy seemed reinvigorated by the presence of business money and various metropolitan developments, the influx of foreign capital was only to "aggravate the imbalance between the industrial centers on the coast and a huge hinterland where the conditions of life continued to deteriorate."[15] It is this kind of modernization process that leads historians like Jacques Gernet to conclude that the prosperity of the urbanized China was "artificial and deceptive," that the Chinese middle class was "a by-product of the foreign colonies in the open ports and in S.E. Asia," and that the growth of Shanghai was "like the swelling of a cancerous tumour"[16] that did not so much prove the progress made by the Chinese as it symbolized their takeover by the West.

Shanghai thus became in the eyes of many an alien China, ideologically and structurally in contradiction to the "authentic" one. This difference must be remembered especially as a conflict in historiography, whereby "Shanghai" has turned into the battleground between sinocentric biases that identify China with the rural, traditional, and thus ethnic "nationalism," and biases of "metropolitan" worlding, which look to modernization and industrialization as criteria with which to judge China as a newborn "nation." Accordingly, the Shanghai urban culture is either seen as something artificially "superimposed on a peasant civilization,"[17] or else as a success from which a new Chinese tradition that seeks integration with world civilization has since developed.[18] For the latter kind of historian, the working-class, intellectual, and internationalistic atmosphere of Shanghai was what made it a true metropolis. Indeed, "the meaning of Shanghai" or the meaning of Westernization from popular perspectives can be used as a way to interpret many Butterfly stories, in which a "traditional" ethics comes into conflict with "modernized" or *wenming* values.

The city where everyone was allowed to come and go without any passport,[19] where foreigners had their respective national settlements in which they were free from Chinese jurisdiction,[20] where opium and gambling houses flourished beyond counting, and where one person in 130 was a prostitute by 1934,[21] was also the city that saw a rapidly booming publishing business. In the first thirty years of the twentieth century, printing in Shanghai expanded sixfold.[22] By the late 1930s, Shanghai's Commercial Press was publishing each year as many titles as the entire American publishing industry, most being, of course, pirated editions.[23] Such figures give us a good idea of the "market" conditions under which Butterfly literature was produced and consumed.

Before the twenties, most of the bestselling stories first appeared in expensive fiction magazines, which numbered more than one hundred in the teens—an example of such magazines was the notorious *Libailiu*, or *Saturday*,[24] from which Butterfly fiction obtained its other label, the "Saturday School" (*libailiu pai*). As Butterfly magazines lowered their prices in the twenties, leading commercial papers also began to run daily columns that serialized some of the biggest hit novels of that decade. Two famous examples of such columns were the "Kuaihuo lin" [Forest of lightheartedness] in *Xinwen bao* and the "Ziyou tan" [Unfettered talk] in *Shen bao*. During the same period the circulation of stories was further aided by their multimedia translation into movies, comic strips, stage plays, and even scripts for traditional-style drum singing. Figures regarding publications and readership size, however, are hard to ascertain. Wei Shaochang's *Yuanyang hudie pai yanjiu ziliao* [Research materials on the Mandarin Duck and Butterfly School] lists a total of 2,215 novels, 113 magazines, and 49 newspapers and tabloids that carried Butterfly fiction.[25] To the list of 2,215 we should add, as Link suggests, serialized magazine and newspaper novels, short stories, translation novels, sequels to popular novels, and the many novels written by unknown writers pirating a famous writer's penname. Link's estimate is that the volume of published popular fiction between 1912 and 1949, including translations, must have reached the equivalent of five or ten thousand average-length (about 200-page or 100,000-character) novels. As for readership size, he estimates the most popular stories to have reached between four hundred thousand to one million people in Shanghai during the 1910s and the 1920s, the years in which the city's population is supposed to have grown from around 1.4 million to around 3.2 million (Link, p. 16).

How should we read Butterfly literature? There are three parts in my response to this question. As popular literature, Butterfly literature is heavily marked by influential readings that are themselves popular among critics and which seek to assimilate the "popular" into more familiar and epistemologically valid realms of discussion. The first part of my response thus involves a critical confrontation with some of the ways Butterfly literature has already been read. The crucial common problem presented by these readings is that of the controlling concept of "tradition," which is alternately present in the invocations of classical Chinese literature, Marxist literary criticism, or Communist revalidations of the "Chinese people." Because of their overriding preoccupation with the coherence and continuity of tradition, none of these readings offers a satisfactory means of coming to terms with the specificities of Butterfly literature, which include its rupturings of, as well as its collaborations with, existing ideologies. I believe that the preoccupation with tradition needs to be challenged through a more materialist reading of Butterfly literature. This is implied in the second part of my response: what is the relation between tradition as such and "woman"? Here, the relation between Butterfly literature as literature on the one hand, and history on the other, must be clarified. I read Butterfly literature not as a mere document of, but in itself a mediated response to, the changes taking place in China around the turn of the century. Butterfly literature's peculiar features—its urbanism, its close relations with the apparatuses of cultural production such as newspapers and magazines, its ambiguous conservatism with regard to the West—are in this way not simply "reflections" but expressions that bear the marks of contradictory historical conditions. What is most interesting, however, is that these features are frequently refracted, sentimentally and didactically, through a focus on "woman" as the locus of social change. How might a reading *by way of* "woman" produce a different understanding of Butterfly literature? Readings of sample Butterfly stories make up the third part of my response.

2. Rereading Some Popular Readings

A

Ever since the early twenties, the volume of Butterfly fiction that was produced and consumed has been equaled in magnitude by the barrage of criticisms that is launched against it. These criticisms spring not so much from the intrinsically inferior nature of Butterfly fiction, as from the difficult and controversial emergence of "literature" as an autonomous yet pragmatic sphere of activity in modern China.

At the turn of the twentieth century, Chinese literature was increasingly given the task of reforming society by discussions that centered dogmatically on the functions of literature. This functionalist orientation dates back to around 1896, the year Liang Qichao began publishing his ten-day periodical *Shiwu bao* [Current affairs journal], in which he was to write continually about the urgency of political reform. Near the back of the periodical, in the section called "Translations from English Newspapers," Liang introduced, interestingly enough, Western detective stories, including *The Adventures of Sherlock Holmes*. Whether or not detective fiction contributed to it, Liang's conviction of the efficacy of fiction was derived from his admiration for the strength of the West. He was eventually to spread this conviction in a famous article called "Lun xiaoshuo yü qun zhi di guanxi" [On the relation between fiction and popular sovereignty], which he published in his journal *Xin xiaoshuo* [New fiction] in 1902. In the article, Liang expounds the theory that fiction could extend the reader's feelings, magnify normal emotions, change ideas and attitudes, or even create all these from nothing.[26]

Following such impassioned belief in the important bearing fiction had on nation building, writers of the May Fourth period continued to strengthen the *pragmatic* approach laid down by Liang. Hu Shi, who studied in the United States, wrote about the "tools" and "methods" of literature, by which he meant a purified language, well-organized "plots," "structures," and "characters."[27] Zhou Zuoren, who was influenced by Japanese literature, emphasized the significant "relation between fiction and life," which should be expressed both in the thought and form of literature.[28] Others spoke of the need to translate Western literature and to fill literature with democracy, attacked the idea that fiction is for "passing time," and criticized Chinese writers' (*wenren*) "basic misunderstanding of literature" in general.[29]

In the 1920s the discussions of literature increasingly centered on "realism," which was to win major support from writers in the decades to come because it represented the principle that literature could not be divorced from life. In his 1922 article "Ziran zhuyi yü zhongguo xiandai xiaoshuo" [Naturalism and modern Chinese fiction],[30] Shen Yanbing (Mao Dun) criticizes traditional-style fiction for being blindly tied to either of two undesirable principles, namely, *wen yi zai dao* (literature as the embodiment of *dao* for moral instruction),[31] and *youxi* (literature as "play" or "amusement"). Accordingly, while authors holding the former view often mechanically record the teachings of the ancients, those who subscribe to the latter view tend to indulge in the description of artificial or unnatural events. Both principles, in other words, suggest to Shen a dangerous departure from "reality," which should be reflected historically and truthfully.

Shen's attitudes strongly resemble those of Georg Lukács at his orthodox, Marxian moments, when the latter's strong distaste for European modernism runs alongside his extremely perceptive analyses. Shen's criticisms of the narrative techniques of old-style fiction in China vividly call to mind, for instance, Lukács's repudiation of modernist modes of "description" in the essay "Narrate or Describe?"[32] Lukács's attacks on naturalist writings were made from the standpoint of nineteenth-century realism, which he upheld as the only genuine artistic tradition in modern times. For the serious writers of the May Fourth period, many of whom had just returned to China after studying in Europe or Japan, "realism" (which Shen in his article strangely calls *ziran zhuyi*, "naturalism"), too, was a correct artistic method to follow. From this perspective, traditional-style literature such as Butterfly fiction had to be condemned as untruthful and behind the times. Shen's central argument against the narrative method of such stories is that it is *jizhang* ("account-keeping") rather than *miaoxie* ("descriptive") — in Lukács's terms, Butterfly stories merely "describe" rather than "narrate." (Note the possible confusion arising from Shen's different use of the term "description," by which he means something similar to Lukács's "narration.") The old-style writers are said to be fond of recording every event in the most detailed manner possible, instead of analyzing actions for a proper description. To illustrate his point, Shen made up a funny example of his own. Someone rising at dawn, he says, would often be portrayed as follows:

> So-and-so opened his eyes and looked out of the window. He saw it was already dawn. Immediately he pushed aside the pillows and the blankets, sat up, put on a small padded jacket, white silk socks and pants, tied up the bottom of his pants, and then got out of bed, slipping into the slippers by the bedside.

Shen's conclusion is that a character thus portrayed is a wooden, unthinking person, whereas the true task of literature is to depict "expressions" (*biaoqing*) that would lead us into the "inner activities" (*neixin di huodong*) of what would then emerge as a living person. He goes on to say:

> The talent of real artists lies in their ability to select from various motions the important one for description, in order thus to express the described person's inner activities. Only a slice of life put on paper in this manner has artistic value. Only this is art!

For Shen, real art consists essentially in the *analysis* of events and in the *investigation* of psychology. In addition, both functions are based on "objective observation" (*keguan di guancha*), a "scientific" criterion against which the old-style writers' craft can only be condemned as "subjective invention from nothing" (*zhuguan di xiangbi xüzao*); in short, as unartistic.[33]

Shen's authoritative views are paralleled by those of another important May Fourth figure, Zheng Zhenduo. In an essay called "Xin wenxue guan di jianshe" [The construction of a new concept of literature],[34] Zheng also attacks writers who write for the *dao* or for "amusement": "Neither group knows what literature really is." The real life and soul of literature lie in "true emotions":

> Literature is the pouring of human emotions into words. It is a reflection of human life that occurs *naturally*. . . . The writer writes for nothing; the reader reads for nothing. To be more clear, *literature is literature*; it is not written nor read for amusement, propaganda, or didacticism. The writer is only writing *naturally* about his observation, feelings, and emotions; the reader is *naturally* assimilated and moved. We need not and cannot *deliberately* spread any lessons through literature. We especially cannot *deliberately* pretend to amuse readers. (my emphases)

Implicit in the May Fourth critics' embrace of disinterested realism is the theory that literature should *in itself create* the truthful social vision by capturing history in its whole. In a detailed response to a reader's inquiries about the merits of Zhang Henshui's *Tixiao yinyuan* [Fate in tears and laughter], the Butterfly bestseller of the late twenties and the early thirties, Xia Zhengnong, another writer, defines the makings of a novel of "social consciousness" in a way that once again reminds us of Lukács.[35] Zhang's novel, says Xia, has only accomplished an "accidental" juxtaposing of events, while a truly great novel should, by contrast, be able to *set off from within* "the progressing action of society." This "progressing action" is in other words the inner reality that would ultimately allow human society to move beyond its outer, temporary contradictions. Thus, in spite of its extremely realistic contents, a work like *Tixiao yinyuan* stops short of being a genuinely "socially conscious" work of literature precisely because of its lack of that "inner" historical motion.

The privilege of hindsight allows us to see that what the May Fourth theorists were clamoring for was not so much a new definition of literature as the autonomy of literature from all previously prescribed categories within Chinese history. For them, literature had to be freed from its low status as craft, and also from its subservient bondage to the *dao*. What emerged was hence the view that "literature is literature." However, as the course of history shows, this independent status of literature, which was assimilated from the readings of Western literature and infused with a Western sense of humanism, led not to an aestheticism in China but rather to the ideal of literature as a new agent for social change. And if the failure of aestheticism could be interpreted as an indication of "the exhaustion of Confucianism, premises and all" (an exhaustion that deprived aestheticism of any tension with its logical opposite, *wen yi zai dao*, and thus of its theoretical thrust, from the very first),[36] the success with which a socialist pragmatism was to be steadily combined with the newly won autonomy of literature demonstrates, paradoxically, the exhausted Confucian ideology's power to linger on. In their attacks on Butterfly literature, the May Fourth leaders came across as modern-day inheritors of the scholastic class in a society that had always revered literary scholarship far above the "professions," inheritors who were helping to continue the traditional demands on literature even as they tried to rebel against them. While the "new literature" that claimed to be rev-olutionary and nationalistic might strike one as purposeful (in rhetoric at least), the threat that Butterfly literature posed was not only that it was immoral or useless, but also that it was unexpectedly implementing a much-longed-for, democratic social reform: mass literacy. The written word, which had hitherto been the privilege of a few, was now robbed of its sanctity and abused by the vulgar masses for such improper ends! The May Fourth objections to this mass literature were hence, on close examination, conventional and traditional, for the view that literature should be related to "reality" in specific ways was at least as old as the May Fourth favorite target, *wen yi zai dao*, itself. It was the May Fourth writers' narrow view of *dao* (as lessons from the classics) that enabled them to define what they themselves were advocating as the "opposite" to tra-ditional attitudes. We need only to broaden the concept of view of *dao* to in-clude any "implicit principles," and the May Fourth writers' alleged claims to free literature from *dao* would, by logic, collapse. The *dao* that literature was asked to embody this time included the Western literary principles of individu-alism, romanticism, objectivity, scientific analysis, naturalism, and so forth. More important, *dao* now took a negative form: it was the principle that litera-ture must *not* embody any *dao* but must be given an independent value of its own. [37]

B

In the contemporary attempts to reinterpret Butterfly literature, it is, once again, this "independent value" of literature that constitutes the core of the problem, often in spite of the authors' explicitly stated intentions. These con-temporary attempts may be classified in terms of two types of approaches — the "literary" and the "sociological."

The "literary" approach, as is shown in the *Renditions* "Special Issue on Mid-dlebrow Fiction" (1982),[38] specializes in tracing Butterfly fiction back to themes and techniques in traditional Chinese literature. Butterfly fiction is defined as the latter-day successor to a long tradition of colloquial storytelling that dates back to the Tang Dynasty, when storytelling took its origins from a then-popular type of Buddhist sermon. Liu Ts'un-yan, the guest editor for the special issue, writes in his introduction:

There is no doubt that many elements of Buddhist literature influenced and enriched Chinese popular fiction, particularly tales of combat between various celestial beings, and the individual characters of a host of originally Buddhist deities. . . .many of the ritual conventions and stereotypes followed by the Buddhist sermons and recorded in their texts found their way into Chinese popular fiction in the form of inserted eulogizing verses, *gathas*, as did traditional poetry and other literary forms.[39]

Liu then mentions the most notorious example of such Buddhist influences, the classic expression of the Chinese storyteller in what is known as the *zhang hui ti*, or the "linked-chapter" form: "If you wish to know what happens next, you are welcome to hear my next exposition." Coined after the style of the Buddhist serialized sermon, the formula continued to be used by traditional-style colloquial fiction well into the twentieth century.

Calling works of Butterfly literature "milder tonics for enlightenment or relaxation,"[40] Liu and his fellow writers in that special issue nonetheless succeed in establishing a great sense of continuity between Butterfly fiction and the rest of Chinese literature. And yet, if continuity is indeed an inevitable fabrication by literary historians regarding their fields of study, we still need to ask in what ways it is established. In this case, the continuity of Butterfly literature is established through a hierarchical organization of the objects under investigation, so that some are "better" than the others. It is not an accident, therefore, that the predominant metaphor that organizes Liu's piece is that of "heights":

> As far as content is concerned, we cannot expect these works to depict in detail the struggle of individuals with the world around them, the eternal problems of human relationships or timeless moral perplexities. These things were beyond their time and environment. But within their confines, and comparing them with works of similar nature produced by their contemporaries in other lands, I would say that they are unsurpassed in their own way. When we choose the word "middlebrow" to describe them, we mean only that they belong to the rank *below the very highest*.
>
> *The very highest* model of imaginative writing in the Chinese context remains Ts'ao Hsüeh-ch'in's unfinished *Dream of the Red Chamber*. . . . Nearly all the authors discussed in this volume shared an admiration for Ts'ao Hsüeh-ch'in. But none of them scaled his *heights*.[41]

Butterfly fiction, referred to throughout as "middlebrow" fiction, is then at best second best, and merits attention as "social history."[42]

The notion that popular literature is fit primarily for the understanding of social history is a notion that follows logically from the early twentieth-century May Fourth clamor for literature as an autonomous sphere of activity. The ascendency of literature to its tautological uprightness ("literature is literature") means that those works of fiction that fail to measure up to specific standards have to be rechanneled in a different way and attributed a different function. What is not purely "literary" now conveniently belongs to "social history," a field of study designed for the messy and unclassifiable. The really "good" works from this second best group, however, must be carefully rescued and reinserted into the canon. In C. T. Hsia's study of Xü Zhenya's *Yü li hun*, which he titles "an essay in literary history and criticism," we sense precisely the restorative urgency of the "literary" approach.

Hsia begins his eloquent essay by pointing out that the general inferiority of Butterfly literature has always been taken for granted, and that the long-entrenched prejudices of the May Fourth critics who have pronounced on Butterfly fiction with "undisguised ridicule and scorn" cannot be removed simply by a sociological understanding of it as "fiction for comfort" (Hsia, p. 200). He is thus discrediting from the start the work of Perry Link, to which I will turn in a moment. Hsia's blatant elitism aside, this opening pronouncement succinctly marks the difference between the "literary" and "sociological" approaches, and serves as a pointer to the methodological problems we face repeatedly in studying Butterfly literature.

In an effort to introduce Xü Zhenya's work as a scholarly achievement, Hsia calls it "one of the most outstanding Butterfly novels" (Hsia, p. 200), a claim he then substantiates through an erudite overview of the "long sentimental-erotic tradition" in Chinese literature (Hsia, p. 201). The literary historian's writing is most striking in its profuse use of a social Darwinist rhetoric of eugenics, which is translated in this context into the rhetoric of artistic value:

> Given the *scarcity* of good fiction in any given age and culture, we can
> safely assume that the majority of the latter [Butterfly novels] are as
> unworthy of serious attention as the majority of Ming-Ch'ing novels,
> but it is not unrealistic to expect that *the most outstanding* Butterfly
> novels . . . may not compare unfavorably with *the best* of Ming-Ch'ing
> novels in artistic worth, and may command comparable interest as
> intellectual and historical documents of their time. Instead of treating
> them *merely as a species of popular literature* (after all, what are the
> classic Chinese novels if they are not works that have achieved
> enduring popularity through the centuries?), we should be prepared to
> examine *the best* Butterfly novels. . . . we should be as fair-minded
> about these works as we have been about *the best* of the Ming-Ch'ing
> novels. (Hsia, p. 200; my emphases)

With *Yü li hun* being cogently defined as "a tragic novel of love" (Hsia, p. 200) that is the culmination of the long and proud sentimental tradition, Hsia steers his arguments clear of the vulgar social facts of the Shanghai commercial book market, with which the tremendous success of Xü's works was, to a large extent, significantly related:

> Far from being a commercial product exploitative of the sentimental
> clichés of the past for the amusement of the public, *Yü-li hun* owed its

tremendous popularity to its astonishing emotional impact upon the
educated reader of its time, and its equally astonishing literary
virtuosity. (Hsia, p. 201)

"Enduring popularity" is therefore unquestionably equated with "emotional
impact" on the "educated reader" and with "literary virtuosity"—reasons that
lead Hsia to conclude that Xü's work "should be rescued from oblivion and restored to a position of honor in the sentimental-erotic tradition of Chinese
literature" (Hsia, p. 203).

This highly ceremonious attempt to "restore" suggests that what is restored is
not the popular work but the proclaimed tradition itself, to which Xü's story now
becomes the latest addition of "individual talent." The tradition may be modified, but will remain intact. It is precisely this unswerving faith in the continuity
of tradition, which to Hsia *must* appear in certain forms, that makes him identify
some of the most interesting aspects of a work like *Yü li hun* as unsatisfactory
rather than disruptive. For instance, in analyzing the strangely restrained behavior of the lovers in the book, Hsia complains of their inability to break down
with genuine physical passion for each other. Looking to Shakespeare and
Goethe as his models, Hsia implies that the Chinese lovers are inferior to
Romeo and Juliet, or Werther and Charlotte:

We may say of *Yü-li hun* that it would have been a work of greater truth
and power if its lovers, who are much more in love, had on rare
occasions yielded to caresses under the power of their emotion. (Hsia,
p. 235)

This example of Hsia's reading reveals not only the naive assumption of a
Western-educated Chinese literary scholar who seems to think that the expression of passion should be universally alike—that is, through the "Western"
mode of "spontaneity"—but also his learned, cultured biases for the canonical.
These biases prevent him from registering the melodramatic excesses of the lovers in Xü's novel, excesses that take the form precisely of physical restraint (a
point to be discussed in detail in my readings below), as constitutive of a way of
signification that requires attention of another kind. Hsia's dissatisfaction with
Yü li hun's failure to be properly tragic explains why, much as he does seem to
think highly of the novel, his ultimate description for it is the "Chinese equivalent of the Gothic novel" (Hsia, p. 225), a genre that is always studied with
"sociological" rather than "literary" interests in the West. In making this connection, Hsia is reintroducing the problems his argument tries to ignore from the
very first. If the value of *Yü li hun* lies in its Gothic-like preoccupation with questions of etiquette and morality, and with society's sickness and decay, then how
is it that a "sociological" reading such as Link's should be discredited, and that
his own rescue attempt has been based on the "literary tradition" alone?

C

In coming to terms with Butterfly literature, Communist Chinese critics, following the post-1949 official doctrine of constructing a "people's China," have largely sidestepped the issues of the strictly "literary" tradition. For, as feudal China is "literati-China or the China of formal intellectual expression," the people's China is "the China of material culture." Against feudal China's "literary" emphases, which made up the previous oppressive "superstructure" that was Confucianism, Communist literary historians, like their colleagues in archaeology, herbal medicine, or popular science, are concerned instead with unearthing tangible materials that would reflect the life of the "Chinese people" in the past.[43] In the two currently standard critical anthologies of Butterfly literature from the mainland, *Yuanyang huidie pai yanjiu ziliao* [Research materials on the Mandarin Duck and Butterfly School] and *Yuanyang huidie pai wenxue ziliao* [Materials on Mandarin Duck and Butterfly literature], the editors explain their work as a way to understand the economic or material "infrastructure" of Chinese society. Butterfly literature is hence defined as the literary manifestation of a particular period in history (*yiding lishi shiqi chuxian di yizhong wenxue xianxiang*), that is, the semifeudal and semicolonial ambience of early twentieth-century China.[44] The restoration of Butterfly fiction is now part of the ongoing reproof to the idealism of feudal culture and an attempt to record "comprehensively" (*quanmian*) the developments of movements, thoughts, debates, and societies in modern Chinese history. The editors thus feel obligated to collect materials, both positive and negative, which were neglected in the past.[45] The emphatic claims to be "scientific," which are said to be in accordance with the "historical materialist" principle to reflect the reality of history "truthfully," become in this way inseparable from the idealist constitution of a "people's tradition."

It is in the light of this kind of materialist idealism that Link's book, *Mandarin Ducks and Butterflies: Popular Fiction in Early Twentieth-Century Chinese Cities*, should be understood. The first book-length study of Butterfly fiction to appear in English, Link's work will, I am sure, continue to be of invaluable use for its ample and conscientiously documented historical data. In discussing the "sociological" methods of his work, what I aim to do is not to slight the admirable scope of his research, but to reveal the unconsciously imperialistic effects of his approach.

In spite of their vastly different strategies, Link's project, like Hsia's, can be called "restorative." The objects to be restored are, however, not quite the same. Whereas Hsia is keen on redeeming the outstanding work of Butterfly literature in order to reaffirm tradition, Link's object of interest is "knowledge." Beginning his book with contemplations on the significance of *min* ("people") in modern Chinese thought, Link explains his research in terms of the need for the "unmediated access to the views of the non-elite" (Link, p. 4). Pleading that "we must now ask what is known, or knowable" about the ideas and attitudes of China's non-elite classes in the early twentieth century (Link, p. 5), he sees his own work as an attempt "to understand" those ideas and attitudes "through the study of the urban popular fiction which boomed during those decades" (Link, p. 6).

The abundance of historical data, much of which includes figures and statistics, must be seen within this assumption about "knowledge," to which the historically obscure is now thought to "contribute." Butterfly fiction is thus more or less neutralized as transparent documents that give us the "truth" of its period: it "expressed genuinely felt concerns of its readership,"[46] and, like popular fiction in general, existed as the "midwife for new ideas" (Link, p. 229). The problematic nature of this argument lies not only in its romantic search for the intrinsic truths about the Chinese, but also in its identification of those truths as *ideas*. Knowledge is constituted when the historian successfully rediscovers these ideas through traditionally neglected "records."

Butterfly fiction is now restored as the handmaiden of truths that are always there, and the truths, not the handmaiden, are what matter. The handmaiden is cast in terms of uses or "functions," among which are those of "blunting" the threat of Westernization, "soothing" a reader's worries about social status, and "introducing" readers to modernization (Link, pp. 20–21, 128). In sum, these functions fall into two broad categories: that of *testing* new ideas, and that of *amusement*. The "truths" that we learn through Butterfly literature are therefore the "ambivalences" in the Chinese attitudes toward modernization.

But while Link's point about the ambivalences in Butterfly literature should be well heeded, it must not be confused with his facile conclusion therefrom, that is, that these ambivalences (identification and rejection; actual and ideal behavior, etc.) are ultimately manageable as a unity, the unity in a "contradictory pose" (Link, p. 235). It is this view that sustains Link's central argument that Butterfly fiction is a "fiction for comfort": the Chinese readers' identification with pro-Western tendencies is ultimately just a matter of "stylishness," while their rejection of the West remains at the "deeper level" (Link, p. 20). Not surprisingly, Link's concluding statement about Butterfly literature is earnestly medicinal: "It seems reasonably clear that the greatest service of this fiction was, in several ways, to make people feel better" (Link, p. 235). With this unabashedly utilitarian stroke, the whole corpus of decadent Butterfly literature is converted into "how-to" guides in modern Chinese life.

I have called the implications of this sociological approach to Butterfly literature "imperialistic" because, in an apparently well-intentioned attempt to salvage canonically obscure materials, the historian seems only to have neutralized those materials for the extension of that empire called "knowledge," which is forever elaborated with different "national" differences. This means that the specificities of a complex cultural form would always be domesticated as merely "useful" by a method that claims to be scientifically objective simply because it is backed up by "factual" data.

This "factual" method, however, also uses the by-no-means factual category of psychological needs to explain the existence of popular fiction: "If modern work routines created time for fiction reading, they also appear to have created part of the need for it" (Link, p. 197). At its worst, the "psychological" explanation dwindles into a nostalgia for the "natural": the lovers in Butterfly stories are "in tune with the immanent ways of nature. Their closeness to nature gives them a purity which sharply contrasts with the confusion and complexity of modern life" (Link, pp. 199-200). The power of the "psychological" explanation lies in this case in its appeal to universal human truths. Because of this, the picture of Butterfly fiction that emerges from Link's work is that it is, after all, just a *conservative* vindication of the official ideology. Link emphasizes this by drawing on traditional vernacular fiction, in which the element of "protest" often signifies not the attempt to overthrow the Confucian value system itself, but a criticism from below of the abusers of power, who should be treating the abused with fairness within what is basically "the same value system."[47] Because human psychology is, for Link, the same regardless of class or time, protest is necessarily deemed to be "remedial" rather than "radical."[48] The Confucian system thus turns into the "nature" that the historian, in spite of his pro-Communist materialist-idealist sympathies, ironically seeks after.

That popular literature is "remedial protest" coheres with Link's view that reading popular fiction is a kind of anxiety-management operation. And, just as reading Butterfly literature equips its contemporary readers with technical, moral, and philosophical "know-how," so Link's rereading of Butterfly literature would lead, not to a radical disruption of Chinese literary history, but to certain additions of knowledge. "History" continues to be progressive enlightenment, a process in which even the most obscure material awaits restoration as "knowable" truth.

The discourse of objective historical knowledge remains incapable of dealing with the specifically "formal" elements of Butterfly stories themselves. When Link discusses individual works and authors, he falls back on the conventional terminology of aesthetic judgments in spite of his overtly nonliterary orientation. To explain the formal characteristics of Butterfly stories, Link refers to a set of features, all of which he italicizes in his text as a way of highlighting their import. These include "*readily understandable form*," "*predominance of action*," "*immediate pursuit of interest*," "*predilection for the weird or unexpected*," "*pretense of truth*," "*primacy of character*," "*division into sympathetic and unsympathetic types*," emotions that are "*familiar*," and "*absence of the disquieting*," a phrase he takes over from Q. D. Leavis (Link, p. 185). The traditionalism of Link's aesthetics is particularly revealing when he discusses writers in terms of their literary gifts. Of Xü Zhenya's fiction, for example, he says that "there is no doubt that a peculiar kind of genius was necessary to produce it" (Link, p. 51). What this means is that Xü had "an unusual sensitivity to human psychology" and "remarkable ability with words," and that his stories are invested with "heightened poignancy" (Link, p. 51). In Zhang Henshui's *Tixiao yinyuan*, he sees an ingenuity of "plot" (Link, p. 35) that accounts for the novel's success. Of Zhang, Bao Tianxiao, and Chen Shenyan, he says that they had an "unusual gift of being able to describe ordinary events in daily life and make them seem lively and interesting" (Link, p. 181); of Bao especially, that he cultivated "fluency, ease, and clarity," combining these qualities with "a keen eye for vivid detail," resulting in a style that is pleasant and "life-like" (Link, p. 182).

In underlining Link's aesthetic terminology, I am not necessarily invalidating its relevance; my point is rather that the uncritical attempt to see popular literature as more or less transparent documents of sociological knowledge inevitably runs up against the problems of literature's opacity or constructedness. The need to attend to this opacity or constructedness, in other words, could be avoided only insofar as it would then resurface in the most conventional form: the scientific rigor of Link's "sociological" project, confronted with the artfulness of the stories themselves, is forced to resort to the tools of, say, Anglo-American New Criticism, which are adopted unproblematically as the "natural" way of discussing the "formal." Ironically, then, in spite of the drastically different approach he takes, it is when Link attempts to deal with the specifically "literary" aspects of Butterfly literature that his arguments most closely resemble Hsia's. A critical discourse couched in criteria such as "literary gifts," "intensity of mood," "lyrical ingenuity," "cleverness of plot," and so on, even as Link emphasizes the "sociological" interest of Butterfly fiction, means that the fundamentals of a sociological approach *as such* do not really differ from those of the "literary." And, as such, Link proves the point Hsia tries to make before launching his own literary recuperation, namely, that a sociological understanding of Butterfly fiction as "fiction for comfort" is hardly designed to remove the long-entrenched prejudices against it since the days of the May Fourth movement.

3. Reading by way of "Woman"

If there is one thing that unifies the various types of criticisms above, it is the neglect of the question of woman. This does not mean, of course, that the critics under discussion fail to notice that there are women characters in Butterfly stories, but rather, that the issue of women does not become for them a point of rupture, an opening into a different type of reading. Women may be mentioned, but only under the "larger" headings of history, society, tradition, and the like.

For instance, a standard description of Butterfly literature is that it consists of sentimental stories centering on the unfulfilled love between scholars (*cai zi*) and beauties (*jia ren*). These stories are typically summarized as follows: "Boy meets girl, boy and girl fall in love, boy and girl are separated by cruel fate, boy and girl die of broken heart."[49] What is thought to be the core of the matter is therefore, rather unproblematically, "the balanced reciprocity of the romantic relationship between lovers."[50] However, the details that remain strangely unaccounted for are, among other things, the melodramatic deaths of many of the women characters, which constitute what are generally and imprecisely summed up as "sad endings." The thing that is not mentioned is that "love" in these stories is more often than not a mere engagement between couples who have never met, or an arranged marriage in which the husband dies before the marriage is consummated, or the adolescent passion of couples who are separated for most of their lives after having made a secret engagement on their own. In the majority of cases, these stories are not about the "balanced reciprocity" of love relationships but about issues of morality, chastity, and the social demands to resist personal passions, especially from the point of view of the women involved. This is probably why, though it is rarely if at all remarked on by critics, these "love" stories often take place in the consistent absence of the women's beloved, who "participate" only by being weak, sick, dead, far away, or a foreigner untouched by Confucian culture. The women are left to struggle alone in the main parts of the dramas. For them, "love" is not a cherished state of being endowed with the meaning of a "completed" life; it is rather a disaster that befalls them in a world in which they are supposed to live by hiding not only their minds, but also their bodies—in short, a world in which their public, positive appearances are often concomitant with their own physical absence or destruction.

Once the interpretative focus is shifted to women, the criticisms that are traditionally made about Butterfly literature become themselves problematic. Take for instance the charge that Butterfly literature is mere "entertainment," and that its authors were passive and lazy, pandering to the low tastes of the public. Why are such qualities objectionable? What general cultural associations do they conjure up? A departure from serious nationalistic concerns, an indulgence in the subjective and physical aspects of life, and in improper and immoral modes of behavior? Pretty soon a cluster of discourses that surround the denigrated aspects of feminine sexuality and emotionality, and that conflate the authors with their narratives, emerge in the powerful denunciations of this popular literature.

Because what is at stake is not simply the neglect of woman, but the neglect of woman in the battle among various critical discourses for the hegemony to consolidate the Chinese tradition, to invoke "woman" as a strategy for critical reading is a complex task. What is required goes beyond pointing out that women's issues are consistently being elided or normalized under "bigger" concerns such as reform and revolution, even though such elisions and normalizations are still commonly the case among Chinese intellectuals and China scholars today. Crucially, the use of "woman" needs to become a tool of formal analysis that would unsettle the very notion of "tradition" itself. In the case of Butterfly literature, "woman" allows for a fundamentally different formulation of what seem to be well-understood relations between "literature" and historical facts. What Butterfly literature creates is a social struggle in the very realm of reading itself, a struggle that, willy-nilly, relegates this type of literature and its authors, all of whom were male, to the position of "woman" vis-à-vis the great Chinese tradition.

The feminist historian Joan W. Scott states that gender, besides being "a constitutive element of social relationships based on perceived differences between the sexes," is "a primary way of signifying relationships of power."[51] Although gender can function as a tool of structural analysis whose terms of difference are sexually defined, what is more important, as Scott's definitions suggest, is when attention to gender alerts us to how the purely structural takes on the meanings of "relationships of power." The focus on "woman" is thus a way of foregrounding the politics of so-called structural, systemic differences, by foregrounding the oppressed existence of those who occupy the low side of the male/female opposition. As a means of formal analysis, "woman" deals not only with gender but also with the power-invested processes of hierarchization and marginalization that are involved in readings of culture. In this latter sense especially, "woman" helps reveal the deep-rooted problems in modern Chinese literary history. This does not mean that it redefines all these problems as misogynistic, but that, on the basis of the conspicuously feminine themes of Butterfly literature, it makes visible subtle connections between apparently unrelated forms of discrimination.

Let me be more specific. There are many aspects to the meaning of "woman" in Butterfly literature. The first of these pertains to an often asymmetrical narrative structure whereby women characters take up the major part of the stories. Rather than being reciprocal, relationships between men and women are simply the pretexts to situations in which women are left alone to struggle with the traumas of life. These women characters willingly resist personal desires or give up their own lives in the names of chastity and morality. This asymmetrical or *sacrificial* structure places Butterfly literature squarely within the Chinese *lie nü* ("virtuous women") tradition, which stresses obedience to unwritten as well as written laws regulating female behavior. The question is, are these popular stories then simply writings that "imitate" or "continue" traditional patterns of oppression against women in Chinese culture? If it were not for the manner in which I am asking this question, the answer would probably be a straightforward yes. And yet, if texts are not regarded merely as mechanical reproductions of real action, but themselves a form of action, then what precisely is the action given in Butterfly literature's consistent, indeed frequent, use of woman as the hinge of narrative? It seems to me that we can locate in this fascination with women a significant clue to modern Chinese society. Because women are the fundamental support of the familial social structure, the epochal changes that historians document are most readily perceived through the changing status of Chinese women. Ironically, however, it is also woman-as-hinge-of-narrative, fictional and historical, that is most often erased, abstracted, and substituted with more "normative" concepts of structure and development in the languages of criticism and investigation.

Second, one of the chief attacks on Butterfly stories is that they are traditional or feudalistic. In contrast to the May Fourth obsession with the creation of new realities, among which was the autonomy of literature, Butterfly authors did not conceive of their writings with the same kind of novelty. Accordingly, while the same May Fourth obsession paradoxically ended up prescribing to the dated practice of art and literature a functionalist role of "serving" society, Butterfly authors' works gave the impression that they were falling short of any utilitarian political purpose. Instead of demolishing the traditional through "new" perspectives such as romanticism and realism, their fiction reads more like an imitation of precisely the "dominant" ideologies at their limits, in a mode of narration that is general, sensational, redundant, and lacking in either individual protest or hope for change. Once again, I offer another way of posing the question: if indeed Butterfly literature is full of the most out-dated, incorrect ideologies, what are its contributions to a practice of reading?

At this point, it is possible to redefine our problem by borrowing from Pierre Macherey's theory of literary production. The "emergence of thought," Macherey says, "institutes a certain distance and separation, thus circumscribing the domain of the real, rendering it finite as an object of knowledge."[52] This formulation of "thought" enables Macherey to develop the relationship between criticism and literature. He does this by building on the account of the relationship between art and ideology already theorized by Althusser. For Althusser, art is, first and foremost, ideological simply because it takes its materials from history. However, by its very existence, art also creates a distance from ideology; this distance accounts for the formal specificity of art, whose effect is, for Althusser, the internal rupturing or silent staging of what it appears to present.[53] Extending the relationship between ideology and literature to that between literature and literary criticism, Macherey describes the function of criticism as what "produces" the literary work through the distance that is set up in the act of reading. Like ideology, literature is at once complete and incomplete; that is, it is a product of history that is already made, and which, in its limitedness, can be "completed" only through critical intervention.

Now, I do not think that these models of artistic and literary production are without problems. However, in the context of modern Chinese literature, I find them useful in offering a way out of the entrenched habits of naturalistic reading that make it impossible for literature to be considered beyond its strictly reflectionist function. If reading and writing involve, as Macherey's formulation of thought implies, processes of distancing and separation from what is read and written, then the problem presented by many critical accounts of Butterfly literature is precisely that the gap from which thought and knowledge arise is dismissed. Instead of seeing Butterfly writers' act of writing as what institutes a distance from feudalist ideology, most criticisms corroborate the notion that Butterfly writings *are* ideology and ideology alone. As such, alternative readings are foreclosed, and any attempt to read differently would easily look like a fabrication out of nothing.

Macherey defines the specificity of a literary work as follows:

First, that it is irreducible, that it cannot be assimilated into what it is not. It is the product of a specific labour, and consequently cannot be achieved by a process of a different nature. Furthermore, it is the product of a rupture, it initiates something new. (Macherey, p. 51)

As we have seen in the discussions in section 2, the problem inherent in the powerful popular readings of Butterfly literature is that they often seek to assimilate it into tradition, either in the form of the Chinese literary canon, or in the form of the "Chinese people." What accounts for Butterfly literature's irreducibility, on the other hand, is that it is itself already a *reading* of modern Chinese society and its ideologies. As a form of labor, this reading is stylized in specific ways: it repeats much that is extremely familiar (ideological, feudalistic); it often closes with a set of morals that warn against Westernization and that support traditional Confucian thinking; it employs recognizable conventions of storytelling as its techniques of transmission. These are not, to my mind, merely formal features that Butterfly literature inherits from or shares with premodern Chinese narratives. More interestingly, they produce the effect of a silent display of, or a problematic nostalgia for, that which no longer "is": "tradition." If there is something obvious and ideological about Butterfly literature, as the charge that it is feudalistic implies, the obvious and ideological are already part of what Macherey calls the "parodic" function of literature (Macherey, p. 53). This parodic function means that literature cannot simply be regarded as the replica of reality but should be understood as a "contestation of language" (Macherey, p. 61).

Butterfly literature provides a wonderful instance of the parodic function particularly because of its popular and marginalized status. In the stories, we often find a collage of narratives that are split between sensationalism and didacticism, between sentimental melodrama and the authors' avowed moral intent. This crude fragmentedness produces the effect not of balance and control, but rather of a staging of conflicting, if not mutually exclusive, realities (such as Confucianism and Westernization, female chastity and liberation, country and city lives, etc.). Juxtaposed against one another, such realities produce narratives that are violent not only because of their subject matter, but more important, because of their mannerisms, which implicitly undermine what they consciously uphold in "content," i.e., a Confucian attitude toward female virtue. This violence, whose theatricality ultimately strips any single reality of its claim to full authenticity, is what can then be rethought as the dispersing, demoralizing, and thus *feminizing* of Confucian culture through storytelling. In the words of Macherey, what needs to be explained in these stories is

> . . . the presence of a relation, or an opposition, between elements of the exposition of levels of the composition, those disparities which point to a conflict of meaning. This conflict is not the sign of an imperfection; it reveals the inscription of an *otherness* in the work, through which it maintains a relationship with that which it is not, that which happens at its margins. (Macherey, p. 79; emphasis in the original)

As I have been trying to show, Butterfly literature's fragmentary, parodic narrative modes have been misread by even the most sensitive critics as signs of its inferiority, its *failure* to become good "canonical" literature. To this extent, rereading Butterfly fiction is not merely an exercise in learning about the mediated nature of fictional discourse, but is crucial for deconstructing institutionalized criticism's erudite and persuasive *mishandling* of popular cultural forms. Within the hierarchy of Chinese letters, Butterfly literature thus occupies a feminized position that carries with it the irony of all feminized positions: while in its debased form it reveals the limits of the society that produces it, it is at the same time devalued by that society as false and deluded. But it is also in the marginality of such a position that the parodic function of literature is, arguably, at play in the most radical fashion. The visible "crudities" of Butterfly literature constitute a space in which the parodic function of literature is not smoothed away but instead serves to reveal the contradictions of modern Chinese society in a disturbingly "distasteful" manner.

The third aspect of the meaning of "woman" pertains to the emotional ambiguities involved in what is commonly thought of as the "traditionalism" of Butterfly literature.

The staging of female traumas in a popular, readable form means that sentimental emotions, which had hitherto been hushed up in a society that considered public demonstration of strong feelings embarrassing, were now released to untried degrees of exuberance. What used to be unutterable, "feminine" feelings were now put on a par with the heroic and patriotic, circulated, and made lucidly "available" for the first time through the mass practices of reading and writing, activities that used to belong exclusively to the highbrow scholarly world. Going hand in hand with the sentimental liberation were increasingly fragmented and commodified processes of production and consumption, which place Butterfly literature not in the "tradition" of Chinese storytelling, but in the expanding channels of mass communications that were making their way into the newly modernized Chinese cities. The serialized form in which many Butterfly stories first appeared, for instance, prefigured and coincided with new cultural forms such as film. In the manner of the cinematic montage, serialization broke up narrative continuity and replaced it with consciously manufactured types of illusion.

On the other hand, although it fully participated in the modernized processes of cultural production, Butterfly literature also incessantly gestured toward "tradition." The conscious deployment of women as figures of change becomes ambiguous in its implications when we see that change itself is often repudiated in conservative attitudes that embrace traditional values through the agent of the narrative voice. However, instead of seeing it as a simple *return to* the past, I think Butterfly literature's recurrent conservatism should be understood as part of the many wishful *reconstructions of* the past that are strewn over modern Chinese culture. The prominence of the representations of women, then, must also be situated against this overriding sense of wishfulness. In this light, the artificially recuperated continuities that surface in many Butterfly stories signify, in spite of themselves, tradition's disappearance rather than its continued existence.

4. Rereading Butterfly Stories

A

The trend of the modern Chinese love story, which for some readers is *the* Butterfly genre per se, began with Wu Woyao's (Wu Jianren) *Hen hai* [Sea of remorse], first published in 1908.[54] According to Hsia, the story "depicts the rapid degeneration of a weak-willed youth and the belated attempts by his devoted fiancée to restore him to physical and moral health. He dies, nevertheless, and she bids her parents farewell to enter a nunnery" (Hsia, p. 216).

Hsia's summary is an example of how this kind of fiction has continually been interpreted on so-called neutral but therefore imprecise grounds, as a portrayal of the love relationships between a man and a woman who both share the narrative focus. What are distorted are the female struggles that take up most of the story's actual space.[55] The "weak-willed youth" mentioned by Hsia is in fact separated from his fiancée for the major part of the story, to be reunited with her in his physically and morally degenerate state only in the last twenty pages or so, which may be described as the "climax" of the story. Hsia also fails to report that the story is about *two* engaged young couples (the two men being brothers) who are separated in the turmoil of the Boxer Rebellion (1900). When reunion finally takes place, the woman in one couple (the one mentioned by Hsia) finds that her unfaithful beloved has reduced himself to a life of opium smoking and begging. He soon dies. His brother, the faithful partner in the other couple, discovers by chance that his own fiancée has turned into a prostitute. The story ends with his lamenting the misfortunes in human fates, that is, the contrasts between his brother and himself, and between his fiancée and his sister-in-law.

Dihua, the faithful woman in the first couple, is clearly the means with which Wu Woyao explores the problem of sentiment. Sentiment as we see it in Dihua's behavior is anything but spontaneous passion: it is rather a proof of her virtues of chastity, filial piety, and faith in her beloved. The story is set up in such a way that Dihua is foregrounded, even though Bohe's absence is brought about in the most improbable manner. Evacuating from their village during the Boxer Rebellion, the engaged couple travel in a cart pulled by a mule; but as they are not yet married, Bohe decides to keep Dihua from feeling embarrassed by walking by the cart himself while she sits in it. When they are attacked by a gang of bandits, the mule runs off in another direction in fright, thus separating the couple by literally removing Bohe from the scene. Obviously crude and ridiculous, this device of separation nonetheless illustrates how essential it is for the novelist to find a way to stage the woman alone. In the events that follow, we see Dihua as the virtuous daughter and wife-to-be, taking care of her sick mother and trying desperately to contact Bohe under the most poverty-stricken circumstances.

That the love story is designed primarily as an exhibition of women is also suggested by the fact that the degeneracy of Bohe remains strangely unexplained. Disappearing when he is still a loving fiancé, sensitive to his beloved's needs (that is why he volunteers not to sit in the cart in the first place), he becomes a very different person on reappearing. The absence of any sense of tragic "inevitability" in the development of this male character serves only as another way to accentuate the permanent virtues of the ideal woman, who, unlike the man, is not changeful at heart. When she is finally hopeless, what she changes is her *style* of living: Dihua becomes a nun, in compliance with the classic Chinese fictional device for endings, which signifies at once a character's "awakening" and "resignation." In this arduous course of female melancholy and moral development, the male would only be remembered as a stage prop.

With Dihua's resolve to enter a nunnery, an interesting question arises. Given the significance of filial piety (*xiao*) in feudal Chinese morality, why is it that she would leave her own father behind for what appears to be a selfish life in nunhood? It is as if the need to prove herself "pure" sexually far overrides even the important duty to serve her own parent. This is a feature that appears again and again in Butterfly stories: as their attempts to be successful virtuous females in sexual relations fail, women characters would sacrifice their own lives *in* society before they would fulfill their filial or familial obligations. Becoming a nun is, at least in the Chinese context where pain-stricken women have traditionally found refuge in Buddhism and Taoism, not entirely separable from giving up one's own life: it is primarily a vow not to participate in the family, the basic ground for social life in China.[56] Dihua's abandonment of her father is therefore really an abandonment of her own life to the empty and colorless (*kong*) world *outside* the home. It is a sacrifice as complete as suicide. For, though the nun is physically alive, her body is supposed to be forgotten and its familially signifying, reproductive powers deadened. In an economical way, Wu Woyao's story introduces us to the ambiguities surrounding the issue of female sexuality that were to reappear in other Butterfly stories.

B

Shen Zhenniang, the beautiful woman in Li Dingyi's *Shuang yi ji* [The story of two hangings], dies a virgin in spite of two marriages. Her first, arranged marriage to Sun Zhongjian takes place while he is severely ill, in accordance with the superstitious custom that a joyful celebration would overcome an illness (*chong xi*). Her husband dies before their marriage is consummated. Zhenniang's own mother and father-in-law pass away too, leaving her alone with her wicked mother-in-law. Ignoring her continual plea to remain chaste for her dead husband, her mother-in-law secretly plots to remarry Zhenniang to a wealthy man in Shanghai as concubine. Powerless to resist and escape, Zhenniang hangs herself on her (second) wedding night. Her act moves everybody as an act of purity and courage. Reduced to poverty and sickness in the countryside, her mother-in-law also hangs herself two years later.[57]

Early in Li's story, we are told that Zhenniang, whose name in Chinese means "chaste woman," has been well versed since girlhood in the *Lie nü zhuan* [Biographies of women],[58] the earliest extant work in Chinese literature using the term *lie nü*.[59] Sometimes translated as the "Biographies of virtuous women," Liu Xiang's book actually contains biographies of both virtuous and virtueless women.[60] The misunderstanding arose from the similarity between the two Chinese characters—both pronounced *lie* and written only with a slight difference in strokes—meaning "series" (or "list") and "virtuous," respectively. It is quite certain that Liu Xiang, who believed in the importance of women for both the prosperity and adversity of a state,[61] did not intend his work to be a "mere" record of female chastity, even though his didacticism on the subject cannot be missed. In the following centuries, however, the title *lie nü* was gradually removed from its first use as "list or series of women" to "virtuous women." This historical slippage in meanings is, of course, poignant with suggestions. Not only did the *Lie nü zhuan* continue to be quoted as the original text for "correct" female behavior in China for the next two thousand years; it also gave rise to a popular genre in which the "courageous" deeds of women—especially those who committed suicide—have been glorified since. Apart from the many folk stories bearing the same title, the genre's wide acceptance by the public can also be seen in its use in the "local gazetteers" (difang zhi), the semiofficial histories of counties (xian) in which women's suicides or lifelong chastity on behalf of their dead husbands were frequently recorded in vivid detail among other "significant" events to make a particular county outstanding.[62]

This tradition of women's biographies tells us something peculiar about the mechanisms of women's subordination in China: they work by means of public celebration as well as suppression. The Chinese practices of recording, praising, and erecting shrines and arches for the lie nü are excellent examples of how the issue of ideological subordination cannot be dealt with simply from the perspectives of the hidden, the mystified, or the unspoken: it is in what we would otherwise associate as the most enlightened forms of human culture—written texts, literacy, and education—that that subordination was accomplished. Because of this long tradition of careful, erudite attention to, rather than simple neglect of, female lives, the public celebrations of women did not have to rely on unique or unusual personalities at all; the typically mundane, domestic realm proved an inexhaustible source for inspiration. Indeed, it was from the familial home that the vast numbers of lie nü were drawn: virgin daughters, faithful wives, loving mothers, filial daughters-in-law, all of whom had nothing personal to define them other than their chastity and their willingness to destroy their own lives when their families' honor was threatened. The Chinese domestic realm was hence anything but a private zone of unspeakable desires; it was precisely here that the public codes of morality were most heavily inscribed, down to a person's—especially a woman's—physical expressions. The publicly glorified lie nü were women who were taught lessons like these:

The female is to the male what water is to fire.[63]

Women should not look around while walking, not open the lips while talking, not shake the knees while sitting, not sway the skirt while standing, not laugh aloud while feeling happy, and not talk loudly when angry.[64]

Women are those who follow the instruction of man; thus do they become capable.[65]

A girl at the age of ten ceased to go out [from the women's apartments]. Her governess taught her [the arts of] pleasing speech and manners, to be docile and obedient, to handle the hempen fibres, to deal with the cocoons, to weave silks and form filets, to learn [all] woman's work; how to furnish garments, to watch the sacrifices, to supply the liquors and sauces, to fill the various stands and dishes with pickles and brine and to assist in setting forth the appurtenances for the ceremonies.[66]

Male and female should not sit together (in the same apartment), nor have the same stand or rack for their clothes, nor use the same towel or comb, nor let their hands touch in giving or receiving. . . . None of the concubines in a house should be employed to wash the lower garment (of a son). Outside affairs should not be talked of inside the threshold (of the women's apartments), nor inside (or women's) affairs outside it . . . (Even) the father and daughter should not occupy the same mat. . . .

Male and female, without the intervention of the matchmaker, do not know each other's name.[67]

Women should not group together by themselves.[68]

To die of hunger is a trifling matter, to lose chastity is a grave matter.[69]

Such quotes can continue infinitely. I have selected them according to certain perspectives that are significant for women's problems in general: myths of women's frightening sexual proficiency; control of women's bodies; prescribed male superiority; women's household obligations; sexual segregation for reasons of purity (women being naturally "unclean"); the dangers of female friendship; the demand for chastity in widowhood. In each case, the Chinese classics are stunning in their didactic explicitness: the detailed pedagogical instructions come across as definitive imperatives that are absurd but powerful and complete. What they produced was the conception of the female whose inferiority has remained proverbial to this day.[70]

This history of nuanced and careful subordination based on texts[71] seems coincident with a recognizably distinct trait among Chinese women, the overwhelming tendency toward suicide.[72] The disturbing figures obtained from contemporary statistics echo the disturbing stories and biographies recorded in traditional *lie nü* literature. Whether the apparent increase in female suicides in modern times[73] is due to the worsening conditions in a society that could no longer sustain but was still tightly gripped by Confucianism remains a matter for speculation. Likewise, we may never know whether these suicides are attempts to emulate a tradition that was clearly laid down in the texts, or whether texts about women's suicides were the results of the same phenomena that had kept occurring throughout the ages. One thing, however, is clear. In a tradition in which the oppression of women is so cogently elaborated through texts, the very instruments of general cultural literacy, the problematization of such oppression must seek other means than a mere reliance on "enlightened" understanding through education. In this respect, the formally excessive, oftentimes vulgar, elements of Butterfly literature take on significantly subversive meanings.

The fantastically oppressive world of Li Dingyi's story focuses our attention on the enigmatic and troubling relations between "texts," literacy, and women's lives. On the almost incidental detail about Zhenniang's education in the classics and the *Lie nü zhuan* hangs a whole cluster of questions regarding Chinese women's existential agency. We would not be exaggerating if we say that it is because Zhenniang is so well-versed in books that she chooses (of her "own free will") death over remarriage. The question that persists from a feminist point of view is: Why does her own life matter so little to her? Is this a specifically female issue, or is this not in fact an issue pertaining to the ramifications of Chinese culture in general, which has caught our attention here in its most palpable, most terrible form—the difficult lives of Chinese women? If the latter is correct, then what can we say about the predominance of "female" content in Butterfly literature?

To theorize the critical import of this predominant content, it is necessary to recognize the ideological horizons against which it emerges. Here, one of these horizons is Confucianism, in the form of interlocking *social* as well as written texts: customs, rules, taboos, and a tightly structured extended-family system in which one constantly runs up not against "God," but against other watching, listening human beings. The ubiquitous nature of Confucianism as a monitoring social system that encompasses all aspects of Chinese cultural life means that "individual" ontological freedom, which remains to this day a valid source of resistance against systemized ideology in the West, is much more difficult to establish in China. Individual "psychology," together with a sense of the rightful priority of one's own physical existence and personal interests, is, strictly speaking, irrelevant. Accordingly, when ideological systems (in the form of social pressures one continues to encounter within one's lifetime) turn unbearably oppressive, it is difficult, if not impossible, to use the notion of "individual truths" to subvert or counteract them. As a "well-bred" woman turns inside to "herself," she runs straight into the two-thousand-year-old definitions, expectations, and clichés of what she always already "is."

This is perhaps why so many representations of women in traditional Chinese literature seem so stereotyped, and so lacking in any deep sense of personal revolt in the direction of life. Conventions preside everywhere, from the onset of tragedies to their resolutions. Instead of encountering revolutionary subversiveness, we are confronted again and again with what appear to be conservative assertions of Confucian culture, which often assume the form of an author's explicitly avowed moral intent to teach his readers a lesson "through" the sorrowful tales of "liberated love." But more important and interesting is how this lesson is conveyed. Often, the dangers of "liberated love" are really the dangers of a female sexuality that departs, or has the chance to depart, from traditional mores. *The conservatism in Butterfly literature hence appears specifically in relation to the woman's body.* In Li's story, Zhenniang is confronted with a choice between nightmares on her second wedding night: should she "lose her body" (*shi shen*, the Chinese euphemism for "being deflowered"), or should she die (*shen wang*)? The trauma of the "love" story consists in a test of the woman's morality against society's requirements, which are fundamentally sacrificial. While readers may be amazed to see Zhenniang willing to devote her whole life to her first husband's memory when she hardly even knows him, it is only when she has been properly sacrificed (in lifelong widowhood, or else in death) that a woman can become a respectable model for others to emulate.

The issue at stake in reading *Shuang yi ji* is not whether it "resembles" and "calls to mind" the *lie nü* tradition. The answer to that question is a definite yes. What matters, however, occurs beyond the safe establishment of this type of canonical resemblance. The airtight oppressiveness of an ideological system like Confucianism means that any alternative reading to such "recognizable" textual patterns needs first of all to overcome the habit of regarding texts as natural, transcriptive, and simply repeating what was "already" written before. Second, it needs to amplify, indeed force, the issue of the text's constructedness for a politically effective criticism. The obvious "reaffirmation" of a problematic, misogynist ideology can then be read, not as another instance of a familiar and immediately comprehensible ideological closure, but rather as a possible "rupture" and point of departure for a different discourse, signifying a distance from that ideology. However insignificant this "rupture" is, it is indispensable for fundamentally different types of questions to be asked about the relationship between ideology and popular literature.

C

Another story by Li, *Qian jin gu* [Thousand-dollar bones], takes these problems still further. Once again the story evolves through a steady deprivation of the heroine of her "protectors." The motherless heroine, Biying, lives with her father, her grandfather, and her father's concubines. She is taught the classics by a resident teacher, Zhao Mingde, whose son Diqing becomes emotionally involved with her. Biying's cousin Fangling, who is also in love with Diqing, becomes a jealous rival. A series of deaths—her father's, her grandfather's, her stepmother's (the only one of her father's concubines who is good to her)—turns Biying into an orphan. Her teacher Zhao, to whom her father entrusted the welfare of the family before his death, is also ordered to leave the house by her father's remaining concubine, who sides with Fangling.

Separated from Diqing and ill-treated by her stepmother and cousin, Biying lives miserably. Her teacher Zhao soon dies too, and Diqing must therefore leave the village to seek shelter with relatives in another town. The two young lovers become secretly engaged before his departure.

Biying is now forced by her stepmother to marry into the Zhang family. On her wedding day, she tries to cut her own throat with a pair of scissors, but fails in the attempt. Only then is she given a chance to explain the fact that she is already engaged to someone else, and allowed to return to her own home. Bearing a grudge for this incident and continuing to be greedy for the money that the sale of Biying would bring, her stepmother and cousin plot to sell her to a whorehouse. After drugging her, they transport her there while she is unconscious.

At the whorehouse, Biying is tortured by the "Madam," who uses different perverse methods to punish those who are disobedient. Biying has her palm pierced through with a nail as she refuses to obey her instructions at first, but upon the advice of another "colleague," she gives in by agreeing to entertain customers during the day, even though she would not spend the night with them. She soon becomes the most famous prostitute in the district because of her artistic and literary talents, and wins the top award in a contest for the best "public woman" (hua bang).

Through the contest she meets Xü, who is at first interested in her sexually but is then moved by her story. He negotiates with the "Madam" and rescues Biying from the whorehouse by repaying all her debts.

Another surrogate father for Biying, Xü soon dies, leaving her in the horrible household with his miserable daughter Liyun and his adulterous second wife, who is having an affair with his son, Liyun's brother. The continual oppressions that Biying and Liyun suffer from the adulterous couple finally drive them to set fire to the Xü home and escape together.

Left on their own, the two women travel to the Shanghai area, placing advertisements in the paper to look for Diqing. Another accident happens while they are staying in a hotel: a robber is caught by Biying in the act of stealing their belongings, and stabs her in the arm. A kind doctor volunteers to see to her wound, and offers the two women shelter when the hotel manager forces them to leave. But the doctor turns out to be another oppressor who is really interested in them for sex. Biying soon dies in sorrow and illness; Liyun is raped by the doctor.

Liyun finally succeeds in finding Diqing, who has tried many times to contact them in vain. Together, the two bury Biying. Liyun resolves to become a nun.

The narrator concludes with the didactic wish that China's family system be changed. But this explicit attempt to moralize only calls attention to the mediated process of the story's telling, which begins when a curious traveler stumbles upon Biying's gravestone one day. Having heard something of Biying's life from his innkeeper, who keeps after him with questions about the value of "love" and "freedom," the traveler asks to be introduced to Liyun. The story that we read, then, is the account that he heard from the nun and which he then passed onto the narrator, who now "reports" it. To further dissociate himself from what in the following would be an extremely involved telling strewn with delicious fictionalities, the narrator *prefaces* his tale by philosophizing on the meanings of love. Not only does he find love to be the most incomprehensible thing in the world, he also considers it a definite evil, which unfailingly brings with it chaos and confusion in what is like "a great flood." A person who is in love, he warns, would be so blind as to go willingly into the "eighteen-storied hell" and not awaken even in death.

The ambiguities of such a stand against love are obvious, for we immediately see that the disasters in the story are far from being caused by love alone, if at all; similarly, the narrator's own concluding wish that the family system in China be changed revealingly contradicts his opening reflections. "Love," then, is only the visible event that exhibits an oppressive reality of codified female chastity at its limits. The disastrous nature of "love" corresponds to the extent individuals, in particular women, are subjected to the control of that reality especially if they are virtuous and *cultured*. Put in another way, "love," being the expression of accidents and disasters, demonstrates the logic of the culture in a negative way: when put at stake, the culture sacrifices not itself but the individuals who challenge it, even (and particularly) if those individuals are otherwise the culture's strongest and most loyal defenders. Being "cultured," "educated," and hence "virtuous" hardly liberates one from the system; it only guarantees the system's reproduction of itself.

If "intrinsic" readings of Butterfly stories such as Li's uniformly confirm them to be "ideological," in that the self-reproductive powers of Confucian ethics they reflect seem to make any effort to undermine it improbable, it is also necessary for us to recognize in them a method of subversion that is specific to a feminized, popular perspective. This method of subversion is fundamentally *formal* in that it exceeds and violates the coherence of cultural forms from within, and replaces that coherence with dislocations, perversities, and crudities. It is in this melodramatic replay of historical realities, a replay that often includes the stance of a fictional didactic Confucianist in the narrative voice, that Butterfly stories emerge as an undermining of Confucian culture in a way that is yet distinct from the monumental iconoclasm of many May Fourth writings.

In *Qian jin gu*, the narrative is divided between an inquiring curiosity about the idea of love and a concurrent reinforcement of the oppressive social norms, between improbable events and an extremely poetic, or lucid interpretation of them. The narrator's position is that of the *obviously* conservative, as is manifested in his overtones, his philosophical summaries of the problems he sees, and the moral conventions he follows. But why does he delight so much in the vivid descriptions of *perversities* if they are "immoral"? The violence of the images and the morbidity of the incidents in the work go far beyond the work's overt didactic intentions. In tirelessly describing to us the details of suicides, the cruel and sadistic practices at the whorehouse, the lewd, animalistic nature of incestuous, adulterous relationships, the macabre surroundings of graveyards, and old, deserted homes, the narrator conjures up a compelling atmosphere of disease and entrapment, whereby even accidents seem preordained. How does a reactionary worldview that is intent on the reinforcement of Confucian ethics accommodate this indulgence in the cruel, or crude, materiality of life? We might interpret this violence—and this is not just the violence of the details themselves but the violence of the juxtaposition of the conservative, ideological economy *against* those details—in two irreconcilable ways. Either we rationalize it as the "means" with which our authors preach their more positive, moralist messages against the dangers of the social evil called "love"; or we place our interpretation on the split and on the *fragmentary* nature of the narrative as it is, without trying to integrate into a meaningful whole the pieces which are crudely juxtaposed. The first way returns us once again to a utilitarian, reflectionist view of literature; the second places us in what Macherey calls the parodic function of literature and what Walter Benjamin in a different cultural and theoretical context exemplifies as the "allegorical" reading of history.[74]

An "allegorical" reading would show us that the subversiveness of Butterfly stories lies not so much in their offering a window looking "out" to the world beyond the one in which they are situated, but rather in the *impossibility* of their narrative mode, that is, in their attempts to force together two traditionally incompatible forms of writings, storytelling and didactic treatises. The fact that Butterfly stories, in spite of their obvious didactic intentions, are held suspect by Chinese critics left and right, suggests that something is amiss in their didacticism: not that it is not there, but that it is out of place. Their didacticism is inconsistent with their lurid depictions of a macabre reality. Butterfly authors were also untrustworthy as they shamelessly regarded their own work as play (*youxi wenzhang*), as a withdrawal into the ideological leftovers of a social and political world that was collapsing but which still constituted, in broken-up forms, the materiality of a people's lives. Their fiction lacked that urgent sense of a complete break with the past, and contradicted the optimism of a liberated and enlightened China. But through them we see a very different *kind* of subversion at work—a subversion by repetition, exaggeration, and improbability; a subversion that is parodic, rather than tragic, in nature.

The fragmentary quality of these stories—"fragmentary" not only because they are episodic rather than tightly plotted, but also because they demand interpretations that are powerfully at odds with one another—means that what they evoke is necessarily a *critical*, and not simply "appreciative," response. This makes them a politically useful way of understanding the problems that accounted for their conception and production in the first place. In other words, this critical response is an awareness not only of what social problems the stories "reflect" or "criticize," but also of how their modes of presentation and contradictions relate to the society that gives rise to those problems and which at the same time censors their representation in this particular form. Before we reject these stories as trash, we must consider what it is that seems to constitute their trashiness. To give one example, consider the often unbelievable sense of fatalism on the part of the characters in these stories. Why do women characters so often interpret suicide as the necessary way out of their trouble? Why do they not value the life they have? From a more prevalent aesthetic point of view, much of the "trashiness" of Butterfly literature seems to arise primarily from a missing sense of "inevitability" in the stories' construction. But, instead of corroborating Butterfly literature's dismissal, can the feeling of disbelief perhaps be the beginning of a productive understanding of Butterfly literature's historical and political meanings? A mode of narration that invites disbelief by inflating a society's addictive ideologies (such as fatalism) to such melodramatic proportions is fundamentally dangerous for that society, which relies on its members' *earnest*, *serious*, and thus *appropriate* involvement with what they read, learn, and study. Butterfly stories' frank operation as mere play, entertainment, weekend pastime, and distraction from "proper" national concerns, meant that they had to be exorcised not because of their subject matter (which is much more homespun than most May Fourth literature) but because of their deliberately fictional stance, their absolute incompatibility with the modern Chinese demands for "reality," personal and social. The excessive images of a story like *Qian jin gu* live on as an inexplicable dream for an enlightened Chinese mind, hauntingly recognizable but rationally suppressed.

D

The novel that became representative of the Butterfly love stories in the first two decades of the Chinese Republic and which subsequently earned its author the title "Master of the Butterfly School" (*yuanyang hudie pai dashi*) was Xü Zhenya's *Yü li hun*, first published in 1912. The total sales of the story, which first appeared in a serialized form in the entertainment section of the *Min chuan bao* [People's rights journal], are estimated by most critics and historians to have been in the hundreds of thousands, including reprintings in Hong Kong and Singapore. Another source claims the total circulation to be over a million, counting continued reprintings in the late 1920s and later (Link, p. 53).

Hsia's well-written summary helps give the reader a sense of the story's main developments:

> Briefly told, *Yü-li hun* is a tragic tale of love and self-sacrifice involving
> three principals: the hero Ho Meng-hsia (Ho Dreaming of Rosy
> Clouds), the heroine Pai Li-ying (White Pear Image), and her younger
> sister-in-law Ts'ui Yün-ch'ien. Meng-hsia, a twenty-one-year-old
> graduate from a normal school, goes from his native city of Soochow to
> teach in a village school near Wusih. While paying a visit to Old Mr.
> Ts'ui, a distant relative, in that village, he is persuaded to stay at his

home to teach the eight-year-old grandson, P'eng-lang, in exchange for room and board. Li-ying, more familiarly known as Li-niang, is the boy's mother who, at twenty-seven, has been a widow for three years.

Though they rarely see each other, the tutor and the widow fall violently in love by reason of their spiritual and poetic affinity and regularly exchange poems and letters with P'eng-lang as messenger. Li-niang, while profoundly touched by and grateful for Meng-hsia's love and returning it in her own fashion, has no doubt where her duty lies. It is only when he becomes ill and vows perpetual bachelorhood to match her determination to remain a widow that she becomes greatly worried and gets sick in turn. She cannot see him wasting his life for her sake when it is his primary duty to get married and produce a son to please his widowed mother. Moreover, with his talent, he should aim higher than being a lover—he should serve the country and, like the headmaster of his school, Ch'in Shih-ch'ih, go to Japan to study. She would exhaust her own savings to bring about the event.

When the seventeen-year-old Yün-ch'ien returns from her boarding school for the summer vacation, Li-niang shows dramatic improvement in health. The two sisters-in-law have always been very close, and to all appearances, Li-niang's recovery is due to Yün-ch'ien's able ministrations and cheerful company. But what restores her health so very quickly is the thought that it would be best for all concerned if Meng-hsia can agree to marry Yün-ch'ien and live with the family as a resident son-in-law. Meng-hsia, too, is duty-bound to go home for the summer to be with his mother and his elder brother due to return from Fukien, but he cannot leave so long as Li-niang remains ill. Fearful that outright rejection of her proposal will further endanger her health, he reluctantly agrees in principle to the match but stalls for time. He returns home and spends a miserable summer plagued by malaria.

When the fall term begins, Meng-hsia returns to the Ts'ui residence, unchanged in his love for the widow. His co-teacher, Mr. Li, suspects the worst and inflicts even greater torment on the lovers by his malicious meddling. This crisis soon brings about the betrothal of Yün-ch'ien to Meng-hsia, with Headmaster Ch'in, on holiday from Japan, serving as matchmaker. Yün-ch'ien, who has set store by her modern education and talked much about women's liberation from feudal bondage, now quits school and resigns herself to her fate as a girl under paternal command to marry a stranger. Upon learning of her misery, Meng-hsia accuses Li-niang of duplicity and avows his love in even more violent terms. Under the unbearable pain of this accusation, the tubercular widow is now determined to die, hoping against hope that, with her out of the picture, the betrothed couple may yet find happiness. She hides her worsened condition from Meng-hsia and dies on New Year's Eve when the unsuspecting lover has already gone home to spend the holidays.

He returns in a disconsolate state. Equally grief-stricken is Yün-ch'ien when she discovers a long letter from Li-niang telling about her unfortunate affair with Meng-hsia, her well-intentioned plan to match him with her beloved sister-in-law, and her determination to leave the world to ensure their happiness. Deeply affected by her friendship and self-sacrifice, Yün-ch'ien wants to offer her life in love and gratitude, and dies half a year later in the sixth month of 1910. After studying in Japan for a few months, the doubly bereaved Meng-hsia dies a patriotic martyr in the Wuchang revolution of October 10, 1911, to topple the Manchu government. (Hsia, pp. 221-22)

The autobiographical nature of *Yü li hun* has often been pointed out. Some of the details in Xü's life are revealing about the strategies that orientate his story. Unlike his brother, Xü was unsuccessful in his attempts to earn the official scholarly *xiucai* degree, which would have enabled him to further his studies abroad. He became instead a schoolteacher in some village of Wuxi upon his graduation from a normal school at Changshu and lived with the Cai family where he tutored the grandson. He fell in love with the boy's mother, who was a widow, and their affair probably ended as he left his post as schoolteacher.[75] As is obvious, this illicit relationship subsequently formed the basis for *Yü li hun*. The representation of love in the tale moves back and forth between propriety and marginality, as we see it most clearly in the figure of the schoolteacher, who is at once a genius (*cai zi*) steeped in traditional classical poetry and a reject from the official scholarly world. Link's explanation of *cai* elucidates its otherworldliness:

> Genius (*ts'ai*) [*cai*] . . . is primarily literary genius, but not the ordinary kind of literary genius which brings official position and fortune. It is a highly independent, almost wizardly genius which obeys only its own standards. . . . The reader is given to know a young man's genius through his brilliant poems and his great powers of understanding and sympathy, especially concerning the natural world. But ordinary society does not recognize the rare genius. He is isolated, and often impoverished. He rejects the normal world because he understands higher things; the normal world rejects him because it does not. (Link, p. 66)

What does not come across in Link's passage is the duality of the genius's existence: he is not merely excluded from society but is also given a very special, at times privileged, status; he is considered the rare, sensitive human being who is "hubristic" by being more gifted. It is therefore wrong to see Mengxia (Meng-hsia) purely as "isolated" from society, for his obviously elitist taste for poetry and writing, which finds its ideal realization in unfulfilled sentiment, puts him squarely within it.

Likewise, Liniang's position as a widow does not itself entirely explain the obstructed path of their relationship. In spite of the common assumption that Chinese widows were not supposed to remarry, the classics as well as actual history show that the old society's stand on the issue has yet to be completely understood. The aphorism by the Song neo-Confucianist Zhu Xi, that it is a small matter to starve to death, but a large matter to lose one's chastity,[76] is often quoted by scholars who take the view that Chinese society was absolutely against widows' remarrying. In her interesting study of widows and remarriage in Ming and early Qing China, Ann Waltner shows that, even though Zhu Xi's instructions were revered, there did exist in the Ming and more strongly in the Qing different ideas about widowhood that granted widows a certain kind of freedom. For instance, according to a set of family instructions, women should not be forced to remain chaste or to remarry.[77] In other words, even though the first marriage was her parents' mandate, the second was the woman's own choice. Waltner concludes that "widowhood was a state in which the first round of familial obligations were fulfilled, but society's position on the widow's future was unclear."[78] Liniang's widowhood therefore represents the marginality of her position, but does not account for the propriety of her response to it. If the decision not to remarry is indeed the woman's choice, it is not a free one—especially not free in the sense of being available to *any, every* woman. The poor widow who has no stable income to back up her chastity is usually not only impoverished materially but also morally; she becomes literally *barbaric* in being called a woman "married to the left."[79] By contrast, Liniang is a widow who can afford a chaste widowhood. Although not extremely well-off, the Cui (Ts'ui) family apparently has enough to support not only the four family members, but also a few servants and a tutor. The determination with which Liniang insists on her chastity is thus not simply a determination to remain morally correct but, in a more complex way, to stay *civilized* and be *noble*. Hence the particular sense of excess—of extravagance and superfluousness—in her passionate relationship with Mengxia.

This is why, although the two lovers do not have any air of "glamour" about them, their relationship must be seen in terms of the extraordinary. Glamour, an essential ingredient in certain forms of contemporary mass entertainment (such as U.S. television soap operas like "Dallas," "Dynasty," and "Falcon Crest," which are exported worldwide in the 1980s), is in the Chinese context substituted by an affluent, aristocratic *mental* culture, complete with its ornate, classical styles of expression. The reader who would identify emotionally with the characters is at the same time distanced from that world by the very things that attract him or her to it—the rare, unattainable spiritual endowments of the *cai zi* and his beloved *jia ren*.

The desires of this exquisite, sentimental world are communicated through a consistent concealment of the lovers' bodies. Although living in the same household, Mengxia and Liniang rarely see each other; they have two nocturnal meetings throughout the entire work, only one of which is fully described (Chapter 18: "Crying Face To Face"). In that chapter, they clear their misunderstandings brought on by Mr. Li, who had tried to expose their affair, then go on to exchange poetry for the rest of the night amidst sobbing and gazing at each other. Hsia comments good-humoredly:

> With all their sobbing and gazing at each other until almost dawn, it seems all quite unnatural that Meng-hsia should still communicate his love through poetry. Before seeing him off, Li-niang sings some verse from *Romeo and Juliet*. Ironically, the brief lines would seem to be taken from Act III, Scene 5, where Juliet is initially urging Romeo to stay even though morning light is already flooding her room. The Shakespearean lovers have spent their night making love; the Chinese lovers haven't even held hands. (Hsia, p. 234)

Hsia goes on to compare this single love scene in Xü's work with the meeting between Charlotte and Werther in Goethe's *The Sorrows of Young Werther*, in which the Germanic lovers embrace with physical passion, and concludes with the implied though unstated judgment that, as a novel about sentimental expressivity, *Yü li hun* is inferior to its Western counterparts. As I already mentioned in Section 2, Hsia's arguments are flawed not only because of their assumption that passion should be expressed universally in the "Western" mode of physical spontaneity, but also because of their cultured biases for the canonical. Interested primarily in giving an overview of the aesthetic precursors of the Butterfly genre and in defending Xü's work as the culminating example of the long sentimental-erotic tradition in Chinese literature—two tasks that he accomplishes with great erudition—Hsia consistently fails to register the melodramatic physical restraint of the Chinese lovers as *signifying* gestures in themselves, which require reading of a different kind.

The lovers' transcendence of paltry passion (*yü*) is the modus operandi of their relationship. Without this fundamental *veiling* of the *bodily* aspect of love, the excitement of the scholarly sentimental world would be entirely lost. Instead of physical intimacy, the lovers engage in an endless series of masquerades: letters, books left behind in the lover's room, lost handkerchiefs, photographs, flowers, the remainder of a burnt sheet of poetry, a lock of hair, inscriptions made with blood—all of which conjure up the presence of the beloved in broken, missing forms, as incomplete traces. This construction of "love" as a fundamentally *empty* process of signification, an artful play whereby gestures could be continually exchanged without any positive goal, is probably what led to the intuitive rejection on some critics' part of Butterfly literature as "dangerous" and "harmful." What is alarming for the morally concerned is not that love is immoral, but that it is fictional and unrealizable. For Xü, on the other hand, the "artistic" meaning of Mengxia and Liniang's affair would have collapsed if (as Hsia would have it) the lovers had allowed their relationship to be consummated physically.

The physical withholding of sentimental desires is thus Xü's most crucial formal aspect. It is what ultimately explains the fragmentariness of the story: while the actual contact between the lovers is almost nonexistent, there is always yet another letter or poem to be written with ever greater lucidity and abundance of emotion. The result of such "playful," self-perpetuating displacements is that every happening in this sentimental world always seems too large or too small, too much or too little, but never coherent and together. Meanwhile, even though the body of the woman remains "chaste" in all this play, her mental excesses become, in this context, the violation of propriety for which she must, by the law of Butterfly narrative, pay.

E

As she struggles through the difficult classical or semiclassical language of the Butterfly story, a reader of the late 1980s is inevitably confronted with the question as to the relationship between popular and elitist culture in early twentieth-century China. At a time when the scholarly styles of writing were increasingly replaced by the use of *baihua*, the vernacular, the *popularity* of Butterfly stories highlights the split between the arcaneness of "production" and the mundaneness of "reception." As the highly literary language of the dying scholar-official class was used to sell entertainment fiction in urban centers, Butterfly literature was unexpectedly helping to bring about a much awaited social reform — mass literacy. For the first time in Chinese history, phenomenal numbers of people were reading as a "public," before which the decadent, beautiful classical language turned more and more into a gimmick of technical virtuosity looking for buyers.

The contradictions of democratization, however, are perhaps best illustrated in what the language of political economy would call the "fetishization" of love as a global currency. "Fetishization" here refers not only not to the "subjective" or "psychological" processes of fixation, but also to the processes of commodification whereby "love" acquires an exchange value. What is fetishized or commodified is precisely the "objectivity" or public transparency of love, which progressively becomes the means with which to "communicate" within the increasingly opaque — because outmoded — world of Confucian culture, and also with the menacingly opaque — because foreign — world of the technological West. Only thus is it possible to understand why an apparently degenerate classical language could so happily participate, at least in the first couple of decades of the twentieth century, in a mobilization of love and of "spontaneous," "revolutionary" feelings for the general purposes of cultural catharsis. It also becomes intelligible as to why one of the most popular translated novels of that period was Alexandre Dumas fils's *La Dame aux Camélias.*

Translated as *Cha hua nü yi shi* by Lin Shu in the 1890s and widely read by Chinese readers of the late Qing and early Republican periods, Dumas fils's novel was what inspired Xü Zhenya's own love stories. This "sentimental bias" (Hsia, p. 219) typical of a "romantic generation"[80] was explicitly acknowledged when, in the epilogue to *Yü li hun*, Xü had another character refer to the narrator (thus, as some critics believe, alluding to himself) as the "Alexandre Dumas fils of the Orient" (*dongfang zhong ma*).

The most interesting aspect of the processes of fetishization has to do not simply with the apparent similarities or equivalent passages in the Chinese and Western texts. While love is fetishized as a global currency, its impact here in fact depends on the successful *translation* of "foreign" paradigms into those which were specific to China at that time. "Love," the "exchange" with the West that is conducted in the name of a universal condition, seems obstinately attached to the familiar modes we have encountered in other "homespun" Butterfly stories. My reading here is therefore a reading of Lin Shu's translation of Dumas fils's text.[81]

As is well known to readers of Chinese literature, Lin Shu's more than 160 translations were all done through the tandem arrangement, whereby a person who could read the original would report a story to him, and he would then rewrite it in good classical Chinese (*wenyan*). In spite of using what sounds in our age like a fantastical method, Lin Shu's prolific productions proved one important point: the eagerness of Chinese readers at the turn of the century to acquaint themselves not only with Western technology, a source of great humiliation, but also with Western culture and literature as ways to "humanize" the barbarians and thus domesticate the immediacy of the latter's technological omnipotence. According to one literary historian, translations from foreign texts took up two-thirds of all the fiction produced in the late Qing.[82]

Lin Shu translated Dumas fils's work with the help of his friend Wang Ziren, who knew French. A comparison of the Chinese text with the French and English versions reveals the ways in which a Chinese reader made use of the foreign text to replay China's specific cultural problems.[83]

In Dumas fils's story, passion is used as a way to bring into play certain structural and ideological contrasts. Armand's interest in Marguerite is from the very first clearly expressed in a language of domination and conquest. This interest is triggered not by Marguerite's simplicity—something he is surprised to realize later and the worship of which he only then becomes "converted" to—but by the *difficulty* of the task facing him:

> Etre aimé d'une jeune fille chaste, lui révéler le premier cet étrange mystère de l'amour, certes, c'est une grande félicité, mais c'est la chose

du monde la plus simple. S'emparer d'un coeur qui n'a pas l'habitude des attaques, c'est entrer dans une ville ouverte et sans garnison. . . .

Plus la jeune fille croit au bien, plus elle s'abandonne facilement, sinon à l'amant, du moins à l'amour, car étant sans défiance elle est sans force, et se faire aimer d'elle est un triomphe que tout homme de vingt-cinq ans pourra se donner quand il voudra. . . .

Mais être réellement aimé d'une courtisane, c'est une victoire bien autrement difficile. . . . Elles sont mieux gardées par leurs calculs qu'une vierge par sa mère et son couvent. (*La Dame*, pp. 137–39)

To be loved by a pure young girl, to be the first to reveal to her the strange mystery of love, is indeed a great happiness, but it is the simplest thing in the world. To take captive a heart which has had no experience of attack, is to enter an unfortified and ungarrisoned city. . . .

The more a girl believes in goodness, the more easily will she give way, if not to her lover, at least to love, for being without mistrust she is without force, and to win her love is a triumph that can be gained by any young man of five-and-twenty. . . .

But to be really loved by a courtesan: that is a victory of infinitely greater difficulty. . . . They are guarded better by their calculations than a virgin by her mother and her convent. (*Camille*, pp. 113–14)

This Western male lover's perspective is that of a warlike conquest, which seeks the courtesan's love in the form of her religious punishment. For Armand, since courtesans have by profession deceived so many, real love from them has to be the passion of total, self-destructive surrender:

. . . quand Dieu permet l'amour à une courtisane, cet amour, qui semble d'abord un pardon, devient presque toujours pour elle un châtiment. Il n'y a pas d'absolution sans pénitence. Quand une créature, qui a tout son passé à se reprocher, se sent tout à coup prise d'un amour profond, sincère, irrésistible, dont elle ne se fût jamias crue capable; quand elle a avoué cet amour, comme l'homme aimé ainsi le domine! . . . ces malheureuses filles, . . . Elles ont menti tant de fois qu'on ne veut plus les croire, et elles sont, au milieu de leurs remords, dévorées par leur amour. (*La Dame*, p. 139)

When God allows love to a courtesan, that love, which at first seems like a pardon, becomes for her almost always a punishment. There is no absolution without penitence. When a creature who has all her past to reproach herself with is taken all at once by a profound, sincere, irresistible love, of which she had never felt herself capable; when she has confessed her love, how absolutely the man who she loves dominates her! . . . these unhappy women . . . have lied so often that no one will believe them, and in the midst of their remorse they are devoured by love. (*Camille*, pp. 114-15)

However, Armand's belligerent assumptions break down when he is confronted with the genuine innocence of Marguerite, who, in spite of her worldly social background, proves herself pure and virginal in her yearning for simple love. Her reasons for loving him, which are entirely disarming, go as follows:

> Je me suis donnée à toi plus vite qu'à aucun homme . . . parce que me voyant cracher le sang tu m'as pris la main, parce que tu as pleuré, parce que tù es la seule créature humaine qui ait bien voulu me plaindre . . . j'avais autrefois un petit chien qui me regardait d'un air tout triste quand je toussais; c'est le seul être que j'aie aimé. . . . Eh bien, je t'ai aimé tout de suite autant que mon chien. (La Dame, p. 177)

> I gave myself to you sooner than I did to any man . . . because when you saw me spitting blood you took my hand; because you wept; because you are the only human being who has ever pitied me. . . . I once had a little dog who looked at me with a sad look when I coughed; that is the only creature I ever loved. . . . Well, I loved you . . . as much as my dog. (Camille, pp. 149-50)

Marguerite thus proves herself an exceptional individual whose love exposes the worldly, sinful nature of Armand's assumptions: it is he who becomes dominated, and finds himself beside himself with "genuine love" for her (La Dame, p. 152; Camille, p. 127). Marguerite's "purity" culminates finally in her willingness to sacrifice her own love for the sake of her beloved's future and for his family's reputation. When the priest who receives her confession just before she dies proclaims that "she lived a sinner" but "shall die a Christian" (La Dame, p. 304; Camille, p. 265), we know that it is her own purity, not any ritual or religion, which makes her "a Christian," that is, gives her "immortality." In the motif of blood spitting—the symptom that leads to her death—the sentimental, sociological, and sacrificial meanings of the story are inextricably welded together: the genuine, passionate woman loves excessively, suffers from pulmonary tuberculosis, and gives up her own life.

In the Chinese Cha hua nü, the interplay between the virgin and the courtesan, which is fundamental to our understanding of the Western texts, disappears. What remains is the emphasis on Marguerite's purity and moral superiority, and her real innocence becomes the primary factor that attracts Armand to her.[84] Whereas Marguerite alludes to the insignificance of her life as being "typical" of courtesans like her, in the Chinese text she has taken up the Chinese concept of "fate" (ming) and describes herself as bo ming (meager-fated), a classic Chinese phrase referring to the unlucky life that is believed to befall beautiful women.[85] In a similar manner, the Chinese concepts of propriety (li), chastity (zhen), and the like are introduced where no such ideas are invoked in the original.[86] The more scandalous suggestions of Marguerite's becoming Armand's mistress, meanwhile, are completely omitted (in spite of the long Chinese tradition of keeping concubines).[87] Another significant difference is the Chinese text's transformation of the essentially sexual nature of Armand and Marguerite's relationship. Passages where physical intimacy is described are consistently shortened, removed, or rewritten.[88] Armand's significant meditations on the delights of conquering a courtesan are also made much briefer.[89]

The result of such *translations* of a Western text is a story whose meanings are much more compelling for Chinese readers. Marguerite is much more like a chaste Chinese woman, and Armand a much less aggressive male lover who becomes closer to the traditional *cai zi*.[90] Consciously or unconsciously trimmed are also the tightly structural contrasts that balance each other with opposite connotations in the Western text: virgin/courtesan, sin/repentance, worldly wealth/unworldly poverty, urban prostitution/rural love. The Chinese text comes across as much more single-mindedly concentrated on the recording of nonphysical sentiment, demanding the reader's sympathy especially for Marguerite.

Lin Shu's translation of "love" should be read as a sociotextual interchange with the West that could not be obtained elsewhere. "Love" in the Chinese *Cha hua nü* is not purely the indicator of a feminized narrative with Chinese women's unsolvable problems as its hidden text; nor is it exactly the fictional play as entertained by the culturally privileged scholar class. It is, literally, the process by which a Chinese reader recast the foreign as familial. Especially because China's relations with the West in the nineteenth and early twentieth centuries were continually conducted on the premises of a xenophobic rejection of foreigners as wicked barbarians, a novel that showed the barbarians as equally capable of sentiment was a significant move toward the increasingly willing, modernizing resolution of cultural compromise. Sentimental love, raised to the level of intercultural "communicability," becomes here first and foremost a survival strategy, an effort in "knowing" that steers clear of the realities of the West as wholeheartedly as it seeks to grasp them.

Ideologically, therefore, a love story like *Cha hua nü* functions as the instance of an effective alibi, providing two alternative modes of meanings that constantly recede into each other according to the contexts in which they are required to work. Love is "mere fictional entertainment" when its effects are charged for being harmful to the pressing concerns of the nation, but it is also "universal human nature" when the reality of the West's disembodiment of China has to be faced. Either way, sentimental love works as a space for escape and for neutralizing the problems before they could be solved—if at all—by other means.

F

Zhang Henshui's *Ping-hu tongche* [Beijing-Shanghai Express], a Butterfly "social novel" written in eminently readable *baihua* in the late 1930s for a travel magazine,[91] tells the story of a traditional Chinese gentleman's "romantic" encounter with a Westernized young lady who, after successfully seducing him with the tale of herself as a pretty woman stricken with misfortune, steals all his money while he sleeps, and vanishes. The main part of the story takes place on a train journey from Beijing to Shanghai in January 1935, with a brief ending that takes us to some years later. Hu Ziyun, the former banker whose career has been ruined by Liu Jichun, the *femme fatale*, is on his way back to Beijing. As the train moves into Suzhou station where he lost all his money years ago, the memory of that incident becomes so vivid that, in a half-hallucinatory state, he begins identifying with every wealthy-looking man who is escorted by a pretty young woman. Finally spotting someone he imagines to be Liu, he lets out a cry at the man who is walking beside her: "Watch out! She is going to steal all your money!" Hu is thrown out of the train for causing a disturbance. The train rapidly moves on, while Hu, a lunatic now, continues to scream behind it.

In a way that illuminates the predicament of a traditional China confronting the modern and the West, Hu's "journey" stands as a fascinating tale of the destruction of one man's perceptual relation with his world. Once again, this tale has as its hinge a woman whose capricious, mysterious "nature" is associated with the cleverness and the relentlessness of a new culture that is increasingly commodified. To this new culture, Butterfly literature's response is, apparently, a resimulation of tradition. The question is, what has tradition become?

In his essay, "The Work of Art in the Age of Mechanical Reproduction,"[92] Walter Benjamin used the concept of the "aura" to describe the changing relations between art and its reception. For Benjamin, the "aura" is a way of talking about the distance that exists between an art object and its viewer, and which allows the former to acquire a unique and irreproducible presence. The nature of this "distance" is complex, as is indicated by one of Benjamin's favorite descriptions: "If we designate as aura the associations which, at home in the *mémoire involontaire*, tend to cluster around the object of a perception, then its analogue in the case of a utilitarian object is the experience which has left traces of the practised hand."[93] This "clustering" of traces and associations in which we behold the art object "as it is" also makes up our perceptual relation with ourselves. While the object shines in its inapproachable, "auratic" presence, it is our involved gaze at it that produces "its" intense, inalienable meaning.

Benjamin's evocation of the "aura" at the time of its alleged decline is really an attempt to articulate the critical change of sense awareness that has been brought about by the possibilities of mechanical reproduction and accelerated by the advent of photography. For Benjamin, writing in the early part of the twentieth century, the camera has destroyed the "auratic" relation between art and perception forever because it "records our likeness without returning our gaze."[94] In other words, our gaze at an object is meaningful only when it is returned or reciprocated, for only then do we feel that a perceptual exchange has occurred: "To perceive the aura of an object we look at means to invest it with the ability to look at us in return."[95]

From this typically modernist, arguably formalistic fascination with "looking," we find a useful method to articulate the relation between "China" and "the West," and also the Butterfly, or traditionalist, interpretation of that relation. The ruin of perceptual reciprocity in early twentieth-century Chinese society is traceable to the way in which the traditional "gaze" at the world increasingly fails to be met by a common, expected "look." As spectacles of the foreign—commodities, gestures, modes of dress and behavior, verbal expressions—multiply, what is returned is more and more a contradiction and a nullification: no matter how hard it gazes, tradition now looks empty.

The irony inherent in this clashing and hollowing of "sights" is aptly expressed in a work such as Shen Congwen's A li si zhongguo youji [Alice's travels in China], in which Alice and her rabbit friend are disappointed to find the Shanghai scene extremely "un-Chinese": "The things displayed in shop windows are foreign merchandise; the houses are European in style; the people walking in the streets or riding in cars are for the most part Europeans."[96] The fact that Shen himself satirized the foreign contents of modernized Chinese life by borrowing, not lessons from the Chinese classics, but the fictional structure of an English author's study in logic and semantics, only emphasizes the irony even more. What is crucial, however, is not only the decline of the traditional "look" itself, but also how that decline is fictionally dramatized and resisted, leading to a re-simulation of the "aura" at the quotidian as well as abstract levels.

Returning to Hu's Beijing-Shanghai journey, one can see that, structurally, the journey suggests the predicament of a man who is unable to return to his old world after he has been destroyed by the new. Beijing and Shanghai represent the old and the new respectively, and their historical differences are put in this schematic comparison by Joseph T. Chen:

> Historically, Peking [Beijing] was a museum city of old Chinese civilization, and an educational and political center. As the capital of China, traditionally it has always been identified with the North. As a non-Western, non-treaty port city, it had no international settlements (except the foreign legations quarter), no large foreign population, and no large modern commercial or industrial establishments. Its population consisted largely of mandarins, intellectuals, bureaucrats, and old-type artisans, merchants, and workers. Shanghai, on the other hand, was a modern, urban, cosmopolitan, and Western-oriented treaty port city. . . . Its society had highly variegated subdivisions, such as foreign

settlements, large commercial and industrial establishments, and heterogeneous social groupings. . . . While the great Chinese heritage gave Peking its quality of simplicity, serenity, grandeur, and imperial stature, the nascent Western influence quickly transformed Shanghai into a lively, mobile, competitive, iconoclastic, and materialistic center.[97]

What helps to dramatize the dissolution of a tradition—the impossibility of its return—is a new object, the train, which was met with violent protestations when it was introduced into China in the nineteenth century. The train changes familiar perceptions once and for all. The narrator in *Ping-hu tongche* begins with an observation of the crowds who seem to have been brought together only because of it:

If one has a job at the railway station, it must occur to one how strange it is that there are such crowds surging into the station as each train arrives. And then each train takes off again with such an uncountable number of people. . . . In the olden days before trains, why did travellers never appear so crowded together, like rising winds and clouds? (*PHT*, p. 1)

The crowds bring with them a ruthless efficiency that alters the rural, flexible nature of interpersonal relationships: the train does not and will not wait for the passenger who cannot catch it (*PHT*, p. 165). As the private individual is required to adapt himself or herself quickly to these new conditions, even the body's responses to sense phenomena alter:

The sensations of the train passenger seem to differ from those of ordinary people. We normally sleep in quiet at home, and wake up as soon as there is noise. On the train, passengers fall asleep even while the sounds of the machine running on the rail strike like thunder. And yet as the train stops and all harsh noise quiets down, human sensibilities seem suddenly reversed: the passengers wake up. (*PHT*, p. 78)

Adjustments to crowds and modern facilities constitute a crisis of experience that is increasingly construed as a proliferation of disparate external objects, none of which leaves any distinct impression. This crisis is described in part in the term "panoramic" by Wolfgang Schivelbusch, who argues that the railway journey in nineteenth-century Europe and America was itself a commodity.[98] The proliferation of disparate external objects experienced on the train is not necessarily "mechanical" in Benjamin's sense, but its effects are no less destructive of the sense of "auratic" oneness that, in retrospective imagination at least, used to shape the world. As the train moves from city to city, Zhang's story supplies its wealth of local details—weather, customs, even snack specialties—in a way that reminds us of what Benjamin elsewhere refers to as the "practical interests" of the storyteller.[99] However, in the age of the decline of the aura, the presence of those "practical interests" that used to give every storyteller his or her uniqueness raises an intricate set of questions. What the reader of a travel magazine obtains from *Ping-hu tongche* are fragmented pieces of information that provide a temporary, transient, orientation, similar to that which a passenger receives on the train. As the passenger in Zhang's story purchases different kinds of food at different stations with only the most superficial ideas about their origins, so the reader of the travel magazine acquires details about different places without really knowing them. An experience of the world becomes more and more a collection of things that one gathers haphazardly—and uncomprehendingly.

As it multiplies nonreciprocating "looks," the experience of fragmentation also intensifies the "look for," the obsession with, the "right" details, and the adherence to familiar methods and perspectives. In this way, a chauvinistic character like Hu is shown to be caught in his own interpretation of the world as much as by the other's premeditated plot to trap him. This "other" is not only "foreign" but also feminine and criminal. The decline of the aura—the crumbling of that perceptual distance that allows us to hold the world in place—is thus inscribed in the crisscrossing of three types of discourses: Westernization, femininity, and the detective mystery. All three discourses function with "objects" to be deciphered. The result is a struggle between the transparent complacency of a sign-reading "subject" and the opaque fascination of "objects" that are construed to be without consciousness. In this struggle, the "objects" are endowed with what I would call a reconstituted or second-order "aura," which may be elaborated as follows.

The kind of knowledge the train offers is not only superficial but relative in value: first class, second class, third class. In the absence of other, more historical information, these divisions take on an immediate signifying function, reintroducing a "self-evident" kind of certainty. For example, the cabin a passenger is in becomes a sign of the passenger's education and financial background. A crude materialism hence emerges as a way of knowing, and anything—from clothes, makeup, jewelry, to a smattering of English—can be invested with an intelligible meaning that lifts it from its haphazard context. As a detective who forces disjointed material messages into a coherent frame of understanding, Hu strikes us as a compulsive interpreter of signs, creating once again a "perceptive" distance between himself and the world.

Here are some examples of how Hu works. On first meeting Liu, he notices that she is reading a book that is bound in foreign style; he concludes that she must be a civilized or modernized person (*wenming ren*) (*PHT*, p. 10). He then notices a diamond ring on her finger, which leads him to think that "naturally, she must be from a well-to-do family" (*PHT*, p. 12). As she says the words "central station" in English, he regrets his earlier speculation of her low-class origins

(PHT, p. 15). After they move into the same cabin together, his curiosity leads him to inspect her belongings while she is out, and, to his delight, he finds that she seems to be rather casual about her money: banknotes in her purse have been put away untidily, which is a sign that she cannot possibly be a scheming thief (PHT, p. 44). Even when he stumbles on Liu and her accomplice talking in secret—to their obvious fluster—Hu still dismisses his observation as a mere result of his own discomfort at his illicit affair with Liu (PHT, p. 99). In his attempt to obtain a second opinion on Liu from a friend who happens to be on the same train, he literally stops their dialogue at the point that fits his own interpretation the best:

> [Hu:] "As far as you can see, do you think she is an honest person?"
>
> [Friend:] "That's hard to say. It can take several layers of analysis. Some people can be very smart and yet still be honest. Others . . ."
>
> [Hu, without letting his friend finish:] "You are absolutely right. Although she is very smart, she treats others in a down-to-earth way. She is in rather unfortunate circumstances, you know, and needs help . . ." (PHT, p. 158)

By contrast, the criminal needs to do very little. In his eagerness to "know" her (that is, to make her submit "her" truth to him), Hu assists Liu's plot by developing a method of detection that precisely blinds him to what she is. When the proliferation of superficial signs in one's surroundings turns every "other" into a mass of impenetrable possibilities, how does one know what is "inside" another, and avoid collapsing into the abyss of the unreturned look? Hu answers by destroying the other's obscurity and molding her in his own shape. The opacity of the modern world is thus accompanied by the individual man's wishful attempt to *forge* a stable perceptual distance from which unknown others appear to be intelligible. Even though he never inspires any sympathy for what he does, the ending of the story seems to portray Hu as a kind of mock tragic hero whose downfall is brought about only because he so unswervingly abides by his own "vision." In his attempt to "domesticate" the other, he ends up being left behind.

In the age of crowds, trains, and uncertainties, the person who can only read others according to his own methodology loses to the person who reads the way the other reads and who turns the other's reading method back on himself. While the former proceeds from a wishful perception of the world by continuing to assume and appropriate its "aura," the latter thrives on makeshift attitudes and crafty surprises, by faithfully following and mimicking the other in a way that makes submission and resistance indistinguishable. If Hu could be read as a representative of traditional China who is clearly ridiculed for being stupid and chauvinistic, then the corresponding association of Liu, the woman, with a kind of shameless cunning that is inseparable from her Westernized attitudes, is equally revelatory. In spite of its ready readability, Butterfly fiction is politically ambivalent. Its politics is here disturbingly divided between its socially relevant content and its "conservative" treatment of disruptive "others." In *Ping-hu tongche*, the sacrificial structure of the love story is both repeated and transformed: the woman is a social outcast whose devastating impact on the world results not simply from heartrending romantic entanglements but from her willing self-debasement as a thief, a prostitute, or someone who leads a pro-foreign lifestyle.

Meanwhile, the presence of recognizable oppositional structures of male/female, Chinese/foreign, and victim/victor unsettles, rather than merely affirms, dichotomizations of power relations as they are traditionally upheld. This impoverishment of tradition is best illustrated by the narration of a crime that no longer functions as the negative proof of a valid morality. Liu's crime does not illustrate the correctness of that mode of behavior which is its structural and moral opposite, namely, the detection of crime; rather, it makes us see the latter's insupportability. As the winner of the game, Liu completes her victory by disappearing into the crowds and thus erasing her own traces. Only by doing so will she be able to catch the train again. Her livelihood echoes that of the train: it is efficient and relentless; it waits for nobody. Whereas Hu remains caught and abandoned where the other has trapped him. The dramatic ending of the story implies that the new world offers "madness" if one cannot catch up with it. But madness is pitied by no one in the new community of anonymous crowds who share nothing except their existence as strangers ignoring strangers.

The manner of the narrator, too, confirms the hollowing of an older order. He tells the entire story in a matter-of-fact tone, juxtaposing observations of touristy details with rhetorical appeals to conventional notions of rationality:

> When a man and a woman go out together, it seems perfectly correct for the man to pay for everything. If the woman should take it upon herself to pay, then the man would not only feel grateful, but sense something unusual . . .
>
> A woman's heart is difficult to see through, as it vacillates so much between fierceness and kindness. The severe mother-in-law often chants Buddhist lessons. Prostitutes can lead honest young men astray by robbing them of all they have, but meanwhile act charitably toward needy strangers on the street . . .
>
> In the olden days, whether one was traveling by boat or by cart, one would always be waited for while one had something urgent to do. Nowadays, boats and trains are the masses' means of transport that operates according to schedules. It is no longer possible for them to wait for one or two people. (*PHT*, pp. 16, 107, 165)

As they resimulate a kind of "common sense," such remarks alert us to a process of masking, in which the crises narrated aesthetically are deemphasized under the voice of communal rationality. Placed side by side with the crime, the narrator's "common sense" is impotent to explain and cohere the modernized, disruptive experience. Like the complacent chauvinism of a Hu that they obviously mock, the conventionally reiterated truths with which Zhang's fictional storyteller prefaces his tale are therefore ironic, indeed parodic, attempts to reestablish an "auratic" space for viewing when that space is disappearing. This endless conjuring of the "aura" that gives rise to its many ideological reconstitutions is a critical way of rethinking the "traditionalism" that is so often deprecatingly attributed to Butterfly literature.

This traditionalism can now be understood as a reconstituted aura that seeks to reinvest with social validity and a marketable value the traditional context just as that context has permanently broken down. Such reinvestment works perfectly alongside a commercial attitude toward literature, attracting buyers/investors precisely with its explicitly didactic or moralist intent. Thus taking on a *new* saleable meaning, tradition refinds its role as one commodity among many on the Chinese market.

The gaze at tradition becomes doubled and duplicitous as a result. Whatever "aura" tradition possesses as the Chinese look at it now is the effect of a reinvented, reinvested set of values, broken up, and reassembled again. As tradition is once again reinvigorated with "the ability to look at us in return," a parallel movement to invest the "foreign" with the same kind of ability is simultaneously in process. When the Chinese market was increasingly filled with foreign commodities that did not really return the Chinese gaze and yet insisted on being there, the associations of impropriety, evil, and barbarism clustered around the "foreign," only to give way subsequently to awe, imitation, and wholesale embrace. In the world of the Butterfly novelist, we see on the one hand the reconstituted aura of traditional moral attitudes, and on the other, the suspect aura of foreign objects, which contradict the novelist's moralist concerns but which are nevertheless registered and narrated with great curiosity.

In this way, as a "new" aura of the native culture lives superimposed on the aura of the foreign, the Butterfly novel shows us how the commercial fiction market offers the means to domesticate the crisis of perception at the same time that it partakes of it (the crisis). The reaffirmation of tradition takes place in this literature in two senses: the novelist tells the readers what they are and makes them buy it, too. Another way of putting this is to say that it is a self-fulfilling moralism: as values are paraded as traditional or "Chinese," everybody buys them; and as everybody buys them, the values "naturally" become "Chinese." Hence, even though a Butterfly story like *Ping-hu tongche* takes as its content the problematic exchange between China and the West, an exchange in which the West is seen to be the inevitable victor, we must also remember Butterfly fiction as a kind of commodity that was itself conducting a powerful and successful line of exchange with urban readers through their emotional and epistemic crises. In other words, the affirmation of tradition as *content*, which easily defines Butterfly literature as "reactionary," must be seen against the phenomenally lucrative exchange of that content in a versatile market, in which Butterfly literature had to remain trendy, liberal, and progressive in order to survive.

The process of reinvesting tradition with aura continues with Chinese people today. Whereas trends on the mainland and Taiwan have remained traditionalist in the sense that a "Chinese" character is emphasized in all "modernizing" undertakings, the metropolitan, Shanghai-style Chinese culture flourishes most evidently in Hong Kong and among overseas Chinese populations with a reinvigoration of the "Chinese heritage" in multiple forms. With the "exiled" Chinese, the marketable quality of "tradition" has long been blended with a pragmatism that justifies modernized life-styles *and* Euro-American living standards. Meanwhile, what remains "Chinese" becomes as intimate as the occasional satisfaction of certain palatal desires: one can do without it, but given the opportunity, one willingly indulges in it even if a little ashamedly. So Butterfly literature in its various genres and multimedia counterparts thrives even today, as supposedly "middlebrow" but nonetheless popular and delicious "Chinese homemade" delights.

Chapter 3
Modernity and Narration—
in Feminine Detail

1

The details of old Chinese clothes . . . were astonishingly pointless.
. . . No artist could, for instance, have hoped for anyone to notice his
intricate designs on the soles of women's shoes, except indirectly by the
imprints left in the dust. . . .

This tremendous amassing of bits and bits of interest, this continual
digression and reckless irrelevancy, this dissipation of energy in things
which do not matter, marked the attitude towards life of the leisurely
class of the most leisurely country in the world . . . .

The history of Chinese fashions consists almost exclusively of the
steady elimination of those details.[1, 2]

Written in 1943 for the English monthly The XXth Century, Eileen Chang's
"Chinese Life and Fashions" calls our attention to the development of modern
Chinese history in a most interesting—if for some irrelevant—manner: through
the vanishing superfluous detail. The detail, whose extravagance and potency as
a method of differentiation mark the ancient Chinese world as a source of intellectual fascination for critics like Jorge Luis Borges and Michel Foucault,[3] is systematically compelled to disappear in modern China. In Chang's essay, that disappearance is not only the result of the reported historical developments, but is
foreshadowed by what is a remarkably conservative attitude on her part in spite
of her otherwise indulgent enthusiasm. After tracing, in detail, the elaborate cor-
respondences between women's status, what they wore, and how they wore

84

them during the period from the Qing to the 1940s, Chang concludes that the proliferation of details is a sign of social stagnation:

> Quick alternations in style do not necessarily denote mental fluidity or readiness to adopt new ideas. Quite the contrary. It may show general inactivity, frustrations in other fields of action so that all the intellectual and artistic energy is forced to flow into the channel of clothes.[4]

In the midst of her fascination with the irrelevant, then, a deep ambivalence arises and a moralism of the "proper" purposiveness of social activity comes clearly to the fore.

In this chapter I will propose, through a series of readings, a critical method that operates with the "detail" in a number of interpretative frames simultaneously. The detail is used as a point of inquiry into the conflictual affective structures that underlie approaches to "history" in modern Chinese narratives. These approaches often appear as the concerted but contradictory preoccupations with "liberation" and with national or ethnic "unity." Details are here defined as the sensuous, trivial, and superfluous textual presences that exist in an ambiguous relation with some larger "vision" such as reform and revolution, which seeks to subordinate them but which is displaced by their surprising returns. As such, details are also the vital joints—produced in the process of reading—at which the coherence of certain modes of narration can be untied. As modernization continues the expectation of an educated class to see literary language as full and serious—as we shall see, for instance, in Ba Jin's emotional or Mao Dun's analytic consistency—the single-mindedness of that expectation is undermined by the persistence of social details, of *the social as detail*. In Lu Xun, the ambiguity of feeling toward superfluous and useless existences leads to a visible, exteriorized fracturing of the narration process. In all three male writers, moments of ambiguity are uncannily connected with femininity, be it in the form of expression, eroticism, or domestic exploitation. The problems of femininity are the central focus in the fictional writings of Eileen Chang, in which an alternative approach to modernity and history arises through a release of sensual details whose emotional backdrop is often that of entrapment, destruction, and desolation. The combination of the detailed and the sensuous with such an emotional backdrop offers an understanding of culture that is defined through powerfully negative affect. Such affect is traceable only in incomplete forms, as deep and ideological "leftovers" embedded in narratives.

In her beautifully written book, *Reading in Detail: Aesthetics and the Feminine*, the feminist literary critic Naomi Schor tracks the career of the detail in modern European aesthetics as one that is bound up with politics and misogyny. Two key moments in the detail's career in the West are its Hegelian sublimation and its Barthesian desublimation.[5] Schor argues that, while for Hegel, a proper aesthetics depends on "a new transcendence which would sublate 'what is itself without significance,' " for Barthes, as for many modern or postmodern thinkers, the fundamental aesthetic imperative is the desublimation of the detail or the reinscription of the detail in the corporeal. Schor's arguments are too refined to be adequately summarized here, but one of the most crucial points she makes is how the assessment of the detail, be it in terms of transcendence or immanence, is inevitably related to the process of gendering—the disturbing fact being, in our age where the detail seems to be enjoying a massive transvaluation everywhere, its new prominence also tends to be degendered.[6] In other words, the history of the detail in which it is associated not only with the prosaic, the mundane, and the ornamental per se, but with the femininity that these realms traditionally connote, has not been given its due attention even by those scholars who now turn to the detail as a means to rethink history.

In the case of modern Chinese literature, very much the same point—the intricately related history of details and the feminine—must be made. "Feminine details" become prominent in a period in China that was characterized by feelings not only of rejuvenation, but more so, of renunciation. "Modernity," writes Paul de Man, "exists in the form of a desire to wipe out whatever came earlier, in the hope of reaching at last a point that could be called a true present, a point of origin that marks a new departure."[7] A paradox arises here: while it is by crushing, leveling, or neutralizing the many figures of femininity that are inextricable parts of an older order that the more heroic forms of Chinese modernity assert themselves, Chinese modernism also consists in the conscientious inventions and elaborations of "new" areas of interest, such as, precisely, women. In the enthusiastic investigations of women, mental and physical, sociological and fictional, a new kind of *voyeurism* surfaces as the other side of solemn patriotism. This voyeurism produces details that are at odds with the solemnity of Modern Nationhood, even though such details are often dissolved in the language of traditional metaphysics, human nature, or revolution.

The conceptual implications of the detail are, then, wide and intricate. I will go on to show how the imperative to modernize and to establish China's international status strives toward a "steady elimination" of details not only in fashion as Chang observes, but also in the conceptions of writing and national culture. As I do this, it is necessary to emphasize once again the ineluctability not only of *what* I analyze (simply because it "already" happened; it is "history") but also of *the ways I go about analyzing it.* It is when the fundamentals of Chinese society were so drastically overturned as a result of China's need for modernization and Westernization that the particular conjuncture of details and femininity stands out, in retrospect, as an effective way of analysis. That the detailed and the feminine, figures that have in common an ambiguous relation to the centrism and purposiveness of tradition, signify epistemological differences to the effect of disrupting the idealist construction of a new China—that this type of analysis can be offered in the late 1980s has everything to do with China's lowly position in the larger framework of modern global cultural politics. While Western intellectuals like Borges and Foucault may pay tribute to ancient Chinese culture, in the modern era it is China as part of the postcolonial context in which nonwhite peoples are massively *cut up* (to use the word "detail" in its etymological sense)—deprived, exploited, discriminated against, and thus "ethnicized"—that makes the interrelatedness of details and femininity an inexhaustibly germane method of reading modern Chinese culture. The ineluctability of *how* I read is thus, also, historical.

Theoretically, how does the management of details become an inter- as well as intracultural project in modern Chinese literature, signifying a modernity that is as intent on self-destruction as it is on self-strengthening? A schematic answer: when "details" are prohibited as "signs" of the decadent "Chinese" tradition, signs of a proclaimed "past." An excellent instance of this is found in Mao Dun's denunciation of the traditional "Mandarin Duck and Butterfly" stories. (I discussed this in the previous chapter.) Here, we need to thematize the notion of "detail" to see its usefulness in the Chinese "revolutionary" context. If details are (by Mao Dun's account) what should be carefully deselected in the proper construction of narrative, and if narrative itself is instrumental in the construction of a new national "identity," then details are a deadly impediment, not only to the new language and new literature as Mao Dun suggests, but to the earnest program of nation building. In what ways does this kind of conflict between "details" and "nation building" structure modern Chinese narratives? This is the question I explore in the rest of this chapter.

As I demonstrate in the previous chapter, the issue that surfaces prominently in the readings of Butterfly stories is the issue of literary subversion in a politically unstable and culturally transitional context. My focus on the formal specificities of popular narratives has been aimed not at reintegrating these narratives into the domain of "respectable" Chinese literature, but at exploring certain feminized, popular methods of cultural subversion that may or may not be recognized as such. For, needless to say, the official representatives of modern Chinese literature—writers of the May Fourth period—operated on the premise that it was they who were the subversive ones, and that the writers and readers of Butterfly narratives could only be regarded as unenlightened minds indulging in feudal ideology and urban book-market consumerism. The valorization of "May Fourth" as "revolution" has long been an unquestioned part of modern Chinese literary history, and writers of that period are generally regarded as cultural "rebels." In the official history of subversion, the greatly interesting methods found in Butterfly literature—methods distinguished by their tendencies toward sentimentality, exaggeration, deformation, vulgarity, didacticism, and melodrama—are bypassed as "merely" fictional and therefore insignificant: Butterfly literature functions at best as entertainment, and at worst in diverting people's attention from "serious" national affairs. Yet our rereading of Butterfly narratives should lead not only to their reinstatement as writings worthy of attention, but also to a revised approach to the May Fourth "classics." In other words: what can be said about the May Fourth literary revolution in the light of Butterfly stories?

From the point of view of the promoters and practitioners of the "new literature" that is to be based on *baihua*, the vernacular, the subversion that the May Fourth experience represents is the subversion of the Chinese literary tradition as a life-crushing authoritarian heritage. The metaphors used in the extremely self-conscious theorizing of language and literature in that period follow a consistently dichotomous pattern: traditional literature is decadent, moribund, and antilife, while the literature using *baihua* is genuine, natural, and living. In the rhetoric of authenticity and nature, the social and historical contradictions of the Chinese literary situation are ideologically erased. *Baihua* literature, being "genuine" and "natural," takes on an *eternal* value: the promotion of it led intellectuals like Hu Shi to reexamine the vernacular literature of the past and only thus reclaim its value retrospectively, as that of *baihua* literature or, to use Hu Shi's phrase, *huo wenxue* (live literature).[8] This historic escalating of the "people's language and literature" to the level of a truly representative national language and literature, which comes with the revolutionary claims of respect for non-elitist developments and linguistic diversity, ironically legitimizes only *certain kinds* of people's language and literature, while others, such as Butterfly narratives, are dismissed as improper.

What are some of the literary qualities promoted along with *baihua* literature? Readers of modern Chinese are familiar with Hu Shi's suggestions in his letter to Chen Duxiu in the October one issue of *New Youth* in 1916. These suggestions were later called the *ba bu zhuyi* ("eight-don'ts-ism"):

> On the whole, the reason for the decay of contemporary Chinese literature is the overemphasis on style at the expense of spirit and reality. This means that writings have form but no spirit. They imitate the ancient works and superficially resemble them, but in content, they are vague. To overcome this defect, we must pay more attention to the meaning and reality of what we write, the spirit which is contained in the body. Our ancients said, "writing without elegant literary style will not spread widely." To this I answer, "If the writing does not mean anything or does not reflect reality, what is the use of having a literary style?"
>
> As a result of my study and consideration of the matter during this year, I have come to the conclusion that we must start with the following eight principles if we now want to achieve a literary revolution:
>
> (1) Avoid the use of classical allusions;

(2) Discard stale, time-worn literary phrases;

(3) Discard the parallel construction of sentences;

(4) Do not avoid using vernacular words and speech;

(5) Follow literary grammar;

(The above are suggestions for a revolution in literary form or style.)

(6) Do not write that you are sick or sad when you do not feel sick or sad;

(7) Do not imitate the writings of the ancients; what you write should reflect your own personality;

(8) What you write should have meaning or real substance.

(The above are suggestions for a revolution in content.)[9]

Hu Shi's literary reforms were accompanied with an openly pro-foreign attitude. Chinese literary methods were declared "incomplete," while Western literary methods were "much more complete, much more brilliant, and hence exemplary."[10] The exaltation of a "cleansed" language as good literature, made ostensibly in the name of national unification, thus went hand in hand with a political program for Westernization.

Characteristic of this marriage of literary reform and political revolution is an idealism that expresses itself in various ways. First, there is a newly found humanism that stresses the dignity of living individuals against the "inhuman" past. It is not, for instance, a mere metaphor that Lu Xun is using when he depicts traditional Chinese society as "man-eating" in his short story "Diary of a Madman." Similarly, Lu Xun's brother, Zhou Zuoren, writes of the need for a "human literature," which must be distinguished by a serious, hopeful attitude toward human life and an angry or sorrowful one toward the antihuman: "Human literature takes human morality as its foundation."[11]

Second, great value is now accorded to the spoken, as opposed to written, language, and also to "Western" grammar. In an essay called "Zhenyang zuo baihua wen" [How to produce *baihua* writing], Fu Sinian singles out precisely these two points as his guidelines: "Pay attention to speech, and directly adopt Western linguistic patterns."[12] This is because, Fu explains, the classical Chinese language is crude and dead. Even works such as Wu Woyao's *Er shi nian mu du guai xianzhuang* [Strange things seen during twenty years] and Liu E's *Lao can you ji* [The travels of Lao Can], which are otherwise praised for their use of the vernacular, are far from satisfactory because they adopt the tone of voice of "women and people of low positions" in a manner typical of traditional fiction, and are thus full of "impurity." Fu advises: "First-rate literature has to be original speech without the least impurity, so that we would have exactly the same feeling whether we read or listen to it. If there is any difference in effect, it is second-rate."[13] In this phonocentric view of literature as pure, original speech, "eternal" and "genuine" literature must be that which exists prior to the written word. As the Chinese literary language has "regressed" to the point at which it is dry and impoverished because all effects are effects of writing, the ideal *baihua* to be created and adopted for literature would be a "Europeanized *baihua*."

The combination of nationalism and intracultural iconoclasm led to the ascendancy of realism in the May Fourth period as the most important literary style, be it expressed personally or socially. As is indicated by the association of adjectives in *New Youth's* slogan, "Opposition to feudal aristocratic literature, approval of popular realistic social literature," realism has become no longer just an aesthetic but a social issue.[14] What results and persists from then on in modern China is a "morally-motivated naturalism"[15] in the arts in general. Traditional Chinese art is now condemned for being "literati art" that tended toward an "art for art's sake" decadence, while modern Chinese art is never again to be severed from "reality." What remain arguable, however, are the implications that this modernist Chinese obsession with "reality" has for a reinterpretation of Chinese literary history.

As we have seen in Mao Dun's denunciation of Butterfly literature, the obsession with "reality" takes a narrative turn inward (to borrow from the title of Erich Kahler's famous work), situating the truth of representation in what Mao Dun calls "inner activities." With the elimination of details that are part of the feudalistic world of old China, what is constructed, at least wishfully, is a semiological transparency among a new set of terms: the New China—inner activities—narrative—reality, with implied subsets of identification between each of the first three terms and "reality" itself. However, in this obsession with reality, May Fourth writers show themselves not simply as the iconoclasts they are generally believed to be, but also—and more disturbingly—as loyal inheritors of traditional *scholarly* Chinese literary attitudes with specific, because deeply cultivated, assumptions about language and literature. This is a very difficult point to prove, as the evidence we have often points to the opposite— namely, that as far as literary forms go, traditional and modern Chinese literature cannot be more different. While the predominant genre for classical China was poetry, in modern times it has been narrative fiction, the genre that used to be despised. So where and how does scholarly heritage persist?

One way of answering this question is by pointing out that the promotion and practice of "womanly and vulgar" speech by Chinese writers since the May Fourth period as the chief means of expression must not be taken superficially. For, in spite of the wide acceptance of *baihua* and of narrative fiction, certain *classical literary* qualities continue to receive investment in the new literature as *socially and nationally valuable*, giving rise to a conservatism that contradicts the official beliefs of the May Fourth cultural revolution. The "classical literary" qualities in question could be described as a set of implicit demands placed on language-as-expressive-form: language is required to be "true" and "precise," not in order to be a faithful reflection of reality, but in order that reality can thus *naturally appear*. This requirement that is made of language-as-expressive-form is evident in the high aesthetic value that is endowed upon terms such as *ziran* (nature, spontaneity, easefulness), or *zhen* (true, real, genuine, and the like).

While it has often been argued that classical Chinese literature (poetry) is distinguished from Western literature for its nonmimetic, nonrepresentational origins, the continual, transhistorical preoccupation in Chinese poetry and fiction with what is "natural," "truthful," or "real," which even the most amateur readers could recognize, flatly contradicts this type of argument. The "nonrepresentation" assertion, often made by sinologists who are interested in showing how completely different the "Chinese tradition" is, cannot account for how the transition from "nonrepresentation" in classical Chinese aesthetics to an emphasis on "realism" with its heavily reflectionist tendencies in the modern period could be possible, except by blaming it on "Westernization." And yet, if the firmness and ease with which realism is able to establish itself in modern Chinese writings are not the signs of novelty, but the signs of the burden and habit of tradition with its preference for the "real," then the assertion of "nonrepresentation" as a unique principle in classical Chinese literature needs to be thoroughly reexamined itself. For my present purposes, I would say that the *traditionally endowed* quality of May Fourth literary beliefs becomes clear as we see that the classical Chinese poetic attitude, with its paradoxical double requirements of the poet's absolute mastery of technicalities and of the poem's natural air, is reproduced in the moderns' desperate search for appropriate literary forms that can present the "truth" of the new reality. The rise of narrative fiction, in this light, is by no means a "democratization" of classical literary culture, but the persistence of that culture in a different guise. If "truth" was sought, in the past, in man's spiritual submission to his ecological fate (as evidenced by the abundance of "nature" themes in classical Chinese poetry and painting), it is sought in the modern world in his engagement with his national and political identity. In both situations the emphasis is on the merger and harmony, rather than the collision and discontinuity, between cognition and reality.

Historically, the extraliterary circumstances that supported the existence of a serious literary culture had changed. With the abolition of the civil service examination in 1905, the men of letters lost the over one-thousand-year-old institution that had justified their dedication to literature. Replacing the imperial channel for intellectual aspirations were now aspirations of nationalism. As a modern *nation*, China must possess a national literature too — this literature would henceforth not be artistic and feudal, but social and international.

The eagerness to align Chinese literature with world literature, which typically uses a future-oriented, progressivist rhetoric, thus produces as its "other" an unenlightened, traditional China, which becomes associated with the metaphors of decadence, darkness, and death. Mao Dun's explicit attempt to organize the "literariness" of literature may thus be seen as symptomatic of the pressure of modernity that has been on Chinese intellectuals since the beginning of the twentieth century. Modernity expresses itself in the struggle between two related but perhaps incompatible notions of autonomy: the autonomy (hence liberation) of literature and culture, and the autonomy of China as a national and ethnic *unity*. On the one hand, as we read in the impassioned theorists of the May Fourth period such as writers of the journal *New Youth*, there is the goal of freeing literature from the traditional fetters of Confucian moralism. The excessiveness of a tautological statement like "literature is literature"[16] signifies the desperateness of the attempt to "modernize" literature by giving it its independence. Consequently, as innovation becomes "theorized as the main quality of cultural production,"[17] everything "Chinese" takes on the ghostly appearance of death and disease. From the denunciation of the customs of the traditional Chinese family in Ba Jin, to the advocacy of an analytic approach to fiction and a recognizably anglicized grammar in Mao Dun, the elimination of details—of all those traditional bric-a-brac—appears as the mark of a new elitism that is self-consciously revolutionary. On the other hand, however, revolutionized literature itself is compellingly associated with the rise of "China" in the modern era. The campaigns to *modernize* the Chinese literary language include not only "new" experiments, but also a revaluation and revalidation of *traditional* vernacular texts.[18] Looming over "autonomy"-as-liberation is thus the preoccupation with the "continuity" of Chinese culture. To use once again C. T. Hsia's phrase, this "obsession with China," which should be more specifically defined as an obsession with the *unification* of "China" in *all* respects, is what gives rise to the Chinese as an "imagined community" in the twentieth century. "Classes cannot assert their hegemony without articulating the people in their discourse," writes Ernesto Laclau, "and the specific form of this articulation in the case of a class which seeks to confront the power bloc as a whole, in order to assert its hegemony, will be populism."[19] In the case of China, the first question we would ask is, which class? The answer to that involves the realization that, in their patriotic attempts to rejuvenate China through language and literature by appealing to the "Chinese people," Chinese intellectuals of the early twentieth century became at the same time a "class" in formation. In the processes of populist solicitations in which the abstract notion of the "Chinese people" is used to invoke feelings of continuity and unity, the autonomy of literature, whose radical implication lies not so much in the severance from traditional bonds as in a necessity to relativize knowledge and values by subjecting them to processes of critical thinking, is consistently being short-changed.

As reality is imagined to be the result of "inner activities," the program of nation building goes hand in hand with an upsurge of interest in autobiographical writings and confessional narratives. As the Czech sinologist Jaroslav Průšek points out, the distinctive features of the literature produced in the May Fourth period are subjectivism and individualism (Průšek, p. 1).[20] From his socialist realist perspective, Průšek considers the growth of these features as indicative of important changes in the social structure and often the sign of "the individual's emancipation from traditional views in the spheres of philosophy, religion or ethics, or even of actual revolt against the inherited social order" (Průšek, p. 1). This emphasis on individual emancipation, which gives to the prominence of lyricism a *revolutionary* significance, is also seen to be concurrent with an increasing "feeling for the tragedy of existence" (Průšek, p. 3), a feeling that, as Průšek adds interestingly, was "very weakly developed or not at all in older literature" (Průšek, p. 3). A look at some of the well-known literary works of this period indeed confirms Průšek's views with respect to formal structures. Guo Moruo, to whom "the essence of literature derives from feelings and ends in them,"[21] translated Goethe's *Die Leiden des jungen Werther* into Chinese under the title *Shaonian wei te di fannao*, a work that quickly became a popular classic. In Guo Moruo's own works we find stories that remind us of the strongly romantic elements of Goethe's novel, such as love and suicide. He even wrote an account of his own life in seven autobiographical novels, of which *Shaonian shidai* [Childhood] is the best known. Highly personal experiences also mark the work of Yü Dafu, whose emotion-charged narratives with their candor about sex make him distasteful to more reserved readers. Yü Dafu's most widely read work is *Riji jiuzhong* [Nine diaries], whose title is once again symptomatic of the autobiographical tendency of his age. The authoress Ding Ling, who was to win the Stalin Prize in 1951 for her novel, *Taiyang zhaozai sanggan he shang* (*The Sun Shines on the Sanggan River*), a work that was later hailed as "a great decisive victory of our socialist realistic literature,"[22] began writing in the May Fourth period in extremely subjective forms. In her early piece, "Shafei nüshi di riji" ("The Diary of Miss Sophie"), the narrator Sophie, like many modern Chinese intellectuals, longs for physical and emotional intimacy and yet is contemptuous of the man she desires. In addition to fiction, autobiographies and memoirs also abounded in a manner hitherto unknown. For instance, there are Hu Shi's *Si shi zishu* [Autobiography of a forty-year old], Gu Jiegang's *Autobiography of a Chinese Historian*, translated by A. W. Hummel, and Shen Congwen's *Congwen zizhuan* [Congwen's autobiography], to name a few. Shen also wrote two memoirs, dedicated to Ding Ling and her husband, Hu Yepin, who was shot by Chiang Kaishek's henchmen (Průšek, p. 8).

Important though they are, the lyrical formal tendencies of the new literature in themselves cannot adequately account for the narrative problems we encounter in much of May Fourth fiction. Here, Průšek's arguments are especially thought-provoking because they are not unidirectional, but waver between two implications of the "lyrical" in the Chinese modern period. As he theorizes the literary transformation of this period as a takeover of the lyrical by the epic, Průšek implies that the new literature is, in its interests, affiliated with traditional *narrative* literature, and that the May Fourth fiction writers are inheritors of vernacular novels (Průšek, p. 42). Hence, too, while traditional Chinese literature is scholarly and aestheticist, modern Chinese literature is social and realist, that is, nonlyrical. And yet, as we have already mentioned, Průšek's main fascination with modern Chinese literature has to do precisely with what he considers its "lyrical" qualities—qualities of subjectivism and individualism that are for him the markers of "modernity" and "revolution." Here, Průšek the critic who is well versed in premodern Chinese literature cannot help but notice that, in their emphases on personal events and personal experiences as the necessary premises for the truthfulness of a literary work, May Fourth writers, even though they are writing in a nonlyrical form, nonetheless share with their literary predecessors a preoccupation with the philosophical and cognitive functions of literature, which were judged in classical Chinese aesthetics against the criteria of *shi* ("fullness" or "completeness") and *xü* ("emptiness") (Průšek, p. 91). Accordingly, "good" literature is by necessity morally sound writing, which is considered "truthful" because "full," whereas "fictional" works, which often foreground the vicissitudes of language, are idiomatically associated with "emptiness" and "falsehood." This classical aesthetics, which Průšek calls "the factographic tradition of the literati" and which he describes as "predominantly intellectual" and "anti-aesthetic" in tendency (Průšek, p. 95), helps to explain the Chinese aversion to artfulness, craftsmanship, and fictionality as alternative and equally valid criteria for judging cultural forms. In modern terms, "fullness" readily translates into "the realistic." One needs only consider the multiple laudatory terms, both literary and moral, that combine and conflate the notions of fullness and reality: *zhenshi, shizai, shiji, queshi, zhuoshi, xianshi, jiao ta shidi*. This is why, in spite of a rich diversity of artistic methods and the highlighting of the artist's personality, all artistic effort in modern Chinese literature is "dominated by the attitude toward reality" (Průšek, p. 83).

What does this persistent attitude toward "reality" mean in our present argument about modernity and narration?

In an essay that discusses extensively the conceptual boundaries of the narrative category in the Chinese context, Andrew Plaks draws attention to the importance of *historiography* and its related emphasis on "truth," both of which underlie the function of transmission of actual or hypothetical fact in traditional Chinese storytelling:

> Any theoretical inquiry into the nature of Chinese narrative must take
> its starting point in the acknowledgement of the immense importance
> of historiography and, in a certain sense, "historicism" in the total
> aggregate of the culture. In fact, the question of how to define the
> narrative category in Chinese literature eventually boils down to
> whether or not there did exist within the traditional civilization a sense
> of the inherent commensurability of its two major forms: historiography
> and fiction. . . .

The point here is simply to acknowledge the fact that historical writing, oriented towards the function of transmission, occupies the predominant position within the range of Chinese narrative possibilities, so that it is fiction that becomes the subset and historiography the central model of narration. (Plaks, pp. 311–12, 314)[23]

While I have problems with the dichotomous manner in which Plaks sets up the conceptual boundaries of Chinese narrative vis-à-vis those of the West—for example, historiography versus fiction; transmission versus storytelling; representational versus nonrepresentational mimetic positions (in narrative)—his discussion provides a useful framework in which to elaborate the conceptual predicaments faced by twentieth-century Chinese writers. In these writers' inclination toward autobiography, subjectivism, and so on, one can argue that there emerges a new primacy of what Plaks classifies as *fictor*, which is in the modern period not so much merely a new narrative "style" as it is the signal of the destruction of the factographic and historiographic bases of the Chinese narrative tradition. And yet, as we have already seen by following the turns of Průšek's arguments, the new "lyrical" tendencies have no sooner struck than they are felt to be haunted, in their very destructiveness, by the familiar preoccupation with "reality" that is typical of traditional Chinese writing. What have been *novelized* are not so much the conventional conceptual boundaries of narrative as the *signifieds* that are attached to the act of writing itself. Chief among them is the signified of a new national identity. In this new signified, the traditional figure of narrative-as-historiography, flanked on the one side by an insistence on the "truth" (or "reality") of representation and on the other by the custom of transmitting that "truth" collectively, once again appears predominant. Only this time, the struggle between historiography and fiction is utterly explosive because the social and cultural circumstances that in the past had made it possible for historiography to subordinate fiction consistently (thus enabling literary historians to see historiography as the "predominant" narrative tradition) have collapsed. The transparency (or naturalistic equation) between "reality" and "fiction," which the factographic impulses of historiography never stop imposing on narration even when such a transparency is meaningless, becomes, in modern times, the point at which the intervening presence of "feminine details" is most acutely felt.

In the following, through a closer look at the works of May Fourth writers Ba Jin, Mao Dun, and Lu Xun, I show how the recurrent obsession with "reality," which sees itself as revolutionary and defines "truth" as personal and historical *at once*, accounts for some of the dilemmas inherent in the "inward turn of narrative" in Chinese modernity. I stress once again that this obsession with reality is indeed subversive on its own terms, but, being akin to the traditional Chinese respect for book learning and classical literary culture, it is demonstrably different from the kinds of subversiveness we have seen in Butterfly literature. The practice of subversion as revolution is essentially tragic, not melodramatic, in structure, because it always posits (a) solipsistic subject(s) against an immobile, indifferent, or contradictory "outside" world. The difficulties of writing that result from this kind of subversiveness easily lend themselves to "deconstructive" analyses, insofar as writing is now always already *ironic*, and predictably always undermining itself. It is precisely as narrative turns "inward" in an (iconoclastic) attempt to "see" the opacities of "humanity," that the monolithic stature of a unified national consciousness is inevitably *cut up*—in detail. Narrative is thus, on the one hand, a new machine of the "human mind," driven in a well-defined direction toward the New China; on the other hand, narrative is an obstacle that makes the transparency between "subject" and "nation," or better still, the identity of subject-as-nation, impossible. In the latter sense, narrative becomes not the means of nation building but the process of detail production that insistently demolishes such a patriotic project.

2

Ba Jin's Jia *(The Family)(1930)*

The popularity of Ba Jin's *Jia* easily leads one to identify it as a Butterfly-type novel.[24] Ever since its publication in 1931, the novel has been well known to most Chinese readers, who were given two sequels, *Chun* [Spring] and *Qiu* [Autumn], in 1938 and 1940, respectively. The playwright Cao Yü rewrote *Jia* as a stage play that has been much performed, and several film versions, including two produced in the mainland in the 1950s and others in Hong Kong, were made. The novel is a family saga based on Ba Jin's own experiences. The Gao family, headed by the despotic, scholarly Master Gao, who has several sons, daughters-in-law, grandchildren, and a great-grandson, is in gradual decline in the age of revolutions and Western learning. The family's own feudal moral rigidities are presented through the lives of the three young brothers, grandchildren of Master Gao's, around whom the novel revolves. Juexin, being the eldest, is weighed down with filial obligations and responsibilities that crush his once enthusiastic attitudes toward new ideas and democratic learning. He marries a woman not of his own choice, causes himself and his old lover great misery, and later loses his wife as he is powerless to protect her from being forced by superstitious practices to go through a dangerous childbirth. Juemin and Juehui, being younger and spared many of Juexin's duties, are more uninhibitedly progressive. They participate in student movements, read journals such as *New Youth,* and write heated articles protesting against the old feudal system. After a series of sorrowful episodes, the novel ends with two uplifting promises. Juemin, who is determined to marry his cousin Qin, with whom he is genuinely in love, successfully turns down the arranged marriage that was once insisted on by Master Gao; Juehui, who is relentlessly indignant about his family's feudalistic ways, leaves his hometown (Chengdu, Sichuan Province) for Shanghai with the support of his two brothers and his friends.

If asked to give a brief description of *Jia*, Chinese readers will tell you that it is a "sentimental," "melodramatic" tearjerker. A close look at the novel, however, reveals that the conspicuous presence of sentimental and melodramatic elements forms part of a larger effort to suppress feminine, traditional modes of expression.

The intricate personal tragedies that afflict the Gao family take place against a background of abundant details of the domestic kind—the New Year's Eve dinner, birthday celebrations, games, gossip, family intrigues, and the funeral of the grandfather. But these details are also clearly subordinate to a narrative action that centers on the untraditional attitudes of several characters, of whom Juehui, with his incessant protests against the old system, is the most uncompromising. Juehui's rebelliousness expresses itself as an emphatically humane and humanist attitude. Of all the family members, he is the only one who refuses to sit in a sedan chair because it is carried by other men. During the New Year's celebrations, when the dragon dance is performed, he reacts coldly to his family members' sense of fun because the performance involves inflicting physical pain on the dancers. Juehui's defense of the dignity of *ren* (human beings) is shared by his older brother Juemin and their cousin Qin, a woman student inspired by liberal ideals. With no irony intended by Ba Jin, Qin once thinks to herself: "I want to be a person, a person just like a man" (*Jia*, p. 215).

This emergent humanism is the sign of an intense subversiveness to which Ba Jin himself attests when he says that his purpose in writing *Jia* was to "cry out my own 'J'accuse' before a dying system."[25] For us to see the problems inherent in this humanism, we must first acknowledge its subversiveness, expressed here in the narrative action, on its own terms. The narration in *Jia* consists in a movement away from the oppressiveness of the family, culminating in the most progressive character's physical departure from home. The denouncement of patriarchy thus constitutes modernity through the plot. What practice of reading does this plot solicit?

First of all, the reader is invited to join a new sense of collectivity that is articulated at the moment of the repudiation of the old China and a wishful announcement of the new. This, indeed, is the official mainland Chinese reading of Ba Jin's novel to this day. However, I am not against the "crudity" of the Communist reading. Something far more disturbing is happening in this novel, which in fact is better clarified by a crude reading. I would describe it once again by way of Althusser's theory of the interpellation of the subject, with the important emphasis that here, the "Ideology" that interpellates, that calls, is a particular kind of literary practice. The reader of literature, as "subject," is "hailed" and formed through the narrative moment of *departure* from the oppressiveness of the family. In other words, we have in this modern Chinese novel a process of radical position forming through *criticism*: the reading subject is positioned already through a subversion, a "flight from" an ideology, in this case the ideology of the feudalistic, Confucian family system. This kind of positioning is persuasive because it derives its strength from a conception and pronouncement of crisis rather than order. It is the institution of crisis both as narrative content and structure that accounts for the "subversive" moments of Ba Jin's "literary modernity."

But, as soon as it is understood that crisis and criticism are themselves inscribed with the force of an ideology that seeks to position the reader in specific ways, a different type of question arises. In spite of the political urgency with which the novel is impregnated, Ba Jin's treatment of the "internal" and "external" worlds of his characters reintroduces the "classical literary" problem of "truth," which is expressed through the novel's imperative to cleanse and purify. Because of this, even though the mood of a "critique of ideology" is clearly present, it remains at an idealist level. I will now elaborate on this.

The narrative mode that Ba Jin's writings often call to mind is that of "autobiography." Autobiography, however, is not simply a matter of the resemblance between the author's "real life" and his or her fictional structures. The compulsion to be autobiographical does not simply mean the "subjective" and "individual" tendency that is characteristic of many May Fourth writings, even though the conventionally "autobiographical" nature of *Jia*, for instance, is well recognized.[26] Rather, it pertains to a confessional urgency that signifies the persistence of a different, inner realm of meanings while the outside world is being narrated in the fullest, most public details. The feeling of self-confinement that accompanies this inner realm of meanings is not simply negative. For the May Fourth writer, the state of autobiographical confinement becomes the point at which truth can be located *in distinction from* the rest of the world. This is so even when events are narrated in the third person, as in *Jia*. Autobiographical narration—narration from the self-same point of view—now functions as a means of revealing the thoughts of different characters, which are tantamount to their *internal reality* (these two words being virtually tautological in this context).

Early in the novel, the servant girl Ming Feng retires to her room after a day's hard work, and we are let into "her mind":

How much longer must I go on like this? she asked herself tragically.
She remembered a snowy day seven years ago. A fierce-looking woman had led her from the side of her father, bereft over the loss of his wife, and brought her to this wealthy household. From then on orders,

exhausting toil, tears, curses and blows became the principal elements of her existence. A life of dullness, of drab, unvarying monotony. . . . Nothing new ever came her way, not even a new hope.

Fate, everything is decided by fate. When she was beaten and cursed she used these words to console herself. Suppose I had been fated to be a young lady too? Ming-feng luxuriated in fanciful imagination: She wore pretty clothing; she had parents who loved and cherished her; she was admired by handsome young gentlemen. One of them came and took her away to his home, and there they lived together happily ever after.

How silly. Of course it could never happen! She scolded herself with a smile. I'll never have a home like that! Her smile faded and her face fell. She knew very well what would happen to her. When she reached the proper age, Madam would say to her, "You've worked here long enough." And she would be placed in a sedan-chair and carried to the home of a man Madam had chosen, a man Ming-feng had never seen. He might be thirty or forty years old. Thereafter she'd toil in his house, work for him, bear him children. Or perhaps after a few weeks she'd come back to serve the same wealthy family, the only difference being that now she would not be scolded and beaten so frequently, and would receive a small wage which she would have to turn over to her husband. Isn't that what happened to Madam Shen's maid, Hsi-erh?

How terrible! That kind of a home is no home at all! (*Family*, pp. 19-20)

As Ming Feng is shown to retire not only to the servants' quarters at night, but also to the private corner of her heart, we notice the investment in "her" of a certain rationalizing, self-reflexive thinking pattern whose "truthfulness" lies outside her, in the interpretative narrative language. By describing "from within" and with uniform meditative complexity a character who is uneducated and simple, this narrative language levels class and gender differences to a point at which they become insignificant or nonsignifying. Ironically, precisely because we are shown the "inner thoughts" of different characters in the *same* meditative manner, they all become facets of the same narrative voice, the voice that in this way turns "autobiographical," writing about itself and no one else.

The revolutionary sympathy for the socially oppressed, which is undoubtedly sincere on the part of Ba Jin himself, must therefore be rethought against his intellectualizing narratives, which are often judged imprecisely as "romantic," "sentimental," "weak in plot," and so on. All these judgments fail to point out that it is the rational, educated leveling of all human beings as sacredly human, and the elimination of the traces of class- and gender-specific conflicts from the psychic reality he seeks to portray, that give his writings their idealist imprint.

As the compulsion to be autobiographical defines truth to be strictly *internal*, the public forms of traditional society are criticized as empty. Love has to be the spontaneous, "genuine" attraction between two individuals: Juexin, whose romantic love for Mei is unfulfilled but who is after all very happy in his arranged marriage to someone he did not know before, would always remain suspect as a passive victim of the old world. Ceremonies, too, have become nothing more than superfluous farces. An example of this is the description of Master Gao's funeral, in which the ritualized mourning that takes the form of loud crying by women is ridiculed as sheer pretentiousness. A theory of emotions that is grounded in criteria of "genuineness" and that rejects the melodramatic as a way of expression is evident here:

> The women behind the curtains were having a hard time. Since guests kept arriving, the number of times they had to cry kept increasing too. At this point, crying had turned into an art; it had, moreover, the function of socializing with guests. For instance, if, while the women were talking or eating, the musicians started playing (to signal the arrival of guests), they would have to burst into a loud cry immediately—the more sorrowfully, the better, of course. But most of the time they were simply shrieking as there were no tears. There had been farces too, when signals of guests' arrival and departure were confused. The women would cry a long time before realizing it was unnecessary, or else, not knowing that guests had come, they remained utterly quiet until the master of ceremony hinted, whereupon they would suddenly explode into a crying noise. (*Jia*, p. 347)[27]

The *detailed* way in which this melodramatic ritual is presented corresponds to the extent to which truthful emotions are now thought to be unutterable. In this Romantic construction of truth—as that which exceeds and defies outward expression—Ba Jin's literary modernity rejoins the allegorical tendencies of classical Chinese poetry, which owes its superior position in the hierarchy of Chinese literary genres to its cultivated reticence, its contrast with popular cultural forms (such as storytelling), which are debased for their frivolous, garrulous, and thus "womanly" expressiveness. The contempt for a traditional ritual that is foregrounded as feminine melodrama therefore unites Ba Jin's canonically "modernist" text with the elitism of classical Chinese organizations of "literariness" even as the modernist text interpellates the reader under the rubric of "antitradition." Poetic reticence now returns in a revolutionary mood, or better still, *as* revolution. In the inward-turning, public-disavowing moments of modernity, the feminine detail of ritualized expression is dismissed twice—as what is traditional and outdated, but also as what has always already been marginalized in tradition itself.

The Romantic construction of "truth" as that which exceeds and defies outward expression means that the intellectual-as-writer takes on a haunted and tragic personality. While "truth" is on the one hand compellingly *natural*, as the revealing titles of many of Ba Jin's novels suggest (e.g., *Fog, Rain, Thunder, Lightning, Spring, Autumn, Snow, Fire, Germs, The Setting Sun*), the writing of truth is, on the other, inevitably reluctant, painful, and thus unnatural. In sharp contrast to the cleanness of a physical departure such as Juehui's, the "release" through writing is always accompanied by the lingering bitterness of memory: "I fear memory. I hate memory. It reminds me of all those things I want to forget."[28] Hence also Ba Jin's repeated image of himself as having been persecuted into writing against his wishes: "I don't write because I want to be an author, but life of the past forces me to pick up my pen" (*Jia*, p. 394). It is as if, once he picked up his pen, he would be doing something extremely unpleasant, which the momentary relief writing brings can never permanently overcome:

> Each time I finish writing, it's like waking up from a nightmare: the heavy pressure on my heart disappears; my body feels lighter. At this time I would have moments of peace and quiet in my heart.
> But such moments do not last long. . . . It's as if that propelling force never wants to let me free. I am tired, but I can't rest. Many times, I almost want to cry, "Spare me!" But I have never been spared. Writing has gradually turned into a punishment, a painful torture. . . .
> I always wish I could forget about the books I wrote, but in reality I cannot. Whenever I sit at my desk and pick up my pen, I would see all those books piled up in front of me—no, piled up on my heart. They are weighing on my heart so heavily that sometimes I suffocate. I said I wanted to be free, and yet I cannot get rid of these dark shadows.
> And so I pity myself, curse myself. I only wish I need never write one word.[29]

It is this masochistic sense of literature as an unavoidable penal experience that ultimately equates it with the mission of social reform, through an unfailing emphasis on the "life" element in writing:

> In 1928, I learned how to write fiction in France. . . . What I learned was to weld writing and life together, and to weld writer and people together. I think that the highest place for a work to attain is the merging of the two, with the author surrendering his heart to the reader.[30]

What results from the self-conscious reflection on writing seems to be a strange division between vivid, memorable impressions of a past oppressive world and dreamy revolutionary idealizations about a future whose outlines are vague and theoretical. Ba Jin's accounts of childhood events, such as his love for a particular rooster and a servant named Yang Sao (to be discussed in the next chapter), are written with the touching naïveté of a young boy who did not yet fully comprehend but was overwhelmed by what was happening around him.

The immediacy of such accounts is in sharp contrast to his "revolutionary" portrayals of "new" characters in his novels, who are always progressive but uninterestingly predictable. Immersed as it is in the effort to criticize and purify, Ba Jin's treatment of the internal (psychical) and the external (social) worlds demonstrates the vestiges of a culture in which "literary" categories are continually projected into the affective realm. The poetic valorization of sparse expressiveness becomes at the same time a reinforcement of so-called virtues such as self-restraint, silent suffering, and emotional control. And yet, while men have for a long time had access to the practice of art, where emotional restraint can find glorification in the past as poetic elegance and now as progressive modernity, women often have no choice but to resort to violent, improper ways of expressing themselves, the most extreme form of which is suicide.

In *Jia*, then, we have in fact another moment of revolution. The maid Ming Feng, who is in love with Juehui and forced to marry a much older man as concubine, throws herself into a pond as the utmost gesture of "departure" available to a woman of a domestic servant position. The violence of this uncompromising, self-destructive act is the opposite of emotional self-restraint, since self-restraint would mean her total submission to the patriarchal order. However, in the novel this feminine violence is subsumed under a more masculine relation to the patriarchal order that directs the narrative action. This masculine relation is defined through our feeling that the old system must be overthrown, so that new youths like Juehui can replace it. As he mourns her, we feel that he is mourning the destructiveness of the "system," not the death of the woman who has devoted her life to him. His revolution is then the revolution based on affective control and a containment of violence—a revolution that in turn positions us, the readers, in a "truthful," because literary, relation to reality. In spite of the fact that this novel is full of melodramatic, sentimental, tear-jerking "details," it is a more fundamental rejection of such details as superfluous that structures the novel's writing. This structure depends for its support on a dichotomy between "self" and "other." Subversiveness is inscribed in writing as a Romantic struggle of truth against falsehood, of revolutionary-minded "human" characters against the inhuman feudal system. Depending on the context, this struggle can be rewritten alternately in so many other ways, as "man versus universe," "youth versus tradition," "woman versus man," and so forth. The inadequacy of the theory implied in this struggle lies in the assumption of unified, wholesome, uncontradictory ideologies, which are knocked down *en bloc* every time "truth" speaks. The pain involved in writing and the torture of remembering the past become in this light arduous "experiences" that the writer, as Romantic Revolutionary Hero, has no choice but to go through in order to produce what are essentially "autobiographical" narratives.

Mao Dun's Hong [The rainbow] (1930)

Mao Dun's novels bear the mark of a mediating subject whose means of under-standing the world is through analytic penetration.[31] The often unpointed and anticlimactic nature of these novels raises the question of why they are impor-tant for a student of modern Chinese literary history. In their attempts to pin-point that importance, critics have used epistemological and literary categories as ways of defining Mao Dun's modernity, such as "contradiction," de Manian "irony," and "allegory."[32] Using Hong, I argue that the undoubtedly correct de-tection of internal distancing in Mao Dun's prose brought forth by these other-wise different critical evaluations has to be supplemented—or further detailed—by an investigation of Mao Dun's approach to "femininity." The interior dramatization of the conflict between tradition and progress that is such an in-herent part of Mao Dun's characters is one that is most acutely felt in the new woman, whose conviction of the ideals of revolution, itself problematized, fur-ther poses the question of how her "traditional" female body should be repre-sented.

The story of Hong may be briefly summarized as follows. Mei, who is forced to marry her cousin Liu Yüchun, decides that her way out of this trauma is by going along with her father's decision and then asserting her own rights after the mar-riage has taken place. Mei is really in love with Wei Yü, her other cousin, who is consumptive, effeminate, and lacking in courage to rebel against what "fate" has in store for him. In a confused state of mind, Mei enters her arranged mar-riage and only then discovers that her plan of not giving in to her husband's sexual demands does not work. A long period of debating with herself convinces Mei of her need to leave home. The second part of the story shows Mei as a schoolteacher in a different town of the same province. There, she almost im-mediately becomes an object of gossip and jealousy among her colleagues be-cause of her unconventional ways of thinking. In the "educational" circles, she once again witnesses the collapse of her revolutionary ideals. In the third part, Mei moves to Shanghai and involves herself with local activist groups. She falls in love with Liang Gangfu, a cool-headed revolutionary, but he does not recip-rocate with passion. The story ends on a day (supposedly in 1928) when Mei and her woman friend join the anti-imperialist campaigns in Shanghai, distributing flyers amid crowds of protesters, pedestrians, and aggressive policemen.

Intensifying with the tortuous inner thoughts of his characters, the "drama" in Mao Dun's fiction strikes one as unendable because it is "intellectual." The preoccupation with "truth" sees truth as a wrestling with "external" reality. This wrestling is what produces the highly *meditated* effects of Mao Dun's descrip-tions. Characters have the vaguest of outward contours, but are all heavily self-reflexive. As their "thoughts" are what they are "all about," these thoughts, rather than external events, constitute the chief type of action in Mao Dun's longer narratives. Some examples of such inner drama in *Hong* are as follows:

Ms. Mei smiled at these wooden boats. She praised the great power of machines; she had not the least sympathy for those snail-like things that were being lashed at by the rapid, machine-generated currents. She very much trusted this gigantic monster that was carrying her. She was deeply aware that this monster, which was the product of modern civilization, was going to bring her a new "future." Although what was ahead was an unknown, unfamiliar world, it would certainly be bigger and more ardent: Ms. Mei believed in this unconditionally. . . .

During the rapid conversations, Ms. Mei once again heard a lot of new terms. Even though she was not very sure of their meanings, each one of them gave her a strong happy feeling and extreme excitement. . . . She felt that a whole new world was spreading out in front of her—she needed only to step in, and there would be light, there would be happiness. . . .

As the spring term began, "new waves of thinking" were sweeping all the schools even more intensely, and also began to reflect on the concrete life of society. Dr. Hu's slogan, "Investigate more problems, talk less of 'isms'" conveniently became a popular saying. Ms. Mei felt that Wei Yü had been poisoned by "isms" too—the "no-resistance-ism." And yet when she wanted to investigate "self" as a problem, she was lost in the deep waters of contradiction. She did not know what direction to turn. She blamed it on her own insufficient knowledge. She wanted more passionately to swallow all the new ideas. She decided not to let that practical question disturb her again. . . .

She thought: all evils could be blamed on the old tradition, and yet all evils were taking place under the banner of fighting the old tradition—this was the glorious, fashionable New Culture Movement! (*Hong*, pp. 9, 25, 46, 74)

The development of a sensitivity that tries desperately to chart a capricious reality that is outside its control often results in a character's feeling solipsistically lonely: for Mei, the truth is that "nobody really understands me" (*Hong*, p. 137). Moreover, solipsism is strongly associated with being a woman. Like the Butterfly writers he condemns, Mao Dun perceptively identifies women's lives as the place where the most intense ideological issues can be dramatized. His spectrum of female characters, from the quiet, conventional Jing in "Disillusionment," to the liberated Sun Wuyang in "Vacillation," the promiscuous Zhang Qiuliu in "Pursuit," and the rebellious and perplexed Mei in *Hong*, points to the vastly diverse roles "available" to women in early twentieth-century China, though none of them holds the promise of being a solution. Urban and Western-educated, these women characters' dilemmas are portrayed as a clash primarily between old and new *ideas*. The distrust of bygone, feudalistic notions of "womanhood" is now accompanied by notions of "humanity" read from foreign authors such as Ibsen and Tolstoy; yet the conviction of the need for female liberation as part of social reform is continually contested by a pragmatic realization on the characters' part of the societal contempt, the physical danger, and the intellectual confusion that they are subject to as "new women."

Schematically, then, Mao Dun's women characters are, as his pen name suggests, his "contradictory" (*maodun*) approach to "truth." As a literary figure, "woman" in Mao Dun's novels begins by being feminist and progressive, and yet as the narrative moves on it is precisely revolutionary criticism as embodied in the "new woman" that becomes more and more dubious. Mei, disillusioned by her first love, Wei Yü, because of his lack of revolutionary enthusiasm, ends up finding exactly the kind of man she wants—the revolutionary Liang Gangfu— only then to feel dissatisfied with not being able to have a tender *loving* relationship with him. This kind of irony is not a simple reversal of positions, but is suggestive of the unfinalizable complexity of "revolution" that is being staged in a new contemplative literary language through the trope of woman.

The meditative quality of Mao Dun's inner monologues equally describes dialogues between characters. With only the most rudimentary reminders of conversations (such as the presence of quotation marks), Mao Dun's dialogues tend to be extremely studied and read more like dramatic soliloquies. For instance:

[One of the women characters to Mei:] "That's because I, too, am a person made of blood and flesh; I, too, am controlled by physiology; I, too, have instinctual sexual impulses. Yes, I fell into it. Regrets, I have none. I have not considered this event as too terribly important. I only hate myself for being too fragile: instead of controlling my emotions, I let momentary passion drown my will power! Now, I think, is the time I should let go. It's not that I feel conscience-stricken, but I don't want to be involved in this black whirlpool." (*Hong*, p. 76)

Or:

[Mei to a woman friend:] "How? I can't say what I understand in my heart. Sometimes even I myself wonder: why is it that I am not as brisk and unconstrained as before, but somehow 'sticky'? Yet sometimes I feel I am still me, without any difference. Sometimes I feel my heart is empty, like a white sheet; but sometimes I seem to feel it's a wrinkled sheet, and not clean. It's as if I overturned a dish containing seven colors; nothing feels right, and all is mad confusion! There is some each of grumpiness, boredom, and anger. All in all, I understand this better recently: all the colors on my life-picture have been matched wrong!" (*Hong*, p. 112)

The ease with which Mao Dun's prose can be translated into English draws our attention not only to his anglicized grammar, but more importantly to what his determination to abandon traditional Chinese narrative methods implies. The discursive, articulate quality of the characters' "thinking" is the effect of an analytic narrative language that turns "thought" into the new object of representation, making it thus available to the readers. What is even more interesting is that such objectification of thought amounts to the conceptual creation of "selfhood" in modern Chinese literature, a creation that is instantly indistinguishable from the feeling of alienation. As they consciously reflect on their own thinking, characters discover an insurmountable barrier between themselves and the world precisely in terms of that thinking and in terms of reflexive language itself. The predominance of person/subject indicators such as "I" and "me," and the corresponding predominance of reportive sentences beginning with "she" in the third-person narration, thus indicate not only the new construction (in Chinese literature) of reality from the vantage point of individual minds and the common "humanity" these "minds" connote, but also all the problems such a construction entails.

As I mentioned earlier, the renunciation of details that signify the old China goes hand in hand with the invention and elaboration of new kinds of spaces that are conveniently visible through the figure of the new woman. Mao Dun's analytic narrative language, then, can be described in terms of a voyeurism that derives its pleasure as well as knowledge from the spectacle of femininity. In a way similar to Ba Jin's *Jia*, the "inward turn" of Mao Dun's narration becomes ambiguous exactly as it tries to be objective and democratic. While earnestly opening up every character's "thoughts" to analysis, it also leaves behind an area that remains purely pictorial, imagistic, beyond analysis: women's bodies. Among the many descriptions of female physiological details, the narrative gaze returns obsessively to the breasts:

> Ms. Mei's face was now radiating with a beautiful red light. And the curves of her breasts were trembling so nicely. . . .
> She felt that her body was hot all over. Unbuttoning her clothes in front and enjoying the moonlight's caresses, she suddenly noticed that her breasts seemed to have grown bigger than before; they were lying full and tight inside her foreign-cloth blouse.
> The drizzles suddenly turned into a heavy pour. As Ms. Mei reached No. 240, her dress, long soaked through and tightly sticking to her body, was outlining her highly-rising breasts. (*Hong*, pp. 55, 59, 227)

In one sense, of course, one could argue that the obsession with women's breasts is not incongruous with Mao Dun's objective narrative modernity. Female breasts were a "new" figure at the time; their visibility in public signifies "progress" and their inclusion in rational prose signifies a legitimation, hence demystification, of an embarrassing kind of detail: one should be able to describe it as one does anything else. In another sense, however, the breasts establish a gap in the narrative language even as the latter tries to subsume them under its relentless progress. This gap is the gap between "woman" as reflexive "mind" and "woman" as sexual "body." In the midst of the most radical change in Chinese literary language—an analytic openness in fiction writing—we are confronted with the return of woman as the traditional, visually fetishized object, which, in spite of woman's new "cerebral" developments, still fascinates in a way that is beyond the intellect, beyond analysis! One cannot conceptualize the breasts without "seeing" or "feeling" them in one's mind; the "intellectual" grip on reality is then loosened, sensuously. As an irreducibly sensuous figure, the female body also unsettles the revolutionary rhetoric when it becomes intimate with other female bodies. Scenes of women intensely engaged in conversation, so much so that the intimacy changes from being intellectual to being physical, are often depicted in a way that is never matched by similar descriptions of exchanges between men.[33] As the women kiss, touch, and hug one another, and as they are facetiously reported to be indulging in "tongxing ai" (homosexual love), what are the implications for the social revolution at large? It is ironic that Mao Dun, who speaks so strongly for the elimination of unnecessary details elsewhere, would also give us moments of such feminine superfluities. The eroticized, because fetishized, images of women's bodies, which no amount of narrative prose can penetrate enough the way it does women's "minds," remain to haunt the liberating rhetoric of revolution, including Mao Dun's new literary language. Existing side by side with the thoughtful constructions of the new Chinese "self," the familiar but tantalizing tableaux of women's bodies highlight the former precisely as verbal language, which, however activated, remains impotent in fulfilling its own revolutionary desires.

Lu Xun's "Zhufu" ("The New Year's Sacrifice") (1926)

In Lu Xun's "Zhufu," we find one of the most compelling encounters between a member of the dominating class and a downtrodden "other" in twentieth-century literature.[34] A short story that forms part of the collection Panghuang (Wandering) (1926), "Zhufu" is a first-person account of the narrator's visit to his hometown, Luzhen, before the New Year, when he happens to see Xianglin Sao, an old beggar woman who used to work for his Fourth Uncle. While he is still disturbed by the riddle-like questions that Xianglin Sao posed to him about life after death, she dies during the night of New Year's Eve. The rest of the story takes the form of a recollection of Xianglin Sao's life. A widow, she first came to the narrator's Fourth Uncle's house as a servant. As she was strong, quiet, and hard-working, she soon won the favor of her master and mistress. One day, her dead husband's family came and took her home by force to be remarried, so that they would have money to buy a wife for their younger son. Xianglin Sao "gave in" after many protests and an attempt at suicide. She became happily married and gave birth to a boy. But her second husband soon died of typhoid fever. As she tried to make a living by gathering firewood, picking tea, and raising silkworms, her son was carried off by a wolf. She was soon asking for work at Fourth Uncle's, only she had become slow, dazed, and gloomy. Because she was twice a widow and thus an ominous figure, she was no longer allowed to have anything to do with ancestral sacrifices. She now tirelessly repeated the story of how her little son was snatched away, and turned herself into a laughingstock with this obsession. Meanwhile, fearful about being punished in her afterlife for having had two husbands, she spent all her savings on buying a threshold in the local temple, which she believed would take her place in being "trampled upon" and free her of her sins. Psychotic, aging, and losing her memory, Xianglin Sao was dismissed by her master and became a beggar.

If Xianglin Sao's existence can be interpreted as a kind of detail, which is eliminable both for the traditionally privileged classes and for the classes propelled by enlightenment and reform, then Lu Xun's story deals with the detail in a way that is ethically more powerful and more disturbing than those of Ba Jin and Mao Dun.

From the beginning, the narrative involvement with Xianglin Sao is inseparable from the contradictions of the narrator's position. Like many of his kind, Lu Xun's intellectual narrator is a "subject" whose access to society is, by tradition, through a thorough subjugation of himself to "learning." The acquisition of a particular consciousness through the Confucian literary education made him at once the privileged beneficiary and the custodian of "culture." In the age of Western imperialism, however, this traditional structure of *privilege through subjugation* was disrupted. The Chinese intellectual was oppressed by two kinds of impotence: first, the realization that "literature" as he used to understand it no longer worked in sustaining his power; second, that as a "Chinese national" he witnessed the fragmentation of his civilization vis-à-vis the West in an utterly helpless manner. It is against the background of such impotence that the many figures of the "other" make their first entries into modern Chinese literature, figures in which an otherwise inexplicable excess of emotion is invested to the point of sentimentalism. These "others," all of whom are socially oppressed, provide the screen onto which a total sense of China's collapse is projected. As that which is unpleasantly present, Xianglin Sao is like an ancient detail about China that cannot be forgotten.

Like Ba Jin's *Jia*, "Zhufu" is suffused with a desire for departure. The narrator returns to "Luzhen, my hometown," but adds that he is only calling it so; as he has not made his home there for some time, he has to put up at the house of his Fourth Uncle. This general, if mild, sense of dislocation from the time the narrator arrives soon turns "homecoming" into an urge for taking off: "Whatever happened I would leave the next day, I decided" (*Complete Stories*, p. 157). Yet what exactly does this wish for departure mean? What form does it take? When he realizes that his Fourth Uncle and he are clearly opposed on the question of reform and modernization, the narrator "departs" by withdrawing to the study, and into the traditional scholastic mode of contemplation. This "departure" sets the tone for the rest of the narrative. While the narrator cannot forget his encounter with Xianglin Sao, his engagement with her is at the same time an evasion that takes the most convoluted and indecisive turns:

"So you're back?" were her first words.

"Yes."

"That's good. You are a scholar who's travelled and seen the world. There's something I want to ask you." A sudden gleam lit up her lacklustre eyes.

This was so unexpected that surprise rooted me to the spot.

"It is this." She drew two paces nearer and lowered her voice, as if letting me into a secret. "Do dead people turn into ghosts or not?"

My flesh crept. The way she had fixed me with her eyes made a shiver run down my spine, and I felt far more nervous than when a surprise test is sprung on you at school and the teacher insists on standing over you. Personally, I had never bothered myself in the least about whether spirits existed or not; but what was the best answer to give her now? I hesitated for a moment, reflecting that the people here still believed in spirits, but she seemed to have her doubts, or rather hopes—she hoped for life after death and dreaded it at the same time. Why increase the sufferings of someone with a wretched life? For her sake, I thought, I'd better say there was.

"Quite possibly, I'd say," I told her falteringly.

"That means there must be a hell too?"

"What, hell?" I faltered, very taken aback. "Hell? Logically speaking, there should be too—but not necessarily. Who cares anyway?"

"Then will all the members of a family meet again after death?"

"Well, as to whether they'll meet again or not . . ." I realized now what an utter fool I was. All my hesitation and manoeuvring had been no match for her three questions. Promptly taking fright, I decided to recant. "In that case. . . actually, I'm not sure. . . . In fact, I'm not sure whether there are ghosts or not either."

To avoid being pressed by any further questions I walked off, then beat a hasty retreat to my uncle's house, feeling thoroughly disconcerted. I may have given her a dangerous answer, I was thinking. Of course, she may just be feeling lonely because everybody else is celebrating now, but could she have had something else in mind? Some premonition? If she had had some other idea, and something happens as a result, then my answer should indeed be partly responsible. . . .
Then I laughed at myself for brooding so much over a chance meeting when it could have no serious significance. No wonder certain

educationists called me neurotic. Besides, I had distinctly declared, "I'm not sure," contradicting the whole of my answer. This meant that even if something did happen, it would have nothing at all to do with me. "I'm not sure" is a most useful phrase.

Bold inexperienced youngsters often take it upon themselves to solve problems or choose doctors for other people, and if by any chance things turn out badly they may well be held to blame; but by concluding their advice with this evasive expression they achieve blissful immunity from reproach. The necessity for such a phrase was brought home to me still more forcibly now, since it was indispensable even in speaking with a beggar woman. (*Complete Stories*, pp. 155-57)

If thought patterns are indicative of "subjectivity," no commentary can recapture sufficiently the ironic, deconstructive quality of the subjectivity in the preceding passage. Evidently troubled by a figure like Xianglin Sao and yet incapable of locating the sources of his feelings, the narrator is beset by a terror that doubles back on the narrative as a constant flight from his own position. Indeterminacy here becomes an indispensable means of self-defense. But defense against what? Why is the narrator, like so many of Lu Xun's narrators when faced with their socially oppressed "others," so terrified? What constitutes neurosis here? The story's narration does not provide an answer.

Instead, this narrative blank is elaborated through a completely different treatment of Xianglin Sao. While the narrator is a "mind" with which we become acquainted through its contradictions, Xianglin Sao remains someone we observe from without, like an animal: she has "big strong feet and hands" and "would eat anything." She is called not by her own name but "Xianglin's wife." She is sold to her first husband's family exactly as a commodity. Her perplexity over life and death is not entertained nor is it articulated collectively to form a larger experience; her obsession with her dead child dwindles into a ridiculous psychosis no one bothers to investigate; her inability to comprehend her own life prevents it from being transcended in any teleological perspective, including that of sacrifice. All the representational channels that could have given her a kind of "subjectivity" are carefully blocked. This hardened "object" undermines the lucidity of the narrative from within, fracturing the "subjectivity" of the narrator in the form of elliptic shifts in narrative mood, which is now melancholy, now hopeful.

In a brilliant article, Marston Anderson defines the narrative patterns in Lu Xun as typical of the short story, in which the realist effect of alienation, which comes from the portrayal of "a slice of life" in its obstinate, meaningless condition, often goes hand in hand with the lyrical effect of a narrator's subjective struggle against that condition.[35] In "Zhufu," it is the impenetrability of Xianglin Sao (which coexists incongruously with the lucidity of her portrayal) that accounts for our feeling of her passivity and victimization. All the events that shape Xianglin Sao's life are presented with the effect of a certain fatality that "happens" to her, and over which she has no control. By contrast, the narrator is extremely active, not only in his physical comings and goings, but also in his thinking and writing. Through the latter activities of mental composition, we are struck with an inescapable sense of guilt and thus of dislocation. This sense of guilt and dislocation in Lu Xun is often the result of first-person narration. As the first-person perspective is frequently that of the intellectual who is con-vinced of the need for social reform, the no less compelling presence of naive characters who are oblivious of such need and to whom Lu Xun's narrators ob-sessedly return produces a sense of futility from within the narrative itself.

As modern China's most famous writer, Lu Xun has been described alter-nately as "satiric realist" and "predominantly reminiscent and lyrical."[36] The conflict between these two perspectives, whereby the mood of a progressive ori-entation toward modernization is challenged by the colorful narration of child-hood and country life with their moving characters, and by a sad awareness of the immobile habits of a long, tortuous civilization, suggests that Lu Xun's work must be considered not simply for its formal innovative significance, but rather for its explorations of the fundamental problematic of writing in modern China.[37] The question that his work as a whole poses for an understanding of "Third World" politics is this: if writing has always been the possession of the educated classes, how might it be justified for social revolution? Clearly, such a justification must be sought beyond the heated slogans for literary reform. In his two early collections of short stories (*Nahan*, or *Call to Arms*, 1923, and the aforementioned *Wandering*, 1926), Lu Xun's fiction remarkably demonstrates that the most powerful formal effect of writing—that is, the effect of represen-tation as *distancing*—never truly alleviates suffering but only compounds guilt. The effect of distancing was indistinguishable from a complicity with the exist-ing political order at a time when "complicity" could not be supported by the kind of leisure that would allow it to be read as its opposite, as the resistance-in-silence that "literature" theoretically provides. If the process of "othering" in "Zhufu" is a process of cognition, it is also cognition as disability. The presence of a "new" perspective, that of reform, against which "others" like Xianglin Sao are set off, is not yet an alternative to the victims of the social order that is being decried. The complicity and disability of the narrator, who is constantly fleeing from the reality he presents, are implied in the strangely lighthearted, peacefully oblivious ending:

> I was woken up by the noisy explosion of crackers close at hand and, from the faint glow shed by the yellow oil lamp and the bangs of fireworks as my uncle's household celebrated the sacrifice, I knew that it must be nearly dawn. Listening drowsily I heard vaguely the ceaseless explosion of crackers in the distance. It seemed to me that the whole

town was enveloped by the dense cloud of noise in the sky, mingling with the whirling snowflakes. Enveloped in this medley of sound I relaxed; the doubt which had preyed on my mind from dawn till night was swept clean away by the festive atmosphere, and I felt only that the saints of heaven and earth had accepted the sacrifice and incense and were reeling with intoxication in the sky, preparing to give Luzhen's people boundless good fortune. (*Complete Stories*, pp. 170-71)

Paradoxically, precisely because Xianglin Sao, like Lu Xun's other "superstitious" and "backward" country characters (such as Old Shuan and his wife in "Medicine," Fourth Shan's Wife in "Tomorrow," Runtu in "My Old Home," Ashun in "In the Tavern"), is an object on which the narrative does not bestow the qualities of a reflexive mind, the view of oppression that Lu Xun is offering is much more uncompromised. We are confronted with the effects of oppression in the most unmitigated, because "thingified," form: that of a useless, hopeless female existence on the lowest rung of the social ladder. As a detail, Xianglin Sao remains unabsorbed by the narrative action, creating a surplus of emotion that is always present as guilt. This kind of surplus resulting from the impenetrability of the oppressed distinguishes Lu Xun's narrative from those of Ba Jin and Mao Dun. By not subjecting Xianglin Sao to the leveling contemplative scrutiny of progressive thought, Lu Xun's story resists the unifying idealizations of language, modernism, nationhood, and human nature. With Lu Xun, a deep sense of disenchantment that is inseparable from a relentless criticism of the Chinese people gives shape to a modernity that recognizes, rather than neutralizes, the differences among different groups of Chinese people that arise primarily from education, the true marker of "class" and thus the true site of class struggle, in Chinese society. It is his refusal to use his own educated tools for the production of a false sense of optimism for the oppressed classes—to "comprehend" them and thus deproblematize their suffering within a class-generated ideology of revolution—that gives his writing its emotional power. Needless to say, this emotional power is often concurrent with the feeling of *wuke naihe*, the Chinese expression meaning "no alternative"; but *wuke naihe* describes the intellectual impasses that structure May Fourth fictional writings more accurately than many other representations.

3

I would like to conclude this chapter by returning to Eileen Chang, whose own narrative strategies differ considerably from those analyzed here.

In an autobiographical essay called "The Guileless Words of a Child," Chang records a scene where her brother was slapped on the mouth by her father for a trivial matter. As she hides in the bathroom, we are given this description:

Sobbing, I stood before the mirror and looked at my own drawn face, watching the tears trickling down like a closeup in a movie. I ground my teeth and said, "I'll get revenge. Someday, I'll get revenge."[38]

Such clear, straightforward articulations of the desire for revenge are not especially modern. In them we discover a distinctive characteristic of Chang's literary method—the refusal to tame or suppress even the ugliest and bleakest emotions. What we often encounter, instead, is an externalization of emotions that is at once refined and direct. The peculiarities of Chang's language deserve a close analysis as they point to the significantly different approach she takes toward history and modernity. A few examples are as follows:

On the ground, two swaying walking children.[39]
   She seems as if she is greedily chewing a with-its-oil-greatly-squeezed-out-of-it cake.[40]
   "These two lips of your new sister-in-law, chop them up and they'd make a big plateful."[41]

I have taken the liberty of translating these sentences in a way that preserves their construction in the original. In doing so, I hope to demonstrate the sense of *literalness* of many of Chang's descriptions. The sensuous details that mediate the perception of even the most abstract events are not merely images "with which" Chang writes. They are there to block the lucid flow of narration by means of an incongruity between the details and what they are supposed to describe. We feel as if what is described is topped with a cover that is somewhat too large and too extreme. Thus marked, the children's walking movement, the female protagonist's greed, and the new bride's lips become inseparable from the details that have accompanied them in an almost arbitrary manner. But the most crucial effect produced by these details is not only that they are incongruous but also that they dwarf the human figures in such a way as to leave these figures off-centered and hollowed of dignity.

   If we now return to Schor's argument about the detail, we would say that the detail in Chang's fiction is neither sublimated nor desublimated. As Schor sees it, sublimation and desublimation flank the detail's movements in the West from theological to secular to political realms of knowledge and power. In Hegel's aesthetics, details become the newly important constituents of art, which replaced religion as a predominant mode of transcendental cognition around the eighteenth century. In Barthes, the detail is "restored," after a long period of subservience to "art," to a kind of physical reality, a bodily presence, the "punctum" in its unexpected revelatory power. Sublimated or desublimated, the detail is the abode where interests in the human remain central. In Chang, however, the interest is elsewhere. First, because she is writing in a literary tradition whose origins are not "theological" in Schor's sense, it would be untenable to see her attention to details as a way of substituting art for theological "transcendence." The task of demonstrating this point is beyond the purposes of this chapter. I will therefore preoccupy myself with the other question: why are details not simply "corporeal" in Chang?

In the preceding examples, we notice that the presence of details does not so much lead to an unveiling of truth-as-the-physical as it deliberately marks and externalizes what is being described. Detailing in Chang is thus more appropriately a process of multiple layering than the uncovering of a concealed corporeality: while it presents one thing, it does so by adding to it another. More examples: in remembering the gluttony that suddenly caught up with everyone in Hong Kong after the Second World War, Chang tells us how a crowd of people, herself included, greedily gulped down some delicious turnip pancake bought from a hawker while a purplish corpse lay next to them on the street.[42] When a terminally ill patient died in the Hong Kong University temporary hospital where Chang was working as a nurse, what swept through the nurses' quarters was a wave of joy, followed by a group celebration with small baked buns that tasted like a kind of Chinese pastry.[43] The juxtaposition of such irrelevant details—details that are irrelevant to one another—empties the descriptions of any sense of human "virtue." In this respect, the narrative direction taken by Chang is drastically different from those we examined earlier. The dramatization—the cinematic blowing up—of details is a kind of destruction; what it destroys is the centrality of humanity that the rhetoric of Chinese modernity often naively adopts as an ideal and a moral principle. In Chang's language, feelings of indifference dominate, giving rise to a nonanthropocentric affective structure that is often expressed through the figures of ruin and desolation:

> Even if individuals can wait, the times rush by. Things are already
> being destroyed, and greater destruction is still to come. Whether it is
> sublimated or hollow, all our civilization will one day become the past.
> If the word I always use is "*huangliang*" [desolation], it's because I feel
> this frustrating threat in the background.[44]

Might there be a way of understanding "ruin" and "desolation" other than through the fatalistic pessimism that is often attributed to Chang? In these figures of destruction, what we encounter is, in fact, the world as a detail, a part that is always already broken off from a presumed "whole." It is this sense of wholeness—as that which is itself cut off, incomplete, and desolate, but which is at the same time sensuously local and immediate—rather than the wholeness of idealist notions like "Man," "Self," or "China," that characterizes Chang's approach to modernity. In her fiction, this nonconformist approach to modernity as wholeness and detail at once can be traced through one of the most conventional aspects of narrative, the construction of characters. The remainder of this chapter discusses a few of them.

Near the beginning of *Bansheng yuan* [Affinity of half a lifetime], a novel about a fatefully unfulfilled romance, we find this description of Gu Manzheng after she has lost a glove:

> In these places Manzheng is almost petty . . . her temperament is such that whenever something belongs to her, the more she looks at it the better it becomes, so much so that she thinks of it as the best in the world. . . . He [Shijun] knows this, because he was once hers.[45]

In the guise of a sentimental passage, the woman character's love for the man is explained primarily through the way she relates to things. What we read, if we read carefully, is that there is no difference between the two kinds of love. This kind of undifferentiating, possessive, and childlike attitude is sometimes expressed in Chinese as *chi*. The key to it is not spontaneity or innovation—two of the most important ways of feeling in the age of reform and revolution—but repetition: "the more she looks at it the better it becomes." The happiness that is derived from repetition is always accompanied by a sense of the trivial, since in its narcissistic relation with the beloved object, it precludes any "public" understanding. But "private" understanding as such is already the ruin of a battlefield over which the most repressive social mores have victoriously swept. This battlefield is the limited psychic reality in which Chinese women traditionally find themselves.

At the beginning of the novel, Manzheng is positioned somewhat outside the oppressiveness of women's conventional domestic lives. The second daughter of a poor family in Shanghai, she has been spared the ill fate of her older sister Manlu, who supports her family by being a prostitute and who later dies in sorrow in her marriage to a rascal. By contrast, Manzheng has an education and an office job, and freely chooses her loved one. But the greater freedom of choice that Manzheng experiences with regard to love does not lead to her liberation as a woman. After she is raped by her brother-in-law, Manlu's husband, and has fatefully lost contact with Shijun, love takes on a hallucinatory character as seeing Shijun again becomes a dream, while the son she bore as a result of the rape forces her to consent to marrying the rapist. The narrative therefore "progresses" in the direction not of liberation but of entrapment, by steadily associating married life with the degradation of women, who are valued in traditional Chinese society in accordance with their physical "intactness." In spite of Manzheng's access to a more "modern" way of life earlier, the loss of physical integrity and the child that follows ultimately return her to conventional domesticity. As a wife, she appears to us totally passive and indifferent—like a thing. The predominance of the inanimate, whether it appears in her narcissistic happiness or in her passive melancholy, becomes the sign of a trivialized and privatized relation that a woman of her standing can have with the world within the bounds of traditional Chinese social mores.

That this "feminine" relation to reality is shot through with class specificities can be argued when we see Chang approach woman servant characters in a different manner. The maid A Xiao in "A Xiao bei qiu" [A Xiao's lament of autumn] lives a life that is hard pressed, but she remains funny, creative, and resourceful throughout the story. While she manages her English master's house with a dexterity that includes keeping his unwanted girlfriends away and serving inexpensive meals to those in his current favor, A Xiao never loses her independence of judgment and interprets her surroundings in an instructively absurd manner. The details of her master's morning face, for instance, are as follows: "The meat on his face looks as if it is not fully cooked; it is reddish, with tiny streaks of blood. He has newly grown a moustache, so his face looks like a specially nutritious kind of egg, already half-hatched and showing a little bit of yellowish wing."[46] The elements of a rural mode of perception are thus marshaled to create a distance between herself and the foreign object in a way that reinscribes a basic resistance in the trivialized and privatized affective structure. Through A Xiao's contrast with upper-class and educated women characters, Chang alerts us to the roots of social oppression in cultured propriety itself.

What about the woman who straddles two classes? The story of Cao Qiqiao (Ts'ao Ch'i-ch'iao) in "The Golden Cangue" unfolds like a mock heroic journey, with her descending steadily into madness as her social-familial power increases. We are first introduced to her in terms of her insignificance. In the nighttime gossip of two maids, Qiqiao's status as an outsider strikes us especially vividly as we realize that she has already been married into the Jiang (Chiang) family for five years. As a woman of a lower class, her body has been traded for profit by her brother, but the sale of that commodity has not conferred upon her the respectable status as the "original owner." Instead, that transaction condemns her to permanent ridicule. The maids, themselves women and of a lower class, despise her:

> "Did you come with her when she was married?"
> Little Shuang sneered. "How could she afford me!" (p. 531)

In the rest of the conversation, we learn that Qiqiao's marriage into the Jiang family is, indeed, purely the result of other people's economic strategies—not so much those of her own family as those of the Jiangs. Why would the latter "stoop so low," as one of the maids asks, as to want a daughter-in-law from a sesame oil shop? Little Shuang answers:

> "Of course there was a reason. You've seen our Second Master, he's crippled. What mandarin family would give him a daughter for wife?"
> (p. 531)

Old Mistress Jiang, having at first decided to take Qiqiao as a concubine for her crippled second son, changed her mind as she realized that, in his condition, he "wasn't going to take a wife." But "it wouldn't do for the second branch to be without its proper mistress." Hence the offer of wifehood to Qiqiao, "so she would look after Second Master *faithfully*" (my emphasis). The rest of the story, then, is an ironic portrayal of how Qiqiao remains faithful to the Jiangs, as a daughter-in-law and as mother to her own children. If the portrayal of Qiqiao indicates anything about Chang's views of "humanity" in China, then Chang is evidently much more fascinated by that humanity's limits than in the lofty ideals that inspire many of her fellow writers to this day. Those limits are manifested in her narrative in the form of *cruelty*.

Indeed, even though as readers we understand that the perversities of Qiqiao's character are arguably the result of her social position, first as a poor, parentless young woman and then as a despised daughter-in-law in a wealthy family, it is the noisy and picturesque malice, and the utter lack of propriety of her behavior, that strike us as the "very stuff" of Chang's narrative. In the foreground of this narrative, as Qiqiao's marginalized status comes across as social content, Chang dramatizes the ways Qiqiao talks. Unlike Chinese women who are well brought up, Qiqiao has no sense of reticence or restraint. Verbal language becomes the means by which she strikes back at a world that is hostile to her, and as such it also relentlessly externalizes the morbidity of her existence.

Returning to the world the cruelty she has experienced from it, Qiqiao's language is consistently abusive—provoking, mocking, embarrassing, and demolishing those who come into contact with her. In particular, she enjoys picking on those who are more marginalized than herself, such as her unmarried sister-in-law Yunze (Yün-tse):

> Ambling over to the veranda, she picked up Yün-tse's pigtail and shook it, making conversation. "Yo! How come your hair's so thin? Only last year you had such a head of glossy black hair—must have lost a lot?"
>
> Yün-tse turned aside to protect her pigtail, saying with a smile, "I can't even lose a few hairs without your permission?"
>
> Ch'i-ch'iao went on scrutinizing her and called out, "Elder Sister-in-law, come take a look. Sister Yün has really grown much thinner. Could it be that the young lady has something on her mind?"
>
> With marked annoyance Yün-tse slapped Ch'i-ch'iao's hand to get it off her person. "You've really gone crazy today. As if you weren't enough of a nuisance ordinarily."
>
> Ch'i-ch'iao tucked her hands in her sleeves. "What a temper the young lady has," she said, smiling. (p. 534)

Or her new daughter-in-law:

> The guests gathered for the "riot in the bridal chamber" surrounded her [the bride], making jokes. After taking a look, Ch'i-Ch'iao came out.

Ch'ang-an [her daughter] overtook her at the door and whispered,
"Fair-skinned, only the lips are a bit too thick."

Ch'i-ch'iao leaned on the doorway, took a gold earspoon from her
bun to scratch her head with, and laughed sardonically. "Don't start on
that now. Your new sister-in-law's thick lips, chop them up and they'll
make a heaping dish!"

"Well, it's said that people with thick lips have warm feelings," said
a lady beside her.

Ch'i-ch'iao snorted; pointing her gold earspoon at the woman, she
lifted an eyebrow and said with a crooked little smile, "It isn't so nice
to have warm feelings. I can't say much in front of young ladies—just
hope our Master Pai [her son] won't die in her hands." (pp. 548-49)

And then her own daughter, whose chance of marriage she tries to block
even while she is sick herself:

Ch'i-ch'iao, convalescing, could get out of bed a bit and would sit in
the doorway and call out toward Ch'ang-an's room day after day, "You
want strange men, go look for them, just don't bring them home to
greet me as mother-in-law and make me die of anger. Out of sight, out
of mind, that's all I ask. I'd be grateful if Miss would let me live a
couple of years longer." She would arrange just these few sentences in
different orders, shouted out so that the whole street could hear. Of
course the talk spread among relatives, boiling and steaming. (p. 555)

Instead of being a subordinate part of the narrative, then, Qiqiao's language
arrests it, forcing us to notice the deadly nature of her "humanity." Near the end
of the story, we are given this description of her as Shifang (Shih-fang), her
daughter's boyfriend, is invited for a visit:

Shih-fang looked over his shoulder and saw a small old lady standing at
the doorway with her back to the light so that he could not see her
face distinctly. She wore a blue-gray gown of palace brocade
embroidered with a round dragon design, and clasped with both hands
a scarlet hot-water bag; two tall amahs stood close beside her. Outside
the door the setting sun was smoky yellow, and the staircase covered
with turquoise plaid linoleum led up step after step to a place where
there was no light. Shih-fang instinctively felt this person was mad. For
no reason there was cold in all his hairs and bones. (p. 557)

In the trajectory of the detail, Qiqiao's existence is that of a detail gone mad.
But her madness is far from complete, for even at her most cheated and heart-
broken moment, there is a residue of the propriety of self-sacrifice that is required of Chinese women. We see this in the scene where her brother-in-law
Jize, who flirted with her many years ago, attempts to seduce her once again so

that she would give him money. After she exposes his scheme, she blames herself:

> She wanted another glimpse of him from the upstairs window. No matter what, she had loved him before. Her love had given her endless pain. That alone should make him worthy of her continuing regard. . . . Today *it had all been her fault*. It wasn't as if she didn't know he was no good. If she wanted him she had to pretend ignorance and put up with his ways. Why had she exposed him? Wasn't life just like this and no more than this? In the end what was real and what was false? (p. 545; my emphasis)

With "pain" retained as a source of meaning, the moment of the greatest disillusionment becomes the moment of the greatest illumination. But this illumination is also the result of self-denial: while she is devastated she still thinks, "It had all been her fault." This enactment of the time-honored womanly virtue of self-sacrifice, even as Qiqiao is one of the most vicious characters in Chang's fiction, returns us to the question of entrapment. In this brief moment of the deepest feeling, Qiqiao is, like many of her counterparts in modern Chinese fiction, trapped as she voluntarily erases the premises of her own indignation. Putting the blame on herself, she becomes an accomplice to the invisible social demands whose power lies precisely in their ability to solicit the woman emotionally *from within* to assist in her own destruction.

Like some of Chang's critics, Qiqiao displaces her problems in terms of "life." The tendency for specific problems to become unspecified as general human problems is especially pronounced in the case of Chinese women. In Chinese society, it is precisely because women were traditionally barred from the realm of "public" undertakings that the problems posed by their existence would lend themselves to being identified, in a facile manner, as "human" problems, the problems of "life," and so forth. The bestowal of a "universal" significance in this sense should actually be seen as part of an entrenched epistemological reluctance to confront the social origins of the struggles of unprivileged groups. Why are women's "petty" psychology, their "wicked" schemings, and all the "negative" aspects of their "womanly" nature, which in Chinese society must be viewed as residues of the domestic circumstances under which they have had to live for so long, always approached in terms of *either* the insignificant *or* the universal? In the terms of this chapter, the problem of women confined to domesticity can now be rethought as the kind of detail that a culture either dismisses point-blank or subsumes under the largest and most irresponsible terms. Under this double process of erasure, we need to learn to read the tracks of the detail in a different way. The passivity of Manzheng, the viciousness of Qiqiao, the cleverness of A Xiao, and the many others in their trapped and privatized states of mind, are "details" of a society that are by definition incomplete, both because these women's lives are overdetermined outside their own will power, and be-cause in their trivialized feelings they continue to *cut up* their society's dream of a collective humanity. Chang's conception of history as "ruin" and "desolation" thus receives its most significant gloss from her descriptions of femininity-as-detail.

The commonly recognized sensual refinement of Chang's writings, in which "big" historical issues tend to recede into the background (for example, the "change of dynasties" around which "The Golden Cangue" takes place is merely mentioned), stands as the opposite extreme of the "revolutionariness" that we often associate with modernity in the Chinese literary context. Chang's modes of narration sabotage the identity that Chinese modernism seeks between "inner subjectivity" and "new nation." Incomplete because ideological, her women characters mock the progressiveness of the rhetoric for such an identity. The technology of the new narrative machine does not work yet, they seem to say, for the fetters of feudal China are still here, in the very way we feel.

Chang's "outdated" narrative direction ultimately determines her fate as a writer. That she was at the height of her career in Shanghai during the last two years of the Japanese occupation, when modern Chinese literature was cut off from its political aspirations, is ironic.[47] But what is more ironic is that she re-mains to this day a writer who is greatly popular with fiction readers, but whose historical and social significance remains largely neglected except by critics who valorize or criticize her for what they consider to be her portrayals of "human nature."[48] In spite of this, the opposition her work poses to modern Chinese literary history has not ceased doubling itself in important ways—in the uneasy relation between history and literary writing, between historical criticism and formal textual analysis. Any attempt to understand these relations must take se-riously the tension with the "historical" that Chang's writings produce. This tension offers us an alternative approach to history by resisting the lures of mon-umental structures of feeling. It forces us to rethink the assumption of moder-nity-as-revolution in the details of form, which are defined not as the technical-ities of aesthetics but as the fragmented symptoms of historically produced but epistemologically unrecognized conflicts.

Chapter 4
Loving Women: Masochism, Fantasy, and the Idealization of the Mother

1

It is said that Lin Shu and Wang Ziren, as they were collaborating on the translation of *La Dame aux Camélias*, wept so profusely that they could be heard even outside the house.[1, 2] No one to whom I repeat this story has failed to laugh, obviously because of the excessiveness of the sorrow expressed by these two men at what was, after all, a piece of fiction. The excessiveness is made apparent by a specific and intense form of physical discharge — the emission of tears. In a way that is directly opposed to the emotional restraint and control that are central to classical Chinese aesthetics, we witness here a conscious dramatization of the emotions. This story about two *readers* captures a predominant feeling surrounding the impression of modern Chinese literature: a profound unhappiness, an unabashed sentimentalism, and a deep longing for what is impossible. The task of this chapter is to explore the cultural premises of this feeling.

Throughout this book I have been emphasizing the significance of Westernization as what constitutes the materiality of Chinese modernity; however, it would be erroneous to assume that the correspondence between Westernization and modern Chinese "subjectivities" as such is a direct one. Instead of naming the West as the "cause" for a cultural practice such as reading, what I can offer as a literary critic are analyses of how Westernization, which is not necessarily present in a visible, thematic form, nonetheless haunts modern Chinese writings in the form of *emotional effects*, which include those of misery, frustration, despair, as well as emancipation. If it is possible to argue for an "unconscious" that

121

structures the language of Chinese modernity, as I believe it is, what are the symptoms of that "unconscious"? To ask this question is to ask how sexuality—not simply in the sense of sex but more so of libidinal energy—is expressed. In what ways is sexuality allowed to appear in modern Chinese fiction? How does sexuality mediate reading?

Lin Shu and Wang Ziren's response to Dumas fils's novel signals a departure from the stoic, militant sternness that is required of Chinese men in the idiomatic expression *da zhangfu liu xue bu liu lei* (a real man sheds blood, not tears). Crying, which is normally construed as a sign of effeminacy and thus of weakness, seems in these men's case to activate a kind of pleasure, which Denis Diderot defines as "the pleasure of being touched and giving way to tears."[3] Being touched by what? On the basis of the attention Lin Shu pays to her as we have seen in chapter 2, we may safely assume that it is by the character Marguerite's "virtue," a quality of which Diderot has also given an appropriate definition: "What is virtue? It is . . . a form of self-sacrifice."[4] The conjunction of sympathetic response, indicated in our present case by crying, and the virtue of self-sacrifice is a complex one. What is it in another person's self-sacrifice that triggers *our* sympathy? What does it mean to cry? As spectators to a fictional drama, Lin Shu and his friend may be described as having fulfilled a certain "lack" created by the events of the drama, the lack of a benign understanding that would help alleviate and vindicate Marguerite's suffering. In this sense, the spectator is completing by his reception the fictional "tableau" that is unveiled before him.[5]

However, it seems to me that before this theoretical *placing* of the spectator in the work's formal structure can be made, we need to focus first on the moment of the psychic transaction between pain and pleasure, the moment of "being touched." "Being touched" suggests a certain identification with suffering: Lin Shu and Wang Ziren felt touched, we might say, because, *like* Marguerite, they felt pain. But we have already observed that this pain is related specifically to Marguerite's virtue of *self*-sacrifice. An identification with self-sacrifice would suggest that the two Chinese men's "reader's response" is also a kind of self-sacrifice. How does self-sacrifice constitute aesthetic reception, and how do we come to terms with its formalism?

These are the questions that are intended by the first part of the title of this chapter, "loving women." If one of the major cultural demands put on women to this day remains that of self-sacrifice, then a formulation of the sympathetic spectator's position such as the two Chinese readers' cannot be made without a consideration of femininity and gender. What does it mean "to love" women and to be "loving women"? Could the space between these two meanings of love, the one being an act and the other a personal quality, be mediated precisely by the virtues of self-sacrifice, self-effacement, and a responsive understanding of others, especially of their *suffering*? It is not women per se, but the psychic states centering on them in terms of these virtues, that would give us the clues to the strong emotionalism characteristic of modern Chinese literature. We cannot therefore approach the sympathetic spectator's position by simply attributing to it the abstract function of completing a work's formal lack, but rather by another, more indirect route, the route of masochism.

The most common definition of masochism is one given by *The American Heritage Dictionary*, and I invoke it in order to show how we should immediately depart from it: "an abnormal condition in which sexual excitement and satisfaction depend largely on being subjected to abuse or physical pain, whether by oneself or by another." First, as with all uses of psychoanalytic concepts for literary purposes, the distinction between "normality" and "abnormality" implied by this definition must be discarded. It is through states of mind that are designated as "abnormal" that we often expose dominant cultural assumptions of what is "normal." This is a critical strategy that is too familiar to warrant further explanation. Second, the term "sexual" should be interpreted to mean, not merely physiology or genital sex, but those areas of psychic life that are excluded from the conscious mind as a result of the pressures of culture and that are available to us only in "irrational," apparently disconnected forms. I want to clarify this particularly in view of the oft-repeated objection that "Western" psychoanalysis, because of its preoccupation with "sex," is useless to an understanding of "Chinese" literature. If sexuality is, as Jean Laplanche puts it, "the repressed *par excellence*,"[6] then it is as valid a means of inquiry into modern Chinese literature as "history" or "revolution." Once we have deemphasized the narrow meanings attributed to "abnormality" and "sexuality," it becomes possible to explore masochism in much more illuminating ways.

The classical Freudian explanation of masochism originates in Freud's elaborate discussion of "instincts" in the essay "Instincts and Their Vicissitudes."[7] Freud distinguishes a stimulus of *instinctual* origin from one of physiological origin. The former "does not arise in the outside world but from within the organism itself" ("Instincts," p. 72). Instincts are further described by way of their "aims" and "objects": the "aim" is "in every instance satisfaction, which can only be obtained by abolishing the condition of stimulation in the source of the instinct"; the "object" of an instinct is "that in or through which it can achieve its aim" ("Instincts," p. 74). For Freud, sadism, the pleasure in inflicting pain on another person, is an "active" aim that attaches itself to external objects. Masochism, on the other hand, is "sadism turned around upon the subject's own ego." In this definition of masochism and sadism, "the essence of the process is the change of the object, while the aim remains unchanged" ("Instincts," p. 77).

As Freud preserves the primacy of sadism in his discussion, masochism remains essentially the passive, feminine side that is simply the reverse of sadism. However, the complexity of his texts points his critics in different directions, in which masochism is read, alternatively, either as *primary* to sadism or as an *independent* structure of its own.

Laplanche refutes the primacy of sadism by emphasizing the significance of *reflexivity* inherent in Freud's formulation of masochism.[8] Basing his arguments on Freud's concept of *Nachträglichkeit* (deferred action), Laplanche shows that there cannot be a pure "aggressive" act upon another person; for the "sadist" to derive pleasure from his act, he would have to know what it is to suffer pain in the first place. But to know what it is to suffer pain means that the subject is already identifying himself with the suffering object; the "sadist" is thus always already constituted belatedly, in masochism. This does not only mean that masochism has replaced sadism in occupying the primary position in the structure of pleasure-in-pain; it also means that masochism is the constitutive moment of sexuality and thus of subjectivity. Repeating after Freud but giving Freud's words an emphasis that was elided in his texts, Laplanche states that masochism is the "turning around of an instinct upon its subject." This "turning around" implies not only the internalization, or introjection, of a suffering object that used to be external, but also the existence of a psychic reality that is neither active (as in "seeing") nor passive (as in "being seen") but reflexive (seeing oneself). The reflexive, a kind of middle voice between the active and the passive, constitutes what Laplanche calls "the very movement of fantasmatization":

> To shift to the reflexive is . . . to reflect the action, internalize it, make it enter oneself as fantasy. To fantasize aggression is to turn it round upon oneself, to aggress oneself: such is the moment of autoerotism, in which the indissoluble bond between fantasy as such, sexuality, and the unconscious is confirmed.[9]

This reinscription of reflexivity and fantasy in masochism allows us to see in what otherwise seems like a condition of passivity a *psychic* activity. Moreover, such psychic activity is not, as some would say, "merely" psychic but vital, in the sense that it is what, in the form of "personal" or "subjective" processes such as memory and fantasy, registers the intense struggles between the subject and the external world.

Also associating masochism with fantasy, but establishing it as an entirely different kind of formal, aesthetic, and psychic structure from sadism, is Gilles Deleuze's study of Leopold von Sacher-Masoch, the historical figure whose name gave rise to the term masochism.[10] Deleuze's theory is that the orthodox Freudian understanding that sees sadism and masochism as reciprocal tendencies, each fulfilling the needs of the other, distorts the fundamental differences between the two. He suggests that while sadism is, in accordance with Freud's Oedipus complex, oriented toward dominating and controlling the other under the father's law, the origin of masochism lies in the preoedipal phase of infancy, where the goal is fusion with the mother and the mother alone.[11] Consequently, instead of domination and control, it is the submission to the mother figure, a submission that is interspersed with suspense, delay, fear, loss, recovery, and punishment, that is central to the masochist's fantasies.

What is most interesting in Deleuze's argument, I think, is his interpretation of Freud's concept of fetishism for a maternally oriented polemic. In Freud, fetishism stems from the castration complex in men. To "disavow" the possibility of castration that he apprehends from the prohibitive law of the father, a man displaces or projects "lack" onto the body of the woman. Freud tells us that, in the imaginary act of looking for the mother's penis, the little boy's optical path is arrested in places of the female body (such as the foot, the shoe, the hair) that become invested with a substitute, eroticized meaning. This investment in substitute objects that "disavow" the lack of a penis in woman (and by implication, the possibility of castration in men) is what constitutes, for Freud, the mechanism of "fetishism."

Like Laplanche, Deleuze makes use of Freud's terms but gives them his own emphases. Deleuze sees in the process of fetishism the possibility of an aesthetic, in which the fetishized woman is not a substitute but an idol. This then changes the significance of the terms that are crucial to Freud's understanding of the fetish. First, in Freud, the fear of castration functions to prohibit incest. In Deleuze, however, not only is castration not feared; it becomes the "very condition of the success of incest" that the masochistic son desires with the mother (Deleuze, p. 81). The pain that a masochist suffers is a sign not of the punishment of the son but of the father: "It is not a child but a father that is being beaten" (Deleuze, p. 58). In suffering, the masochist "liberates himself in preparation for a rebirth in which the father will have no part" (Deleuze, p. 58). "To become a man is to be reborn from the woman alone" (Deleuze, p. 86).

Second, instead of understanding "disavowal" in a derogatory way as the denial of reality, Deleuze attributes to disavowal the positive significance of the *imagination*: "Disavowal . . . is nothing less than the foundation of imagination, which suspends reality and establishes the ideal in the suspended world" (Deleuze, p. 110). Putting it another way:

> Disavowal should perhaps be understood as the point of departure of an operation that consists neither in negating nor even destroying, but rather in radically contesting the validity of that which is: it suspends belief in and neutralizes the given in such a way that a new horizon opens up beyond and in place of it. (Deleuze, p. 28)

In other words, disavowal has for Deleuze the strategic importance not of disavowing castration itself (which confirms the law of the father) but rather of disavowing the law of the father that is represented in the fear of castration and that determines the existing reality.

If the split caused by fetishism in Freud means that a vital part of man that is being cut off psychically comes back to haunt him in the form of automatized external objects, the split in Deleuze takes the form of irreconcilable but equally dominant sensibilities: "On the one hand the subject is aware of reality but suspends the awareness; on the other the subject clings to his ideal" (Deleuze, p. 30). The displacement of desire onto the fetish of the woman therefore becomes not the "substitute" of lack that it is in Freud but rather a process of fantasy in which the subject clings to his ideal of being fused with the mother. While the notion of fetishism in Freud implies a "control" of the other by using the other to amend for what one fears is missing in oneself, fetishism in Deleuze suggests a passionate submission to the other. As Gaylyn Studlar, who uses Deleuze's theory for her analysis of cinematic pleasure, puts it: "In masochism, . . . pleasure does not involve mastery of the female but submission to her. This pleasure applies to the infant, the masochist, and the film spectator as well."[12]

Hence, although man and woman occupy the same positions in Deleuze as in Freud—man being the subject and woman the object—the implications of these positions are entirely different. The male subject is no longer the active, sadistic, aggressive master that he is implied to be in the orthodox readings of Freud, but rather is a passive, masochistic, submissive, infantile character. It is by reconceiving male subjectivity in these terms that Deleuze is able, in turn, to give to the fetish its idealized, maternal power. Woman-as-fetish in Deleuze assumes the same kind of archaic and supernatural potency that primitive people are said to invest in their talismans.

However, once we have grasped the altered emphases Deleuze puts on Freud's fetishism, an important question arises. The aesthetics of fetishism that is valorized by Deleuze requires that its fetish be *unmoving*. As he puts it, the fetish is "a frozen, arrested, two-dimensional image, a photograph to which one returns repeatedly to exorcise the dangerous consequences of movement, the harmful discoveries that result from exploration" (Deleuze, p. 28). For Deleuze, this "static" quality of the fetish, a quality he associates with the coldness and cruelty that Sacher-Masoch demands of the women he loves, is what enables the neutralization of reality and the protection of fantasy. But this way of reading also freezes the mother as a picture and a picture alone, while the relation to her can only be described through the terms of aesthetic *distance*. Although woman is no longer "mere" substitute for man's penis but phallic power itself, she is now a deified *tableau vivant*, constituted solely by his waiting, his need for suspense, his enjoyment of delay, and his demand for the postponement of the final moment of union with the mother (since that union means death). If the conception of male subjectivity has undergone profound change from Freud to Deleuze, the two paradigms of fetishism still have one thing in common: the exclusion of the fetishized woman's psychic life. And this, I think, is what is ultimately limiting about Deleuze's account—*not* the idealism masochistically attached to the mother but the aesthetic form that this idealism assumes. That aesthetic form prevents the mother from speaking and thus cannot provide the terms for psychic and narrative *reversibilities* that constitute the relation between "mother" and "subject."

On the other hand, if, once again, we return to Laplanche's notion of "reflexivity" and see the mother not in terms of a picture that is "frozen" for the projection of our ideals but rather as an *object* whom we introject in our own subjectivity, then what emerges is a very different way of "idealizing" — or fantasizing. As an object, the mother is both passive and active, submitting to our infantile, anal-sadistic wishes while having the power to protect us or torment us. The introjection of the mother in our fantasy has to imply both of these qualities. Such an introjection is, I think, descriptive of Lin Shu and his friend's reaction to *La Dame aux Camélias*. In the suffering Marguerite appeared the figure of the woman who, like a mother, is continually subjected to sacrifice while she actively charms and loves. The internalization of this "mother" constitutes the moment of masochistic identification with the Other: as they see Marguerite suffer, they also suffer. With this response, a space is opened up where the apprehension of suffering becomes reciprocal and reversible. Why? It is because Marguerite is responded to not only as the mother, but also as the powerless infant to whom the reading subject becomes the understanding mother. At the center of the movement of fantasmatization is not the mother herself, but a psychic process in which she no longer occupies a fixed position. Instead of being only that aesthetic spectacle, that frozen picture that the reading subject beholds from a distance, the "mother" is also what has been *activated* in the reading subject as the capacity to see; what is seen now, with emotional excitation, is not a phallic mother but an infant in the picture. This mutual shifting of positionalities between "maternal" and "infantile" is what accounts for the fantasy involved in the idealization of the "mother," and for the pleasure-in-pain that is fundamental to masochism. Because it is enabled by suffering, the fusion with the mother cannot be imagined to be "preoedipal" but should be recognized as grounded in culture.

Lin Shu and Wang Ziren's excessive crying, then, can be read as a sign of that "turning around" of external aggression upon the subject's self, which I have further specified as a masochistic introjection and fantasy of the "mother." Tears, as Steve Neale argues with regard to melodrama, not only signify a response of "powerlessness" but also "inscribe a position of narcissistic *power* in implying an Other who will respond."[13] This "Other" is the mother whom the infant loses with pain, but to whom he or she addresses the demand for the reparation of loss. For Neale, the mother is thus "situated in fantasy as a figure capable of fulfilling that demand."[14] But in the light of our present argument, we should add that, in crying, a reader is not only crying as an infant would to the mother, but as an infant who has internalized the mother's responsiveness to her suffering, and therefore as a mother as well. Whether or not a "mother" is actually present, crying always has in it the twin aspects of performance and response, signifying an identification with a responsive Other who is herself the receiver of pain.

In the rest of this section, I read two stories by two modern Chinese women writers that enlarge and elaborate the terms of our discussion. These stories present the problem of suffering in the form of unmitigated victimization. At the level of formal narrative structure, the sustained revelation of cruelty or sacrifice can be defined as a kind of "aggression" that is deliberately directed against the protagonists, an aggression that is, furthermore, intensified by their seemingly uncomprehending or unprotesting attitude toward their "fate." Might we call such characters "masochistic"? If so, what are the elements of fantasy that are essential to their masochism?

In an autobiographical essay, Xiao Hong tells of the sorrows she suffered as a motherless child and of how she learns about "warmth" and "love" from her grandfather. "And so," she writes at the end of that essay, "it is this 'warmth' and 'love' that I perpetually fantasize and pursue."[15] On first reading, the brutal quality of her short story "Hands" ("Shou," 1936)[16] flatly contradicts this author's sentimentalism. A story about the ordeals that a young girl from a poor Chinese family goes through to obtain a modern education, the dominant impression created by "Hands" is that of an airtight structure of oppression. The title refers to what stigmatizes the protagonist Wang Yaming—her hands, which are brought to our attention in the first opening lines:

> Never had any of us in the school seen hands the likes of hers before: blue, black, and even showing a touch of purple, the discoloring ran from her finger tips all the way to her wrists. (p. 456)

From the beginning, thus, the portrayal of Wang Yaming is inseparable from a fetishism that isolates her as an object of attention, excitation, and disgust. She is maliciously rejected by everyone in the school. The principal, who herself has "bloodless, fossil-like transparent fingers," spitefully and regularly orders Wang Yaming to wash her hands:

> "Can't you wash those hands of yours clean? Use a little more soap! Wash them good and hard with hot water. During morning calisthenics out on the playground there are several hundred white hands up in the air—all but yours; no, yours are special, very special!" (p. 458)

And yet even as Wang Yaming indicates that she would compensate for her "specialness" with a pair of gloves that she has sent for, it does not satisfy the principal:

"What possible good would that do? What we want is uniformity, and even if you wore gloves you still wouldn't be like the others." (p. 458)

On a day when the school receives visitors, Wang Yaming is singled out for more severe indictment. The oversized gloves that she has tried to use to conceal her hands become the objects that are physically attacked in place of her:

As she mentioned the word "gloves" the principal kicked the glove that had dropped to the floor with the shiny toe of her patent shoe and said: "I suppose you figured everything would be just fine if you stood out there wearing a pair of gloves, didn't you? What kind of nonsense is that?" She kicked the glove again, but this time, looking at that huge glove, which was large enough for a carter to wear, she couldn't suppress a chuckle. (p. 459)

As if in a determined effort to compound Wang Yaming's miserable condition, the narrative continues to present us with other characters' discriminating actions against her. When she returns to the school after the summer, no one is willing to share a bed with her because it is "unsanitary" to sleep with someone "with those vermin all over her body." These words come from the housemother, another "authority" figure, who has picked up some "Japanese customs" and whose speech is "forever dotted with terms like 'sanitary,' 'ludicrous,' 'filthy,' and so on." As far as this housemother is concerned, "If someone's filthy the hands show it" (p. 460). Finally, as no one would accept sleeping next to her, Wang Yaming has to sleep on a bench in the corridor.

The steady narrative construction of unmitigated cruelty is not only the result of stigmatizing attitudes toward the girl's "hands." The discrimination against her exterior condition is paralleled by another kind of cruelty, with which Wang Yaming is shown to be a failure in her mental condition as well. In spite of her strenuous efforts, she cannot retain what she learns and fails in even the most simple matter of answering the English teacher's roll call with the correct pronunciation. But her real failure lies in her total oblivion of the others' mockery:

Her quaint pronunciation made everyone in the room laugh so hard we literally shook. All, that is, except Wang Yaming, who sat down very calmly and opened her book with her blackened hands. Then she began reading in a very soft voice: "Who-at . . . deez . . . ah-ar [What . . . these . . . are . . .]."
During math class she read her formulas the same way she read essays: "$2x + y = . . . x^2 = . . .$"
At the lunch table, as she reached out to grab a man-t'ou [Chinese steamed bread] with a blackened hand, she was still occupied with her geography lesson: "Mexico produces silver . . . Yünnan . . . hmm, Yünnan produces marble."

At night she hid herself in the bathroom and studied her lessons, and at the crack of dawn she could be found sitting at the foot of the stairs. Wherever there was the slightest glimmer of light, that's where I usually found her. (pp. 456-57)

As the story progresses, we have the feeling that it is precisely this kind of persistence that makes Wang Yaming pathetic, because with that persistence is the outdated belief that learning is a matter of mechanically accumulating facts. During her last class, she tries to save up "knowledge" in this way:

She worked up quite a sweat in this final hour of hers. She copied down every single word from the blackboard during the English class into a little notebook. She read them aloud as she did so and even copied down words she already knew as the teacher casually wrote them on the board. During the following hour, in geography class, she very laboriously copied down the maps the teacher had drawn on the board. She acted as though everything that went through her mind on this her final day had taken on great importance, and she was determined to let none of it pass unrecorded. (p. 464)

Ironically, the narrator afterward discovers that she has "copied it all down incorrectly." But the point is clear: the girl studies with the idea that knowledge is a mental *storage* of information, a storage that she tries to accomplish by copying and reading aloud.

Both externally and internally, thus, Wang Yaming is victimized. What is remarkable about Xiao Hong's text is the way these two forms of victimization are brought together by Wang Yaming's position in regard to her family. Like the rest of her family, her hands are discolored because of what they do to make a living—dyeing. But unlike the rest of her family, she is the only one who is attending school:

"Aren't your younger sisters in school?"
"No. Later on I'll teach them their lessons. Except that I don't know how well I'm doing myself, and if I don't do well then I won't even be able to face my younger sisters. The most we can earn for dyeing a bolt of cloth is thirty cents. How many bolts do you think we get a month? One article of clothing is a dime—big or small—and nearly everyone sends us overcoats. Take away the cost for fuel and for the dyes, and you can see what I mean. In order to pay my tuition they had to save every penny, even going without salt, so how could I even think of not doing my lessons? How could I?" (p. 463)

There is, in other words, an economic basis to her persistence in learning. Learning is, literally, earning: the whole family's labor is exchanged for the time that Wang Yaming spends at school; in return she would distribute what she has learned/earned to her sisters. As such, knowledge becomes an acquisition that is rationalized in countable terms. And it is this victimized attitude toward knowledge—victimized because it is the result of extreme poverty—that, in the end, makes it impossible for Wang Yaming to acquire it. The item-by-item mental storage to which she subscribes is a storage that finds its parallel in the manual labor to which she and her family are subjected. But just as dyeing clothes article by article, which is based on an outdated concept of labor time, makes them victims of society's economic exploitation, learning by rote memorization makes Wang Yaming the victim of society's traditional pedagogical exploitation. In terms of both manual and intellectual labor, Wang Yaming is doomed to failure.

The harshness of this story seems to leave no room at all for what we would call fantasy, if by "fantasy" we mean simply the idealization of something beautiful. On the other hand, if what fantasy involves is the masochistic "turning around" on the self of external aggression, there is, I think, a moment in Xiao Hong's story where we can locate the brief eruption of such a fantasy, even though it is, ultimately, of no significance to the narrative movement that determines Wang Yaming's "fate."

To trace this moment, we need to isolate a series of episodes that begins one day when Wang Yaming and the narrator are studying next to each other. The narrator, who has up to this point kept a rather matter-of-fact profile, is reading her novel—"but very softly so as not to disturb her [Wang Yaming]" (p. 462). This piece of additional information gives way to a slight curiosity that the narrator directs toward herself: "This was the first time I had been so considerate and I wondered why it was only the first time" (p. 462). The implication of this self-questioning is: "Why did I not think of acting considerate before now?" It is as if this "first" action of considerateness occurs belatedly, and its belatedness allows the narrator to understand, even if only in a glimpse, what her previous lack of considerateness is—namely, a part of the collective cruelty that is inflicted on Wang Yaming.

This moment of self-reflection is followed by Wang Yaming's asking the narrator about the novels she has read. The subject of books makes Wang Yaming feel conscious about her inferiority to the others, who do not have to worry about exams even if they do not review their lessons. She expresses her wish to take a break and read "something else for a change," but concludes that "that just doesn't work with me" (p. 462). In the next episode, the narrator is "reading aloud the passage in Upton Sinclair's *The Jungle* where the young girl laborer Marija had collapsed in the snow scene." There is the suggestion that Wang Yaming has heard this, for she is standing right behind the narrator even though the latter is unaware of it. Contrary to what she claimed earlier, she now expresses the wish to borrow one of the narrator's books: "This snowy weather depresses me. I don't have any family around here, and there's nothing to shop for out on the street—besides, everything costs money" (p. 462). The narrator lends Wang Yaming her copy of *The Jungle*.

The next time they meet, Wang Yaming has read the novel. The conversation between the two characters goes as follows:

> "Did you like it?" I asked her. "How was it?"
> At first she didn't answer me; then, covering her face with her hands and trembling, she said: "Fine." Her voice was quivering . . . her face still buried in hands as black as the hair on her head . . .
> "Marija is a very real person to me. You don't think she died after she collapsed in the snow, do you? She couldn't have died. Could she? The doctor knew she didn't have any money, though, so he wouldn't treat her. . . . I went for a doctor once myself, when my mother was sick, but do you think he would come? . . . as soon as I told him we were dyers he turned and walked back inside." (p. 463)

The clumsiness that Wang Yaming has shown in learning everything else is here replaced by an ability to relate to a fictional situation out of sympathetic reading, but this sympathetic reading is possible because Wang Yaming does not see the book as fiction but as a reality she can recognize: "Marija is a very real person to me." The reality of Marija is the result of a series of identifications and introjections. The fictional event of the doctor not treating Marija because she didn't have any money has a powerful effect on Wang Yaming not only because Marija "is" her mother, who was sick (like Marija), but also because Marija is she, Wang Yaming, whom the doctor refuses to help. Thus the "identificatory" moment is constituted not simply by comparing Marija and her mother, but by a transition that returns her thoughts to herself:

> "The doctor knew she didn't have any money, though, so he wouldn't treat her. . . . *I went for a doctor once myself*, when my mother was sick . . ." (p. 463; my emphasis)

Marija is here the "object" that Wang Yaming "introjects" and includes in herself, and it is as a result of this introjection that the rejection of her own mother by the doctor in the past triggers her suffering at the moment of reading. It is in this way that her mother becomes once again accessible to and indistinguishable from her: "Marija is a very real person to me." In her own narrative, the rejection that leads to the mother's death is followed, not by the mention of the mother's death but by her own "becoming" mother to her younger siblings:

> "[The doctor] said to me through the door: 'I won't be able to take care of your mother, now just go away!' So I went back home . . .
> "From then on I had to take care of my two younger brothers and sisters." (p. 463)

Wang Yaming's reading of the novel thus "reveals" for the first time this identification with the suffering, rejected, but also caring mother. That revelation is made possible by the fictional suffering object Marija, in whom Wang Yaming recognizes her own reality with emotional excitation. This emotional excitation is then transferred to the narrator, who gives to it a higher value than her own feeling: "her tears were much nobler than my sympathy" (p. 463).

Of course, this brief series of episodes that gives us the glimpse of a "movement of fantasmatization" does not alter the overall direction of the narrative structure, which concludes by showing Wang Yaming going home with her father, because the principal told her that she would not be able to pass the exams even if she were to take them. Narrative in this story is thus a kind of sadistic action, which has as its goal the complete annihilation of a character within its "aggressive" trajectory. Completely consumed by a cycle of merciless treatments, the character is exposed as completely powerless. However, what we have seen in this story is a moment in which sadism as narrative action is arrested in its course by a particular kind of reading. This reading is the masochistic "turning around" of aggression on the subject's self, a turning around that happens as the subject's reflexivity is interlaced with the figure of the mother. If it is the reader's reception that activates and completes a narrative, then this reception must be situated, not outside the story, but inside, as part of the series of reflexive fantasmatizations that is triggered by Wang Yaming's reading. These fantasmatizations are what produce the transparent effects of identification and accessibility that are associated with strong emotionalism.

The victimization of a woman from a class much higher than Wang Yaming's is the focus of Ling Shuhua's "Embroidered Pillows" ("Xiu zhen," 1928).[17] Like "Hands," the title encapsulates a victimization through fetishized objects that are closely related to the victim. "Embroidered pillows" are the products of the time- and energy-consuming sewing that Eldest Young Mistress, the first daughter of a certain family, does. From the beginning, there is an uncanny suggestion of a close resemblance between Eldest Young Mistress and what she sews. The excellence of her craft matches her physical beauty in a way that is almost too perfect to be real. Her amah Chang Ma comments:

> "I used to listen to people tell stories, and I'd think that those pretty young women in the stories, so clever and bright, were just made up by the storyteller. How could I have known there really is such a young lady, as fresh and delicate as a scallion, able to embroider like this!" (p. 197)

Once finished, the embroidered pillows are sent by Eldest Young Mistress's father as gifts to another house to entice conjugal interest in his daughter. Eldest Young Mistress's hard work is, thus, an attempt to "sell" herself into an order of life to which Chinese women are assigned by tradition. Herself a gift, she is the maker of a second gift that would promote her. Yet as the second part of the story begins, we are told that "two years passed quickly. Elder Young Mistress was still at home doing embroidery." Her labor has been performed in vain.

The "aggressive" nature of this narrative, then, hinges upon the cruel discrepancy between Eldest Young Mistress's dedication to and the futility of her labor. This discrepancy is chiefly the result of attentive and elaborate descriptions of her dedication, which transforms the embroidery from a mere pastime into a physically demanding and vital activity:

> Eldest Young Mistress, her head bent over, was embroidering a back cushion. The weather was hot and humid. All the little Pekinese dog could do was lie under the table and pant, his tongue hanging out. Flies buzzed against the windows, spinning lazily in the sullen air. Perspiration trickled down the face of Chang Ma, the amah, as she stood behind her mistress waving a fan. She would blot her face with her handkerchief, but was never able to keep it dry. If she blotted her nose dry, then beads of perspiration appeared on her lip. She saw that her mistress wasn't perspiring as much as she, but her face was flushed in the heat. Her white gauze blouse clung to her damp back. (p. 197)

More details of this dedication come to us through Little Niu, Chang Ma's daughter, who expresses a sense of incredulity at the taxing nature of Eldest Young Mistress's work:

> "Mother, yesterday Fourth Sister-in-Law told me that it took Eldest Young Mistress half a year to embroider a pair of back cushions—on just the bird alone she used thirty or forty different colored threads. I didn't believe her that there were so many different colors." (p. 197)

The irony of Eldest Young Mistress's existence is that however hard-working she is and however excellent the products of her labor, her "fate" is beyond her control. She is not only kept permanently where she is by the embroidery, but embroidery itself has become her living while she is perpetually waiting. In this sense, her "dedication," much like Wang Yaming's persistent efforts in learning, is precisely the narrative's means of exposing a character at her most vulnerable, when she attempts wholeheartedly and positively to engage with what is available in, or what is prescribed by, culture. The sense of sacrificial suffering is most overpowering as we feel that it is when these characters comply with society's demands by putting their "best foot forward"—to get "educated" in one case, to prepare herself for marriage in the other—that they are crushed the hardest.

For Eldest Young Mistress, society's cruelty is most conspicuous when she discovers by chance that a pair of pillow covers she sewed a couple of years ago have since been soiled, trampled on, dismembered, and reassembled in a bizarre fashion by people she hardly even knows. Matching and mocking the fine details of her embroidery at the same time, the narrative shows us the utterly mindless ways in which the pillows were ruined:

> A drunk guest vomited all over a large part of one of them; the other one was pushed off onto the floor by someone playing mahjong. Someone used it as a footstool, and the beautiful satin backing was covered with muddy footprints. (p. 198)

The sadistic aggressiveness of the narrative comes to a climax with this fateful chance discovery. It is here, therefore, that the process of masochistic reflexivity begins. The latter makes us aware of the intensity of sacrifice for the first time by shifting our attention to Eldest Young Mistress's memory, in which her past self that once slaved over the pair of pillows becomes the suffering object with which the present self identifies. The minutiae of the physically involved domestic labor now appear especially vivid:

> She thought back to two summers ago when she had embroidered a pair of exquisite pillow cushions—there were a kingfisher and phoenix on them. When it was too hot then during the day to work the needle, she had often waited until evening to embroider. After she had finished, her eyes bothered her for more than ten days. . . .
>   Eldest Young Mistress just stared at the two pieces of embroidery.
> . . . She began to recall that when she had made the crest she had had to embroider it, then take it out, altogether three times. Once her perspiration had discolored the delicate yellow thread. She didn't discover it until she was through embroidering. Another time she used the wrong color of green for the rock. She had mistaken the color while embroidering at night. She couldn't remember why she had taken it out the last time. For the light pink of the lotus petals, she didn't dare just take up the thread after washing her hands. She had sprinkled her hands with talcum powder before touching it. The large lotus leaf was even harder to embroider. It would have been too uninteresting to use only one color of green so she had matched twelve different colors of green thread to embroider it. (p. 199)

All the hardships the Eldest Young Mistress conquered in order to accomplish an impeccable piece of work now become part and parcel of an understanding of herself as a powerless victim to a situation that is likely to imprison her permanently. Like what Marija collapsing in the snow is for Wang Yaming, the ruined pillows are, for Eldest Young Mistress, the external artistic constructs that bring about the movement of fantasmatization, but unlike Wang Yaming, who sees another figure, her mother, in her fantasy, Eldest Young Mistress sees only herself. The introjection of an external suffering object that is fundamental to masochistic reflexivity receives here a disturbing turn. For if what is introjected is simply that part of the self that is "past," introjection leads not to a potentially sympathetic response but rather to a narcissistic self-closure. We see this as Eldest Young Mistress's memory of how she embroidered gives way to the memory of a dream:

> After she had finished the pair of cushions and sent them to Cabinet Secretary Pai's house, many relatives and friends offered flattering words and her girl friends made jokes at her expense. When she heard these remarks, she would redden and smile faintly. At night she dreamed she would become spoiled and proud, wearing clothes and jewelry she had never worn before. Many little girls would chase after her to take a look, and envy her. The faces of her girl friends would radiate jealousy. (p. 199)

This dream is, in the terms of our argument, a fantasy within a fantasy, for it is a dream recalled in the very act of fantasmatization. It contains not the slightest trace of an introjection of another person as object. Instead, the fantasy consists primarily in having others chase after the self "to take a look." Like Eldest Young Mistress's pretty pillows, this self is also embroidered, "wearing clothes and jewelry she has never worn before." Eldest Young Mistress's reflexive "turning around" thus takes place not through the identification with another's suffering but through seeing, as others are imagined to see, herself as a fetishized object. However, because the self's relation to the Other is, even in the depths of fantasy, based exclusively on *others'* looking, this self is incapable of responding to reality in ways that differ from what the dominant culture has prescribed for women. It is in this sense that the self can be said to be completely closed.

2

So far, we have made a number of observations about the problem of responding to suffering. I argue that this is, first of all, a problem of reading. However, as a problem of reading, it cannot be solved simply by positing an abstract "sympathetic reader" who responds to the characters of a text from the outside. Exactly what happens when the reader is touched? I approach this question by showing how sympathetic responses can be seen as a form of masochism involving a fantasy of the mother, which, rather than being simply located in the process of fetishistic idealization, needs to be understood in relation to reflexive introjection. Xiao Hong's "Hands" gives us an example of a fantasy of the mother in the midst of a young woman's experience of social and economic exploitation in early twentieth-century China. By contrast, the absence of another suffering object in the act of reflexive introjection in Ling Shuhua's "Embroidered Pillows" returns the subject to the place to which she has always been assigned in dominant culture.

Before we discuss the formal complexities of a "mother"-centered sympathetic response further, I want first to distinguish these complexities from certain traditional processes of idealizing woman that often take the path of the mother also. What are the psychic mechanisms that accompany such traditional processes? As a way of clarification, I explore in this section the problem of "loving" women from several masculine perspectives, beginning once again with Freud.

In an interesting essay, "The Most Prevalent Form of Degradation in Erotic Life,"[18] Freud analyzes the origins of what he calls "psychical impotence" in certain men's relations to women. A "normal attitude in love," he says, means the union of two currents of feeling—"the tender, affectionate feelings and the sensual feelings" ("Erotic Life," p. 59). When the confluence of these two currents is not achieved, the result is neurosis. Freud attributes the origins of "tender, affectionate feelings" to what a man experiences in childhood; these are feelings that begin early and determine a man's choice of love objects. However, the obstacle of incest taboo means that he must not seek the satisfaction of his love life among the family members that he loves, but rather from new objects who are not "prohibited." If, however, the new objects are not readily available at the time of puberty when the libido seeks its advancement, and if the attraction exercised by the infantile objects continues to be strong, then a neurosis will form in which "the libido turns away from reality, is absorbed into the creation of phantasy (introversion), strengthens the images of the first sexual objects, and becomes fixated to them" ("Erotic Life," p. 61). While the incest taboo guarantees that these images can only remain fantasies, the overwhelming continuance of these fantasies means that the libido cannot be successfully applied "externally to the real world" ("Erotic Life," p. 61). The sexual activity of people afflicted like this hence takes on the characteristic of a restriction in object choice:

> The sensual feeling that has remained active seeks only objects evoking
> no remainder of the incestuous persons forbidden to it; the impression
> made by someone who seems deserving of high estimation leads, not to
> a sensual excitation, but to feelings of tenderness which remain
> erotically ineffectual. ("Erotic Life," p. 62)

Freud's idealism is clear and insistent. Having set up affection and sensuality as incompatible terms because of the incest taboo, he nonetheless repeats that "real," "normal," or "proper" love must equal a fusion of the two and that this fusion is really only possible with the *first* objects of love: "Whoever is to be really and happily in love must have overcome his deference for women and come to terms with the idea of incest with mother and sister" ("Erotic Life," p. 65). With incest being impossible, "the ultimate object selected is never the original one but *only* a surrogate for it" ("Erotic Life," p. 68; my emphasis). This insistence on an originary, primary, fused, irreplaceable first experience of love makes everything else that happens afterward simply a matter of "discontents," as is evident from the statement that has become popularized in various ways: "The lack of satisfaction accompanying culture is the necessary consequence of certain peculiarities developed by the sexual instinct under the pressure of culture" ("Erotic Life," p. 69).

What concerns us here is that, unlike the totally passionate submission to woman-as-fetish that we have encountered in Deleuze's masochistic man, the path of love outlined by Freud is that of an inevitable division of women into two types, those that are "familial" and revered, and those that are exciting and degraded. This division is greatly disturbing because it leads not only to a separation of male libidinal energies, but to a trenchant moralism in masculine conceptions of women. Women are either the recipients of affection and impotence, or the recipients of sensuality and contempt, because idealization and erotic passion are mutually exclusive:

> In only very few people of culture are the two strains of tenderness and sensuality duly fused into one; the man almost always feels his sexual activity hampered by his respect for the woman and only develops full sexual potency when he finds himself in the presence of a lower type of sexual object. ("Erotic Life," p. 64)

In the next three stories, each by a different modern Chinese male writer, we see fictional dramatizations of the conceptual division regarding woman in ways that amplify the implications of Freud's problematic.

In a passage that is interestingly germane to our discussion, C. T. Hsia draws attention to the peculiarities of Yü Dafu's fiction by describing his characters as "by turns voyeur, fetishist, homosexual, masochist, and kleptomaniac."[19] Yü Dafu's "Sinking" ("Chenlun," 1921)[20] gives us a character whose behavior illustrates the difficult meanings of some of these terms. If sex is, as critics unanimously agree, of primary importance in this story, *how* is it important?[21]

"Sinking" begins with an unmistakable feeling of alienation that we associate with Yü Dafu's enthusiasm for German romanticism. We meet the lonely, nameless protagonist in the midst of an unspecified pastoral scene, where he finds solace in the sky, the sun, the breeze, and the fields. Unlike the "philistines" who "envy" and "sneer" at him, Nature is the "refuge" that allows him to be what he is. Moreover, Nature is sexualized and imagined as at once mother and beloved:

> He felt as if he were sleeping in the lap of a kind mother, or else reclining his head on the knees of his beloved for an afternoon nap on the coast of southern Europe.

". . . when all the philistines envy you, sneer at you, and treat you like a fool, only Nature, only this eternally bright sun and azure sky, this late summer breeze, this early autumn air still remains your friend, still remains your mother and your beloved." (p. 125)

Sharing the same status with idealized, feminized Nature as a refuge is also, in a strongly Romantic fashion, his own reading. Among the Western authors who fill his mental landscape are Wordsworth, Emerson, and Thoreau. Here, what is interesting is that a listless, drifting attitude characterizes his relationship to books, to which he becomes passive rather than active. His reading is not the reading for knowledge, but a random, distracted excursion that relies for its pleasure on *incompletion*. The first impulse of impatient *incorporation* of the text gives way to a more "aesthetic" savoring:

It had been his recent habit to read out of sequence. With books over a few hundred pages, it was only natural that he seldom had the patience to finish them. But even with slender volumes like Emerson's *Nature* or Thoreau's *Excursions*, he never bothered to read them from beginning to end at one sitting. Most of the time, when he picked up a book, he would be so moved by its opening lines or first two pages that he literally wanted to swallow the whole volume. But after three or four pages, he would want to savor it slowly and would say to himself: "I mustn't gulp down such a marvelous book at one sitting. Instead, I should chew it over a period of time. For my enthusiasm for the book will be gone the moment I am through with it. So will my expectations and dreams, and won't that be a crime?" (p. 126)

The imagined oneness with Nature-as-woman is therefore associated with an equally dreamlike relationship with books. What is indulged and idealized in both relationships is a kind of involuntary, spontaneous union with the Other that is not the result of conscious cultural effort. In both, too, time is of no importance—one does not hurry, but wanders, loiters, and slowly savors. However, if the protagonist's male subjectivity can be described at this point as "aimless," that aimlessness soon becomes attached to particular objects.

We realize this when we are told that the protagonist does not like going to school. The reason for this, apart from his dislike for textbooks, is that he does not like being looked at:

And when he was in school he always had the feeling that everyone was staring at him. He made every effort to dodge his fellow students, but wherever he went, he just couldn't shake off that uncomfortable suspicion that their malevolent gazes were still fixed on him. (p. 127)

Why, we should ask, is it so uncomfortable to be looked at? What the others' gazes are performing is in fact the process of *self*-constitution. The discomfort derives from the feeling that, as he imagines others to be staring at him, he cannot help but become "self-conscious." The term "self-conscious" is illuminating because it refers in this case both to his unease and to the way he is compelled, soon afterward, to give specific shapes to his hitherto uncomprehended feelings of loneliness, listlessness, and melancholy—in other words, it refers to the way he is forced to "become himself." What are the "specific shapes" in which he becomes self-conscious? There are two: the "shapes" of patriotism and "masculinity."

The protagonist's resentment toward his fellow students leads to our awareness, for the first time since the story begins, that he is in Japan: "They are all Japanese, all my enemies. I'll have my revenge one day; I'll get even with them" (p. 127). But the formation of the "self" through national differences that were intensified by historical events is already beset by a sense of self-doubt: "They are Japanese, and of course they don't have any sympathy for you. It's because you want their sympathy that you have grown to hate them. Isn't this your own mistake?" (p. 127). Thus, as the "shape" of a nationalistic self—of being "Chinese"—is in the process of forming, it already meets with great difficulties. The protagonist's subjectivity is caught between the previous aimlessness, to which he cannot return except with the most self-conscious unease, and the elusive ideal of "China," which is receding from his grasp. This impossible position finds an outlet in what I call the second "shape" of self-consciousness: masculinity.

In the narrative, the reader's awareness that the protagonist is in Japan is immediately followed by a scene in which, walking back to his inn one day, he meets two Japanese girl students "in red skirts." Three Japanese boys walking alongside him amuse themselves by accosting the girls. The protagonist is greatly agitated by this, and we witness an amazing shift between several important subjective positions in his reaction. First, "He alone hurried back to his inn, *as if he had done the accosting*" (p. 127; my emphasis). Second, this wishful attempt to put himself in the other boys' place soon gives way to the realization that he did not really do it. With this realization comes a bitter condemnation of himself as a "coward." Third, however, the remembrance of the physical beauty of the girls triggers a new sense of illusion, only to be replaced, finally, by a fourth position—the self-consciousness of being Chinese. These second to fourth positions appear in the text like this:

> "*You coward fellow, you are too coward!* If you are so shy, what's there for you to regret? If you now regret your cowardice, why didn't you summon up enough courage to talk to the girls? *Oh coward, coward!*"
>
> Suddenly he remembered their eyes, their bright and lively eyes. They had really seemed to register a note of happy surprise on seeing him. Second thoughts on the matter, however, prompted him to cry out:

"Oh, you fool! Even if they seemed interested, what are they to you? Isn't it quite clear that their ogling was intended for the three Japanese? Oh, the girls must have known! They must have known that I am a Chinaman; otherwise why didn't they even look at me once? Revenge! Revenge! I must seek revenge against their insult." (pp. 127–28; emphases in the original)

The twin "shapes" of nationalism and masculinity working together finally produce the two particular longings of this man:

"China, O my China! Why don't you grow rich and strong? I cannot bear your shame in silence any longer!

"Isn't the scenery in China as beautiful? Aren't the girls in China as pretty? . . .

"What I want is love.

"If there were one beautiful woman who understood my suffering, I would be willing to die for her.

"If there were one woman who could love me sincerely, I would also be willing to die for her, be she beautiful or ugly.

"For what I want is love from the opposite sex.

"O ye Heavens above, I want neither knowledge nor fame nor useless lucre. I shall be wholly content if you can grant me an Eve from the Garden of Eden, allowing me to possess her body and soul."
(p. 128)

The question that comes to my mind at this point is: what is China to this man? Yü Dafu gives us a deceptively unproblematic autobiographical answer in these words from Chanyü ji [Repentances]:

"I have lived my lyrical period in a whimsical, cruel, militarist and despotic island empire [Japan]. I have seen with my own eyes the drowning . . . of my own country, I have felt in myself the humiliation of my own country. . . . There was nothing else but sorrow. *I was like a husband mourning the death of his young wife.*"[22]

Is China simply a "young wife" though? If the protagonist's longing for a woman seems straightforwardly "manly" at first sight, his longing for China is not. His wish that China grow "rich and strong" signifies that the position he is adopting toward China is a passive, feminized, infantile one; it is a position that needs to depend for its own integrity on the Other's strength. If so, is China's otherness masculine? Or is China the phallic mother to whom this protagonist becomes Deleuze's masochistic man? The way China is idealized and pictorialized would suggest that it is the latter. But if China is the phallic mother to whom a man submits with his strongest emotions, then his longing for love from "the opposite sex," which is juxtaposed with his longing for China, also becomes ambiguous. If we now look at the lines from "Sinking" I just quoted, we would notice a very distinct characteristic in the qualities he demands of this opposite sex. If China has been turned into a fetishized woman, the woman he wants in actual life is one who would love "sincerely"—that is, in a way that involves feeling and understanding—rather than being simply physically attractive. In this sense, the wish to possess that woman "body and soul" is reversible: it means he also wants to be possessed body and soul himself. But this wish, when juxtaposed against the terms laid down by Freud in "The Most Prevalent Form of Degradation in Erotic Life," is blatantly impossible, for it signifies precisely that congruence of affection (understanding) and sensuality that, according to Freud, can only be a fantasy in civilized life.

Sections 3 through 5 of Yü Dafu's story explore the impossibility of this wish by identifying the opposition and mutual exclusion of its two components. First, the protagonist is cut off from all sources of "affection." He severs ties with his Chinese friends on account of their failure to understand him (p. 133) and with his elder brother after a quarrel (p. 136). He moves to a quiet cottage in the countryside, so that he can be as far away from other people as possible; he also moves mentally, by changing his course of study from medicine to literature, as a way to retaliate against his elder brother, who had urged him toward medicine. Such instances of the severance of family and friendly ties take place against scenes that concentrate on the one component of the protagonist's fantasy that is much more readily available—sensuality (and by implication, "masculinity")—even though he has access to it only through (1) masturbation and (2) voyeurism.

The first, masturbation, is conducted under a great sense of guilt and fear. The cause for guilt and fear is that he might ruin his own health, which supposedly belongs to his parents. Harming oneself in this manner violates a particular kind of "law of the father," filial piety:

> He was ordinarily a very self-respecting and clean person, but when evil thoughts seized hold of him, numbing his intellect and paralyzing his conscience, he was no longer able to observe the admonition [from the Confucian classic *The Book on Filial Piety*] that "one must not harm one's body under any circumstances, since it is inherited from one's parents." Every time he sinned he felt bitter remorse and vowed not to transgress again. But, almost without exception, the same visions appeared before him vividly at the same time the next morning.
> (p. 132)

The excitement and fear brought about by the act of masturbation are paralleled by those brought about by the acts of voyeurism. There are two instances of the latter: once, when he peeks through the bathroom window at his innkeeper's daughter taking a shower; the second time, when, out on a walk, he overhears a couple having sex by a growth of tall reeds. What the exclusive focus on sensuality achieves, psychically, is the effect of pleasure-in-pain. The protagonist would, after masturbating, "go to the library to look up references on the subject" and find to his fear that all the books condemn the practice as harmful to one's health, but the pain of such discoveries does not deter him from repeating the entire experience. Similarly, after he plays voyeur and eavesdropper, he is haunted by agony and filled with contempt for himself, but at the same time greatly excited. In all of these roles, he puts himself in a masochistic relation to prohibition.

The protagonist's condition is aptly summed up by a phrase that is richly resonant in our context: "self-abuse." In this phrase we recognize once again that "turning around of aggression upon the subject's self" and the basis of fantasy in Yü Dafu's story. The last two sections of "Sinking" demonstrate the movement of this fantasy superbly in two thematically related, "climactic" scenes—the protagonist's visit to a brothel and his walk along the seashore.

The first of these scenes picks up from the strong sensuality that fills the immediately preceding sections. On one of his usual aimless walks one day, the protagonist finds himself in front of a villa where he expects to be greeted by prostitutes. A waitress leads him to a room and serves him wine and food, and he is intoxicated by the sensual atmosphere created by "the fragrance emanating from her mouth, hair, face, and body" (p. 139). He wishes to "confide in her all his troubles." But the neurotic division felt by men toward women that Freud discusses helps explain why this wish is immediately transformed. Instead of confiding in this waitress, an act that would have turned her into an affectionate friend, the protagonist's desire becomes predominantly visual, focusing instead on the waitress's hands resting on her knees and "that portion of a pink petticoat not covered by her kimono" (p. 139).

What follows, in a manner that casts the waitress in classically fetishistic terms, is a detailed description of Japanese women's way of dressing. But the process of fetishism ends with a turn toward self-abuse:

> For Japanese women wear a short petticoat instead of drawers. On the
> outside they wear a buttonless, long-sleeved kimono with a band about
> fourteen inches wide around the waist fastened into a square bundle on
> the back. Because of this costume, with every step they take, the
> kimono is flung open to reveal the pink petticoat inside and a glimpse
> of plump thighs. This is the special charm of Japanese women to which
> he paid most attention whenever he saw them on the street. It was
> because of this habit too that he called himself a beast, a sneaky dog,
> and a despicable coward. (p. 139)

The intense gaze at the other as a sex object therefore ends as a gaze that is directed instead against himself as an object of self-curse. This intricate psychic process is then played out externally, as the external object of his gaze, impatient at his tongue-tiedness, asks the fateful question: "Where are you from?" With this question, the external object recedes from the picture and what comes fully to the fore, from this point on until the end of the story, is that other, real object of his gaze — himself and his national identity:

> "Where are you from?"
> At this, his pallid face reddened again; he stammered and stammered but couldn't give a forthright answer. He was once again standing on the guillotine. For the Japanese look down upon Chinese just as we look down upon pigs and dogs. They call us Shinajin, "Chinamen," a term more derogatory than "knave" in Chinese. And now he had to confess before this pretty young girl that he was a Shinajin.
> "O China, my China, why don't you grow strong!"
> His body was trembling convulsively and tears were again about to roll down. (p. 139)

Instead of making love with a woman, the protagonist's adventure in the brothel climaxes with his chanting aloud a poem about the love for one's country, in retaliation against some Japanese men in the next room singing Japanese songs.

In the last scene, the protagonist is walking by the seashore, where he suddenly has "an inexplicable urge to drown himself in the sea" because, we are told, "I'll probably never get the kind of love I want" (p. 141). The mood of self-pity turns once again toward "China." Looking west, the protagonist says:

> "O China, my China, you are the cause of my death! . . . I wish you could become rich and strong soon! . . . Many, many of your children are still suffering." (p. 141)

The fantasy structure of male masochism is here completed by a psychic submission to the "mother" that is looked upon as the savior to her children. This return to an infantile position accounts for the sexual impotence that the protagonist experiences with actual women. At the same time, we can also say that because "China" is resented as what weakens, shames, and humiliates him, it is ironically identified with the actual women with whom he cannot be a potent man. The submission to "China" is hence not simply a submission to a loving "mother," but a submission to the protagonist's own narcissism, in which are images of woman that he creates, desires, but fails to control. The specific cultural makeup of Yü Dafu's story extends the implications of the masochistic idealization of woman by showing it to be at once active, passive, longing, and resentful — also at once masculine, feminized, and infantile. Superimposed upon a discourse of nationalism, the mobility between polarized psychic states and between conventionalized sexual positions in "Sinking" makes it a poignant story in the context of Chinese modernity.

If Yü Dafu's story gives us a man who lives in the margins of society psychologically, Xü Dishan's "Big Sister Liu" ("Chuntao," 1934)[23] looks at a woman whose existence is marginal, economically as well as culturally. The story of Chuntao, a scrap-paper collector, partakes of the fascination with social outcasts that runs through European and American Romantic literature of the nineteenth century and Chinese literature of the twentieth. The aimless wanderings of Yü Dafu's protagonist take place in Nature and in his mind; in those wanderings, "woman" becomes a fantasy that structures yearnings not only for sex but also for national identity. Chuntao wanders too, along city streets, but she wanders to make a living. Her occupation, we are told, is that of "poking through rubbish heaps on street corners and lanes' ends . . . buying old written matter for which she gave boxes of matches in exchange" (p. 112).

Xü Dishan's portrayal of Chuntao's marginality is thought-provoking and warrants an elaborate discussion. As we do this, the question we want to bear in mind is: what does the fascination with a lower-class woman's marginality accomplish in terms of the dominant cultural politics vis-à-vis femininity?

Chuntao, we are told, was married for one night. As she was brought to her groom's home as a bride, the news of an army's invasion of two neighboring villages reached town and disrupted the supposedly blissful time of the wedding, forcing husband and wife to flee with fellow villagers. Chuntao's husband disappeared mysteriously after their second night on the road, when everyone scrambled to hide from approaching bandits. Left on her own, she went to Beijing, became a nursemaid and soon afterward a scrap-paper collector. Since Chuntao needs help with her paper collecting from someone who can read, she rents a room with Liu Xianggao, a man who was once a fellow refugee. When the story begins, Chuntao and Xianggao have been living together for three years.

The marginality of Chuntao's position, as both a woman who has lost her husband and someone who is occupationally at the lowest stratum of society, is staged as a radical way of redefining society's conventional mores. As the collector of scrap paper, she treats "culture" as garbage and thus overturns society's hierarchical distinctions between the educated and the uneducated. In a business that deals with culture as scraps, the man who knows how to read becomes merely the collector's assistant; the skill of reading now helps the improvement not of knowledge but of sales:

> Since Xianggao could read a bit, he was able to sort through the paper that Chuntao collected and pick out the relatively valuable pieces, such as inscribed paintings or letters or scrolls written by some famous figure. With the two cooperating, business improved. (p. 113)

As a domestic woman, Chuntao also overturns social mores drastically, by openly living with a man who is not her husband. In the beginning scene, as she arrives home after a day's work, we hear Xianggao call her, half teasingly and half affectionately, "wife." Throughout the story Chuntao resists this. This resistance continues even as Xianggao tells her that a policeman came by earlier to check up on the tenants and demanded that every family report exactly the relationship of those staying with them. Xianggao confesses that, to keep from causing trouble, he filled out a blank wedding certificate that they had collected but could not sell, and showed Chuntao and himself as a married couple.

Interestingly, Chuntao's resistance to being called "wife" does not result in further protests. And this is one of the most significant meanings of the marginality her character embodies. It is a marginality that asserts its independence without being ostentatious and without fear of public disapproval. This independence is most evident in Chuntao's physical relationship with Xianggao. We see the two characters behaving toward each other like a married couple, but all the gestures that could otherwise be interpreted as having a sexual meaning are desexualized. After they cook and eat, it is time for bed:

> Chuntao undressed, draped herself in a thin coverlet and lay face downwards on the bed. According to their nightly habit, Xianggao massaged her back and legs. As usual, she gradually relaxed, a faint smile on her lips, as Xianggao kneaded her weary muscles in the light of the oil lamp's flickering little flame.
>
> Already half asleep, she murmured, "You come to bed too. Don't work tonight. You have to get up early tomorrow."
>
> Soon the woman was snoring faintly. Xianggao put out the lamp. (pp. 120-21)

The dissociation of affection and sensuality, attached to a female figure who is living in the margins of society in every sense, carries with it the meaning of a criticism of society's "normal" standards of morality. The obvious physical intimacy between a man and a woman that is shown here becomes the opposite of society's expectation of it—"sex"—and serves as the narrative means of *defying* society's narrow conception of such intimacy. In this way, Chuntao's lowly status has the significance of being a "clean" truth that exposes society's unclean (that is to say, pretentious) standards. We are given the clue to this meaning of her marginality early in the story:

> From morning till night, beneath the blazing sun or in the icy gale, she tramped the streets, eating her full share of dust. *But she had always loved cleanliness.* Winter or summer, each day when she returned home she washed her face and bathed her body. (p. 112; my emphasis)

Structurally, therefore, the device on which Xü Dishan relies to put his meaning across is that of an inversion of society's normal expectations. The idealization of Chuntao through inversion reminds us of Xü Dishan's other story "Luo hua sheng" [Peanuts, 1922], in which homegrown peanuts are praised for their earnest, practical usefulness. However, once we have understood this device of inversion, other questions begin to surface. The radicalness of Xü Dishan's moralism becomes problematic when a particular kind of inversion—desexualization—is closely examined. If we reinscribe into the apparently desexualized relationship between Chuntao and Xianggao their separate and specific psychic concerns, the "radicalness" of desexualization becomes disturbing in a way that is very different from what is authorially intended.

The narrative takes a significant turn when Chuntao's husband, Li Mao, hitherto assumed dead, suddenly shows up one day. Having lost both his legs during the turmoil of warfare, Li Mao is now a beggar. Chuntao and he are happy to see each other again, but soon the problem of marital propriety arises. Whose wife is Chuntao? While she has no difficulty telling Li Mao that she shares the same bed with another man simply because they are living together, he is profoundly unsettled. As we can expect, Chuntao's response is much sharper and more clearheaded:

> "Everyone must be laughing at me for being a cuckold," he said at last in a low voice.
> "Cuckold?" The woman's face hardened a bit at the word, but she spoke without rancour. "Only people with money and position are afraid of being cuckolds. A man like you—who knows that you're even alive? Besides, cuckold or not, what's the difference? I'm independent now. Whatever I do can't have any effect on you." (p. 126)

But the defiant and determined attempt to assert her own independence is not easy for Chuntao to sustain. Tugging at her heart is also her concern for Li Mao, who cannot make a living on his own. She finally comes up with a solution: "Why don't we all just live here, and no one think about who's supporting whom, what do you say?" (p. 127). The practical, down-to-earth quality of Chuntao's attitude is clearly contrasted with the worldly and wary attitudes of the men. As Xianggao and Li Mao meet for the first time, with mutual unease, their conversation soon turns to the topic of their rightful relation to the woman. Out of a sense of desperation, Li Mao offers to leave, which triggers this earnest exchange between the two men:

> "That's not right," replied Xianggao. "I don't want to be known as a wife-stealer. And, thinking of it from your angle, you shouldn't let your wife live with another man."
> "I'll write a paper disowning her, or I'll give you a bill of sale. Either way will do," Li Mao said with a smile. But his tone was quite earnest.

"How can you disown her? She hasn't done anything wrong. I don't want her to lose face. As for buying her—where would I get the money? Whatever money I have is hers."

"I don't want any money."

"What do you want?"

"I don't want anything."

"Then why write a bill of sale?"

"Because if we just agree verbally you won't have any proof. I might be sorry later and change my mind; that would make things awkward. Excuse me for talking so frankly, but that's the best way to get this thing settled." (pp. 130-31)

This manly preoccupation with wife ownership and with their own social reputation eventually leads to the drawing up of a contract of sale, which Chuntao discovers when she comes home one day:

"Who does this red card on the table belong to?" Chuntao asked, picking it up.

"We talked it over today," said Li Mao from the brick bed. "You go to Xianggao. That's the contract of sale."

"Oh, so you've got it all settled among yourselves! Well, and I say it's not up to you two to dispose of me!" She walked over to Li Mao with the red card. "Was this your idea, or his?"

"It's what we both want. The way we've been living, I'm not happy and neither is he."

"We talk and talk and it's still the same question. Why must you two always think about this husband and wife business?" Angrily, she tore the card to bits. "How much did you sell me for?"

"We put down a figure just for the look of things. No real man gives his wife away for nothing."

"But if he sells her, that makes everything alright, does it?" (p. 135)

Chuntao's voice is loud and clear. In its direct and fearless mockery of society's scholastic propriety, with which the two men are trying to comply, this marginal female voice makes way for the pedagogical voice of the narrative. Merging with Chuntao's, this narrative voice delivers its moral unambiguously:

The institution of polyandrous marriage after all hasn't too many adherents in the world, one of the reasons being that the average man cannot rid himself of his primitive concepts regarding his rights as a husband and father. It is from these concepts that our customs and moral codes arise. Actually, in our society, only the parasites and exploiters observe the so-called customs; people who have to work for a living have very little respect for them in their hearts. . . .

From the earliest days, real control over the people has been exercised not through the teachings of the sages but by cursing tongues and blows of the whips. Curses and blows are what have maintained our customs. (pp. 133, 136)

At the end, as a result of Chuntao's firmness, a change is accomplished: the two men agree that the three of them should continue to live together. Depending on whether they are in the city or the country, one of them would be the resident-in-charge while Chuntao is wife to both of them.

To return now to the question I ask at the beginning of our discussion of this story: what does the fascination with a woman's marginality accomplish in terms of the dominant cultural politics vis-à-vis femininity? Potentially, the unmistakable idealization of Chuntao opens up many possibilities for change. Chuntao's status as a scrap-paper collector, her unconventional relationship with the two men, the two men's emotional and economic dependence on her, and her defiance of scholastic moral value—all these narrative elements signal fundamental challenges to traditional Chinese society. On the other hand, we must ask whether the idealization of a marginal feminine figure's amoral stance toward the world is not in fact at the expense of something else, namely, Chuntao's "sexuality"—that is, the socially inscribed, gendered psychic complexities that would have been, if the narrative were fully invested in marginality, part of Chuntao's defiance toward the world. If the idealization of woman in "Sinking" is accompanied with a thorough exploration of the male masochist's psychic realities, the idealization of woman in "Big Sister Liu" can be described in terms of a thorough *exclusion* of those elements that are necessary for the same kind of exploration. For some readers perhaps, this may be exactly what a feminist reading should affirm: the man in Yü Dafu's story is sick, the woman in Xü Dishan's story is healthy! "So why are you complaining?" they ask. My complaint is that much as Chuntao is idealized as a strong woman who lives by her own moral code, her independence is in fact in strict compliance with the most fundamental rule in Confucian patriarchy—the demand that a woman remain sexually "clean." When Li Mao tries to give her back their original marriage certificate so that she can be free of her obligation to him, we hear Chuntao say:

"Take it back, Mao dear, I don't want it. I'm still your wife. 'One night of marriage, a hundred days of bliss'—I can't wrong you like this. What kind of a person would I be if I threw you over because you can't walk or work?" (p. 137)

A more literal translation of the Chinese original for "I can't wrong you like this" is "I can't do something that is so lacking in morality [*que de*]." What morality? The text is ambiguous. It could be the morality that says "one does not abandon a crippled person," or it could be the morality that says "a married woman does not leave her husband." The ambiguity does not obstruct our reading, though, but assists it by fusing the two possible meanings smoothly. But in such a fusion, Chuntao's act becomes yet another affirmation of exactly the kind of self-sacrificing virtue that is traditionally demanded of Chinese women. Her marginality is simply an *inverted* way of showing how, in fact, it is in the debased margins of society that the essence of that society's teachings is preserved: the woman scrap-paper collector is more chaste, more virtuous, and thus more faithful to Confucian standards of behavior than those who have studied them. Xü Dishan's text says: this woman's "inner beauty" attests to this.

The possibilities for change that are opened up by the idealization of this lower-class female figure are thus foreclosed precisely on those issues that are fundamental to the cultural constructions of femininity and gender in China. In what is meant to be a complimentary account of her and her kind, Chuntao's psychic life is barred from entering the narrative by the same voice that otherwise uses her speech and action to deliver its morals:

> Work was part of her very being. Even though she was depressed and unhappy, she still wanted to work. Work is the only thing Chinese women seem to understand. They don't seem to understand love. All their attention is concentrated on the routine problems of life. Love's flowering is only a blind, stifled stirring in their hearts.
>
> Of course love is merely an emotion, while life is tangible and real. The art of talking learnedly of love while reclining behind a silken curtain or sitting in a secluded forest glade is an importation brought on ocean-going steamers — the "Empress" of this, the "President" that. Chuntao had never been abroad, nor had she ever studied in a school run by blue-eyed foreigners. She didn't understand fashionable love. All she knew was a dull, unaccountable pain. (p. 139)

These morals occupy a similar kind of theoretical space as that of Freud's argument about the dissociation of affection and sensuality. Freud's conclusion, we remember, is that such a dissociation is an inevitable part of culture. Xü Dishan's story offers us a comparable picture, while at the same time complicating Freud's libidinal terms with cross-cultural and class emphases. The structure of "affection versus sensuality" or "reverence versus eroticism" here assumes the forms of "Chinese women" versus "an importation brought on ocean-going steamers"; and of "work" versus "love." In both, the idealization of a woman depends on a conception of her as clean and untouched by sexuality. This idealization means that woman cannot have a psychic life, for it is precisely the meanders of a psychic life that would, as it were, make her swerve from her place and become the kind of object that, *pace* Freud, no longer deserves man's high estimation.

Put side by side with Freud's model of love, Ba Jin's "Zuichu di huiyi" [My earliest memories, 1931][24] would seem on first reading to inhabit a libidinal space

that is yet free of the turbulence of "sensuality." Written with a delightful simplicity and spontaneity, Ba Jin's autobiographical piece strongly suggests the
memorable quality of a privileged childhood that was filled with care and love
from elders and servants alike. Interestingly, however, the brief sketches of the
author's first objects of love show how the child's relations to these objects are,
even as they inspire in him the deepest affection and tenderness, already characterized by psychic divisions and ambiguities.

At the center of the child Ba Jin's memories is the figure of his mother, both
a face and a voice:

> Every time I think back to my most distant past, my mother's face
> appears in my mind. My earliest memories are inseparable from my
> mother. In particular I cannot forget her gentle voice. (p. 10)

This first object of love is remembered in the most vivid details, none of
which is irrelevant to the child's mind. In a way that reminds us once again of
the process of fetishism, the picture of mother is made up of specific parts of her
that stand out concretely without the mediation of explanatory language:

> A gentle round face, hair that looks bright as a result of *pao hua shui* [a
> conditioner], lips that are always wearing a smile. Pale-indigo, big-
> sleeve short jacket with broad ripple-style borders; no collar. (p. 10)

The magical quality of his mother's presence is also the result of her mesmer-
izing storytelling. Ba Jin and his siblings listen tirelessly to her telling about his
own birth: one night, a fairy came into her dream with a baby that was originally
intended for her sister-in-law, but since her sister-in-law would not take good
care of it, the baby became hers—"The next day, you were born!" adds Ba Jin's
mother every time she repeats this story. With his mother overseeing every major aspect of her children's life, including the study of music and poetry, Ba Jin's
father is displaced emotionally. Ba Jin tells of how disturbed he is once, when he
sees that his father, a local magistrate who holds his office at home, issues orders
for the severe physical punishment of criminals. He takes his discomfort to his
mother, and she solves his problem ably by persuading her husband to change
his punitive methods.

However, two incidents cloud the peace and quiet of this sheltered childhood. The first relates to a group of chickens that the young Ba Jin calls his
"companions" or "troops," among which his favorite one is Big Freckled Hen.
As their commander, Ba Jin would carefully count them every day to make sure
they are all safe and alive. But one day, he discovers that one of the chickens is
missing: it has been killed and served for dinner! This sad process repeats itself
continually, until Big Freckled Hen disappears as well.

The second incident relates to a servant called Nanny Yang. When a little
sister is born, Ba Jin and his older brother are entrusted to the care of Nanny

Yang, who soon develops an intimate relationship with the boys, feeding them rice cakes, making their beds, helping them undress, and telling them bedtime stories. Ba Jin says: "During this time we could not, of course, be without our mother; yet neither could we be without Nanny Yang" (Link, p. 294). But this happy relationship with a surrogate mother ends as Nanny Yang becomes ill and finally dies.

If the child's world is at first one of fused harmony, then these two incidents of death, both representing a severance from the first objects of love, indicate a powerful intrusion of very different emotions. As the chicken dishes are served at dinner, Ba Jin refuses to eat them. He also refuses to believe the adults' talk about the dead chickens' afterlife and instead continues persistently to feed and play with the remaining ones, in spite of his knowledge of their impending fate. In this way, the little boy stages a confrontation with death, in defiance of the adults who smooth over death with ease, through the rituals of cooking and eating. This attitude of resistance characterizes Ba Jin's response to Nanny Yang's death as well, but as we shall see in a moment, this response is more mediated because it is aestheticized.

The ominous feeling of death surrounds Nanny Yang's deserted condition even before she dies. When Ba Jin and his older brother visit her for the first time after she became ill, what greets them is the sight of a lonely, neglected patient:

> Quite to our surprise, we found that there was no other person in that dark room, nor was there the slightest sound. Nanny Yang lay very still on a low bed, the lower portions of her body covered by a thin quilt on which brownish stains were apparent. One side of the bed's mosquito net had been let down and dropped to the floor. Not far from the bed there was a little stool on which rested a bowl of thick, black herb medicine, already cold. Two flies were crawling up the side of the bowl. (Link, p. 295)

At this point of Ba Jin's memories, the idealization of his own mother is difficult to sustain as it is more and more conflicted by her alliance with an adult world that is not kind but cruel. This adult world exploits both the chickens and the servant, and the mother, who is at its center, is "responsible" in both cases. It was she who gave orders for the chickens to be killed, and she who announces Nanny Yang's imminent departure:

> "Nanny Yang is not going to recover," Mother tearfully told Father one day. "Let's get her a really nice coffin. These years she's been with us she's treated our Third and Fourth so well—almost as if they were her very own." Her words suddenly made me cry. It was the first time I understood what death meant. (p. 297)

Ba Jin's reaction to the adults, who all hope for Nanny Yang's speedy death so that she can stop suffering, is an explicitly stated disbelief and incomprehension:

> That the good intentions of so many people should lead them to hope for another person's death — the death not of a person they hated but of one they loved — was something beyond the understanding of a child like myself. And I'm afraid it's probably something *I won't understand* even when I'm forty or fifty. (p. 298; my emphasis)

What we have up to this point is an argument that, by following the grain of Ba Jin's story, opposes the child to the adult world. In this opposition we find a rudimentary form of protest against the exploitation of powerless classes by the powerful, and the suggestion of the child's unconscious wavering between loyalty to his mother and loyalty to oppressed figures such as the chickens and Nanny Yang. However, Ba Jin's text indicates the possibility of a different reading, a reading that, I would suggest, is much more in keeping with the problematic nature of his sentimentalism that I already pointed out in a different way in the previous chapter.

In the statement "I won't understand" lies not only the meaning of potential social protest but also the form of an aesthetic. And it is this aesthetic that accounts for the structure of fantasy in Ba Jin's recollections. What does it mean to say he "won't understand"? What is it that he won't understand? To answer these questions, we need to go back to the scene when the child himself sees the servant sick in bed.

At the sight of Nanny Yang, Ba Jin's primary reaction is that of disbelief. His narrative shows us not simply the transformed appearance of this object of love but simultaneously the child's transformed way of looking at her. Much like the scenario of fetishism described by Freud, the child's optical path toward this mother figure is now marked by a particular kind of attention, an attention that "sees" her as uncanny:

> My mind stood still. I stared at her face with every ounce of concentration. Very slowly a sound began coming from her nose. The hand that had been clutching the edge of the bed gently relaxed. Her body shifted, ever so slightly, and some inarticulate sound came from her mouth. Then her eyes slowly opened, closed again, then reopened wider than before. . . .
>
> [Nanny Yang] lowered her face and gulped down the medicine. As we listened to the gulping noise, it almost seemed we could watch how the medicine passed through her esophagus and into her stomach. . . .
>
> Gradually, before my very eyes, Nanny Yang's face began to change. I saw the face of a goblin: the long, disheveled hair, the pallid, meager face, the high cheekbones, and big, blood-red eyes — this was just like

the goblins' faces in the stories Nanny Yang used to tell. (Link, p. 297)

This process of fetishizing the body of the beloved object to the point at which it is no longer familiar and recognizable is, I think, the most remarkable part of Ba Jin's story. It points to the mechanism of "disavowal" that is essential to the idealism that, as we have seen in Freud and Deleuze, is attached to the mother as a fetish. Instead of believing the reality of death that is in front of him, the child creates in his imagination a new object, partitioned in fetishistic detail, onto which the unpleasantness of the loss of his loved one is safely displaced. What he "won't understand" is therefore not simply, as Ba Jin's explicit statements would have us believe, the other adults' attitude toward Nanny Yang. It is rather the more basic and more overwhelming fact of Nanny Yang's disappearance from his life. In "defamiliarizing" her in what amounts to a grotesque aesthetic, he accomplishes two things at once: the neutralization of his pain at seeing Nanny Yang's reality, and the preservation of her image as he wants to remember her—the potent and gratifying mother.

It has been observed, in regard to European literature, that the social exclusion and the lowliness of female servants become what arouse sexual desire in the young males that they take care of, and that it is to these women that these young males return imaginatively throughout their careers as writers and artists.[25] The imaginative return to a servant figure is also true in our present context, but the linkage between lowliness and the restricted sense of "sexuality" has shifted. Ba Jin's reminiscence of Nanny Yang has more to do with an emotion that associates lowliness with service and thus with maternal power. Nanny Yang is not lusted after but idealized. It is in this female servant that the fantasy of the mother, which initiates Ba Jin's recollections at first through his own mother, receives its most complex psychic representation.

3

To summarize our arguments up to this point, we can say that when idealization is the result of a dissociation of libidinal energies, it leads to the fixed pictorialization of that which is idealized. The various masculine scenarios we have discussed all partake of a particular kind of psychic structure: the idealization of a mother figure that is inseparable from the *rejection* of certain aspects of her. In "Sinking," the mother that is rejected is the China which is weak and humiliated and which is internalized in the male protagonist as his own impotence and masochism vis-à-vis actual women. In "Big Sister Liu," the marginality of a lower-class female figure undergoes an inversion to become what is revered, but this reverence works by a moralistic exclusion of Chuntao's sexuality. In "My First Memories," a child holds onto an idealized memory of a surrogate mother figure by consciously, aesthetically distancing himself from her sickness and death.

The rejection of parts of a figure that is otherwise passionately longed for resonates with Freud's argument about the "dissociation" between affection and sensuality. In that argument, as we have seen, the dissociation of the two forms of love comes about as a result of the incest taboo; a part of the libido that used to be attached to the first objects of love in total fusion is hence broken off and redirected to external, unprohibited objects. However, Freud also insists, with profound idealism, that the original fusion with the first objects of love is the only and most perfect form of happiness. That being impossible, libidinal adjustments such as dissociation, rejection, and redirection become surrogate but necessary mechanisms of survival.

We now see why Deleuze, in using Freud's argument about fetishism, would want to place such importance on "disavowal." In doing so, he brings to the fore the psychic element that is fundamental to Freudian idealism. Deleuze's theory of masochism "solves" the problem of Freud's "unhappy" separation from the first objects of love *aesthetically*, by explicitly turning woman into a divine fetish whose immobile condition makes it possible for the male masochist to retain all the "original" infantile desires he has for her. The protagonist's "impotence" in "Sinking," the narrative exclusion of Chuntao from "love," and the little Ba Jin's disavowal of Nanny Yang's death all demonstrate the structure of this kind of aesthetic structure. As woman becomes an unmoving pictorialized mother, what *move*, psychically as well as textually, are the "active" processes of subjectivity that, because of their tendencies toward dissociation, disavowal, and neurosis, *become* masculine.

The question to ask now is: if we are to retain the idealism of this wish for the "fusion" with the mother, might there be ways of realizing it without involving the mechanisms of disavowal, dissociation, and rejection that are typical of the male scenarios we have followed? Might an idealization of the mother be affectionate and sensual at the same time? Might a masochistic submission to the mother not be synonymous with turning her into an unmoving picture?

These are the questions that Kaja Silverman takes up in a persuasive argument in *The Acoustic Mirror: The Female Voice in Psychoanalysis and Cinema*, under the term "negative Oedipus complex."[26] The Oedipus complex, we recall, works by the mutual implication of taboo and desire. For Freud's little boy, desire for the opposite sex (beginning with the mother) concurs with the prohibitive law of the father, the "same" sex with which he eventually identifies. Desire and identification are thus, in a way that is characteristic of Freud's binary oppositional thinking, dissociated: desire for one parent means identification with the other. However, according to Silverman, Freud had another understanding of the Oedipus complex, which she locates in a brief passage from *The Ego and the Id*. In this passage, Freud divides the Oedipus complex into the positive and the negative, and problematizes the notion that boys are only "masculine." As Silverman quotes (p. 120):

One gets the impression that the simple Oedipus complex is by no means its commonest form, but rather represents a simplification or schematization which, to be sure, is often enough justified for practical purposes. Closer study usually discloses the more complete Oedipus complex, which is twofold, positive and negative, and is due to the bisexuality originally present in children: that is to say, a boy has not merely an ambivalent attitude towards his father and an affectionate object-choice towards his mother, but at the same time he also behaves like a girl and displays an affectionate feminine attitude to his father and a corresponding jealousy and hostility towards his mother.[27]

In other words, in the negative Oedipus complex, desire and identification are no longer dissociated the way they are in the positive Oedipus complex, but rather fused in the boy's attitude toward the same parent, his father. As Silverman comments, while the positive Oedipus complex is "culturally promoted and works to align the subject smoothly with heterosexuality and the dominant values of the symbolic order," the negative Oedipus complex is "culturally disavowed and organizes subjectivity in fundamentally 'perverse' and homosexual ways" (Silverman, p. 120).

In what I think is the most insightful part of her argument, Silverman goes on to show that when the negative Oedipus complex is considered *from the female perspective*, which Freud left unexplored, it becomes possible to see women's relation with their mothers not only in terms of identification, but also in terms of erotic desire: "The girl's aspiration to occupy the place of the mother does not imply the latter's exclusion from her erotic economy, but the endless reversibility of their relative positions" (Silverman, p. 153). Although the negative Oedipus complex often gives way, eventually, to the positive Oedipus complex under the pressure of the dominant culture, its formulation lends important insight into the central role played by the mother in the history of female sexuality, especially in regard to the conjunction of identification and eroticism. "It is," Silverman says, "this conjunction of identification and eroticism which I would describe as the 'censored, repressed element of the feminine,' and which I believe to have a vital relation to feminism" (Silverman, pp. 150-51).

In what follows, two stories by two modern Chinese women writers demonstrate, each in its own way, the conjunction of identification and eroticism from a woman's point of view. I will give a close reading of these stories, before concluding with a summary of the issues we have raised in this chapter.

Near the beginning of Bing Xin's "Di yi ci yanhui" [The first dinner party, 1929],[28] we read about a fantasy of the newly married Ying's, who has just agreed to host a dinner party for her husband. The content of this fantasy can be described in terms of conventional domestic bliss:

> The newly married Ying—or Ying before she got married—had
> fantasized the first dinner party at her little home: pine twigs burning in
> the fireplace; the red, happy flames making the fine furniture shine
> with a solemn black light; a light blue lamp sitting on the table at the
> corner of the room with a shade that has tassels; in this mixture of mild
> light from the fire and the lamp all the furnishings—the carpet, the
> curtains, the book shelves, the flowers, the paintings on the wall, the
> incense—look appropriate and sweet. As for the housewife, she is
> dressed tidily and properly; her big black eyes are bright with pride; a
> smile she cannot hide appears on her slightly made-up face; she talks
> with a clear, bell-like voice, chatting and socializing with the guests.
> (p. 257)

The sentimentalism of this fantasy should be specified as a sentimentalism about what Silverman refers to as "heterosexuality and the dominant values of the symbolic order." Domesticity, as Ying dreams about it, is a picture of order, peace, and sweetness, with her, the impeccable housewife, at the center. Remarkably, this fantasy is destroyed when Ying arrives in her new house. Her mother's illness, we are told, has delayed her plans, so that when she arrives, she is greeted by a house full of painters, carpenters, and other workers still busy with setting things in order. Ying becomes convinced that her dream party can never come true.

When she finally, in spite of the obstacles that stand in her way, puts the house in presentable shape, she discovers a package that she brought home unawares. As she opens it, a few flower holders come into sight and, "As if by lightning, she sees her sick pale mother lying in bed." The narrative now changes its focus and returns to the time when Ying was with her mother before she arrived at her new home. The flower holders, it turns out, are a gift that her mother insisted Ying take home in order to make up for the small dowry her parents were able to afford to give her. For Ying, what the flower holders call to mind is the self-sacrifice that her mother has made her entire life: "Whatever she could, she gives to her daughter, and yet she still never feels it was enough" (p. 261).

The significance of this "flashback" can be described in the following terms. Into her preparation for the party, a preparation that is symbolically her initiation into society as a married woman and thus into "normal," "mature" femininity, Ying's memories of her mother intrude with that desire for the parent of the same sex that is the crucial part of the "negative Oedipus complex." Intertwined with Ying's entry into heterosexuality is an intense emotional involvement with her mother, whose physical nature is expressed in sentences like the following (which I translate literally):

This painstaking love from her mother fills Ying's heart with a deep, acidic feeling. . . .
Such incidents [of her mother's love] have left their marks on her heart like bloody scars carved with a sharp-pointed knife, making her weep whenever she thought of them. . . .
Her heart was completely broken. . . . Oh poor, excessively loving mother! (pp. 262, 263)

The rhetorically strained way in which Ying's feelings toward her mother are expressed is echoed in many of Bing Xin's other writings, which are known to readers of modern Chinese literature as consistently centering on her love for her own mother. She refers to the latter as "the first and the last person I love." Her mother's love, she says, "makes me seek death in life by obligating me to shoulder other people's suffering, and makes me seek life in death by obligating me to forget my own."[29]

Such sentimental remarks are in part what lead some critics, including those who are interested in women's writings, to consider early twentieth-century Chinese women writers like Bing Xin in a pejorative light. In her essay "Women as Writers in the 1920's and 1930's," for instance, Yi-tsi Feuerwerker writes that these women writers were "unable to move on to a broader vision of reality"[30] because of their "emotional narcissism." Feuerwerker's argument is, I think, flawed by her reading of Chinese women writers of the 1920s and 1930s in the light of "objective" literary criteria against which their works can only appear to be failures. Beginning with the observation that the literary achievement of this period is often disparaged by critics as modest, and using that as her entry into the problem of women's writings, she offers some sympathetic analyses, only to conclude, however, that most Chinese women writers of this period, with the exception of Ding Ling, were unable to transcend their personal experiences:

Too much of their experience, overwhelming and inextricable from the historic upheavals around them, entered their writing in a half-processed state. They lacked the balance, the mature detachment, the finality, that make for great works of literature.[31]

Rather than challenging the criteria by which these women writers are judged to be failures, then, Feuerwerker's conclusion endorses those criteria. But "balance," "mature detachment," and "finality" are not ideologically innocent but patriarchal demands; the aesthetics of transcending-the-personal they inscribe is, arguably, also an aesthetics of transcending-the-personal-as-gendered. If a consideration of women writers cannot be divorced from their relation to patriarchy, which functions precisely by reducing women to the "private," the "emotional," the "imbalanced, " and so forth, why should these conditions not be the ones to which women writers obsessively return? And if they do, why should this be used to devalue their accomplishments in what amounts to a teleological method of judging, which presupposes in an a priori manner what is "great" literature? The task involved in reading the women writers of this period in China, it seems to me, is not one of explaining "sociologically" how they fail by the standards of "great" literature, but rather of deconstructing the notion of "great" literature by the limits — personal and therefore social — that are accentuated in their writings.

If we disengage the words of this kind of critical judgment from the typological, derogatory meanings that they are intended to carry, and rethink "not being able to move on" in terms of the negative Oedipus complex, then a new way of seeing Bing Xin's psychical topography opens up precisely with sentimental remarks of the kind that I just quoted. These remarks are interesting because of the excessive and obsessive nature of their manner of utterance. What is it, we should ask, that calls for such extreme emotional expressivity?

The passion in these remarks stems from a sense of debt to the mother's *un-repayable* love. In Chinese, this love is sometimes called *en*, meaning kindness, favor, or grace. But to conceive of love in terms of indebtedness is to give to an abstract emotion an economic base; parents become in this way our creditors. The teaching of *xiao* (filial piety) that is handed down in Chinese families from day to day should therefore be seen as a teaching of the compensation for what is perceived to be a fundamentally unequal transaction between children and parents. In a discussion that offers points of comparison with the Chinese teachings of filial piety, Jochen Schulte-Sasse points out that "compensation" and "sacrifice" share a *common* economic basis in eighteenth-century European religious thinking, in that both contain the notion of reward in suffering. "Even sacrifice," he says, "could be called a means of compensation in the economic sense."[32]

A focus on the mother's role and the significance of *self*-sacrifice it involves changes the nature of the linkage between sacrifice and compensation as described by Schulte-Sasse. What redefines that linkage is the simple but essential question: who is sacrificing for whom? Is the one who sacrifices, the "subject" and the one who receives, the "object" — or the reverse: the one who receives, the "subject" and the one who sacrifices, the "object"? Could sacrificer and receiver *both* be subjects? For that to happen, sacrifice would need to become *self*-sacrifice, which would need to be practiced by two parties mutually, and not only by one party for the other. However, once we perceive the possibility of this alternative conception of sacrifice, "compensation for suffering" would no longer be a matter of "(one) filling (another's) pain with (one's) sympathy," but instead could be reformulated as "(one) filling (another's) pain with (one's) pain." In other words, the binary oppositions that underlie the common understanding of sacrifice and compensation in the form of "giver versus receiver," "sympathy versus pain," or "fullness versus lack" are dissolved in the notion of sacrifice as both self- *and* mutual practice. This elusive alternative meaning of sacrifice is, I think, what constitutes the turn toward the mother in Bing Xin's story.

What precisely happens in this "turn"? Thematically, "Di yi ci yanhui" gives the traditional Chinese preoccupation with *en* and *xiao* a feminine emphasis by placing the self-sacrificing mother at the center. And yet, if what occupies "center stage" now is the mother whose truth is the decentering and effacing of herself, how does one know and learn? What constitutes cognition?

This question can only be answered if we see that Bing Xin's idealization of the mother partakes of masochism in the sense defined by Laplanche. Loving another, the mother, becomes a way of introjecting into one's own self-formation that other's suffering. Hence the mother's self-sacrifice, as a sign of the sadistic "castration" that is demanded of domestic Chinese women, is "turned around" on the daughter's self as this self responds actively to the mother's love. The idealization of the mother as such cannot simply "pictorialize" the mother the way Deleuze's male masochism does; instead it takes place in narrative. It is Ying's memories of her mother's actual and psychic movements—her words, her sorrow, her illness, her insistence that her daughter accept the flower holders, as well as her obliviousness to her own needs—that constitute the space of idealization. Instead of the conventional Chinese understanding of the parent-child relationship, in which parents are assumed to be givers and children receivers, mother and daughter in Bing Xin's story share a certain reversibility: as the mother sacrifices for the daughter, the daughter reciprocates that sacrifice in the pain she feels, not for herself, but for the mother. This chain of signification can be written as: the daughter effaces herself for the mother, who effaces herself. The economics of "sympathetic understanding" is thus no longer a matter of (one's) sympathy for (another's) suffering, or (one) compensating for (another's) sacrifice, or (one's) presence for (another's) lack, but instead could be reconceptualized as (one's) suffering for (another's) suffering, as one "lack" filling another "lack," as self-sacrifice "mirroring" self-sacrifice.

Defined this way, "sympathetic" and "sentimental" understanding in Bing Xin becomes the site for that "conjunction of identity and desire" that Silverman describes as the "censored, repressed element of the feminine." For with understanding comes the most intense feelings of physical interaction with the mother, feelings that are in turn expressed in ways that violate the decorum of proper aesthetic restraint and come across as what some would call "purple prose." With this physical interaction come the tears that are the sign of a mutuality not only between mother and daughter as such, but between mother and daughter as self-effacing psychic capacities. It is this mutually masochistic, but therefore mutually responsive, interaction that forms the basis of that *other* fantasy in Bing Xin's story—not the one about domestic bliss with which the story begins, but the one which, "as if by lightning," surges forth with the flower holders.

When everything is ready for the dinner party, Ying's servant reports that the only thing that is missing is a pot of flowers to be put in the center of the dining table. The mother's gift thus fills the need exactly and *completes* the scene of the daughter's "initiation" into womanhood without claiming attention for itself. As the servant comments, the flower holders match the rest of the silverware "as if they were a set."

The overpoweringly enabling presence of her mother produces a sense of guilt in Ying. Her cultural "normality" haunts her as something she should not have entered: "She regretted that she got married. Otherwise she could have stayed and served her mother permanently" (p. 263). Heterosexuality, symbolized by her bond to her husband, is thus intercepted by a bond with her mother that obsessively reasserts itself precisely at the moment of Ying's change of status. And it is the intricacy of this latter bond that explains the final narrative turn.

If the "negative Oedipus complex" makes it possible for us to see once again the daughter's physical desire for the mother, it also shows us how difficult, if not impossible, it is for the female subject to escape the equally strong tendency to identify with the mother and, furthermore, to identify with the mother in the way society has prescribed it. If our argument about self-sacrifice firmly situates the mother's position *in* culture rather than outside it, in the sense that the need to sacrifice herself is already a social, moral demand that is imposed on the woman, it also necessarily deflates the kind of idealism that is possible only when the mother is immobilized as a picture or assigned to the so-called pre-oedipal realm.[33] The self-sacrificing mother is neither omnipotent nor free. In the interaction with the daughter is also the passing on of precisely that identity that is recruited by culture. As Ying desires her mother, she also comes to re-semble her. Resembling here means she will, like her mother, sacrifice herself to the social order.

Her inheritance from her mother is therefore split in two. Toward her mother, Ying's sense of guilt gives way to a wish and a prayer:

> She could not help sobbing, and in desperation she knelt down by the bed. She gave thanks; she repented; she prayed to Heaven: "May what my mother has sacrificed, may the sweet and gentle air that mother's sacrifice has brought return to her through the sweetness of prayer, ripple by ripple." (p. 268)

Toward her husband, resembling her mother means Ying's self-effacement for the stability of the heterosexual contract. The story ends with Ying thinking to herself what a good husband she has, and how, if he discovers her thoughts, it would spoil his day's peace and happiness. Hence, when he approaches and asks what was bothering her, her response is: "No, nothing—I just feel too happy today!" (p. 268). This evasiveness, this attempt to make her own problems disappear behind a calm and undisturbed surface, is then ironically the practice that she has, because of her desire and identification with her mother, adopted for her own life. While the longing for the mother persists, the bond with the husband assumes its centrality in the married woman's life.

In a way that is, on first reading, remarkably different from Bing Xin's motif of self-effacement, Ding Ling's "Miss Sophie's Diary" ("Shafei nüshi di riji," 1928)[34] firmly puts the psychic/sexual life of the protagonist/narrator, Sophie, in the foreground. To the distaste of critics who are concerned with traditional moralism or with the mission of social realism, "Miss Sophie's Diary" signifies only an early, passing phase in Ding Ling's writing career when she was trapped within a suspect "bourgeois" ideology.[35] Sophie's psychic activity is thus easily dismissed in terms of an immature sickliness and as the sign of a privileged class that is indifferent to "real" social and political problems. This condemnation of Ding Ling's early fiction is usually accompanied by a disapproval of the so-called pro-foreign tendency in May Fourth literature, a disapproval that lately transforms itself, by way of a particular kind of feminist interpretation, into a disparaging view of the *Westernized femininity* in Ding Ling's early fiction. For instance, in an essay called "Gender and Identity in Ding Ling's *Mother*," Tani E. Barlow writes that Ding Ling's early fiction "always included references to foreign ways of being female."[36] In the context of Barlow's essay, this emphasis on the "foreign" is part of a hierarchy of value that opposes the West to China. Accordingly, Ding Ling's work is organized along a gradually ascending scale, with her maturity as a writer measured in terms of her ability to abandon the subjective, Westernized, "merely" feminine concerns of her early writings for the "more important" ones of political revolution and *sinicized* consciousness.

In Barlow's study of Ding Ling we find an attempt to argue for a "Chinese" feminism. Because I find this argument highly problematical for my own feminist understanding of modern Chinese writers, I want to comment on it before continuing with our discussion of "Miss Sophie's Diary."

Barlow reads Ding Ling's unfinished autobiographical novel *Muqin* [Mother] as one that marks a significant turning point in Ding Ling's development as a woman writer. According to Barlow, *Muqin* is no longer preoccupied with the subjective, Westernized notions of female sexuality that are apparent in Ding Ling's earlier works, but instead turns toward a concept of female identity that is rooted in Chinese culture. Meanwhile, Barlow uses her reading of Ding Ling to reprimand "Western" feminism for its assumption of the centrality of sexuality in critical practice. In place of sexuality, she proposes "the discourse of kinship" for her analysis.

The paradigm of "kinship" leads Barlow to the following conclusion about Ding Ling's concept of feminism: feminism is the alliance among women as "political sisters." While I find this conclusion remarkable, the premises on which Barlow arrives at it are, I think, misconstrued. An opposition between "sexuality" and "kinship" works only because sexuality is understood in the restricted sense of "sexual physiology" (p. 124 of her essay). Because of this, although it is meant as an alternative to sexuality, "kinship" (as Barlow proposes it) would still need to account for the sexuality that is clearly present in Ding Ling's novel in the form of a *desire* for the mother. Barlow's argument accomplishes this by eliding this sexuality under another type of critical language — one that prioritizes revolution and sinicization. Thus, for Barlow, while the desire for the mother is comprehensible under the term "political sisterhood," "political sisterhood" itself is the expression not of "mere" feminism (i.e., one that concentrates on sex and self) but of "Chinese" feminism.

The nativizing and nationalizing of feminism in this case spring from a need to decenter the West, and as such it is a type of critique of the hegemony of Western discourse. And yet the critique of the West cannot be achieved by elaborating the reactionary, nationalistic notion of "China" with the newer term "feminism." Conversely, the attempt to deconstruct the hegemony of *patriarchal* discourses through feminism is itself foreclosed by the emphasis on "Chinese" as a mark of absolute difference. To my mind, it is when the West's "other women" are prescribed their "own" national and ethnic identity in this way that they are most excluded from having a claim to the reality of their existence. The assertion of a "Chinese feminism" in the nationalistic sense does not really create avenues for modern Chinese women to come forth on their own terms, but rather compounds deep-rooted patriarchal thinking to which "Chinese woman" is now added as the latest proof of the continuity of a pure indigenous tradition.

On the other hand, if Ding Ling's work as a whole is read in terms of the psychic, ideological contradictions that are embedded in a Westernized Chinese woman writer's attempt at self-representation, contradictions that include, in particular, her subsequent rejection of the West and her submission to Chinese culture, then her "Chinese" female identity is much more complex than one that is readily conceivable within the paradigm of nationalism. It is in such contradictions, and not in what might be called the "allochronism" of a sinicized female identity, that the meanings of modern "Chinese" feminism should be located. Instead of following this type of teleological reading that maps Ding Ling's development in terms of dichotomizations such as subjective versus objective involvements, personal versus national concerns, pro-foreign versus pro-Chinese literary interests, and Westernized, sex-oriented versus sinicized, kinship-oriented conceptions of femininity, I would like to show by my reading of "Miss Sophie's Diary" how an "early" work by this woman writer demonstrates an acute perception of the problems of sexuality and subjectivity that are intensified by a woman's attempt at self-representation and that have continued to be crucial to Chinese literature to this day.

Like many May Fourth writers, Ding Ling tells the story in the first person. More important is her use of the diary form, which sets up the contrast between two incompatible orders—the chronological (which directs the progress of events in an objective, linear fashion) and the psychical (which is fragmented, shifting, and elusive, doubling on itself and contradicting its stated thoughts and desires). The diary form heightens our awareness of Sophie's confinement to her mental world but shows, at the same time, that this confinement is the source of her deepest perceptions. As we enter her narrative, we find Sophie referring to herself as being "wrapped up in my quilt." This is a condition she wants to leave but to which she repeatedly returns in the course of the story. In spite of literally moving to a new room a couple of times, her sense of paralysis follows her. This overwhelming sense of paralysis is, of course, precisely the kind of symptom that leads certain readers to criticize Ding Ling's early fiction as "bourgeois." But once we abandon the dichotomization between intellectual and manual labor, between private suffering and social awareness that is the assumption behind this kind of criticism, there emerges a very different picture of Sophie's condition.

In her first entry on December 24, Sophie remarks, "I wish I could find something new to get miserable over and fed up with. But everything new, whether good or bad, is too far away from me" (p. 15). This longing for the new gradually takes concrete shape in the form of a heterosexual object of love. On January 1, Sophie meets, through two of her friends, "a tall young man," Ling Jishi from Singapore. Her attraction to him is expressed in a remarkably unconventional language, unconventional not because of its content of fascination but because of the way it overturns the paradigm of man-as-gaze and woman-as-sex object. In Sophie's confessions to herself, the reader is invited to play vicarious female voyeur side by side with Sophie, and look at Ling Jishi:

> The tall man's a real good looker. It's the first time I've ever been aware of male beauty: it's not something I'd ever noticed before. I always thought that there was nothing more to being a man than being able to talk, read people's expressions and be careful. Now I've seen this tall man I realize that men can be cast in another and a noble mould. . . .
>
> How can I describe the beauty of that stranger? Of course, his tall body, his delicate white face, his thin lips and his soft hair would all dazzle anyone, but there's also an elegance about him that I can't express in words or put my hands on, but sets my heart aflame. For example, when I asked him his name he handed me his card in an incredibly relaxed way. I looked up and saw the corners of his soft, red, and deeply inset mouth. Could I tell anyone how I looked at those two delightful lips like a child longing for sweets? (pp. 21-22)

The emergence of a subversive way of dealing with a man—by looking at him directly, fetishizing his physique, and recognizing in that process the meaning of sexual desire—is immediately contradicted by a socially oriented self-consciousness:

> But I know that in this society I'll never be allowed to take what I want to satisfy my impulses and my desires, even though it would do nobody else any harm. That's why I had to control myself, keep my head down, and silently read the name on the card: Ling Jishi from Singapore. (p. 22)

The attempt to conform to sexual propriety leads Sophie to the opposite extreme of her desire. Instead of playing it out, Sophie acts in an "awkward and humorless" way until her friends, mistaking it to mean her dislike for Ling Jishi, take him away. Self-mockingly, Sophie comments:

> Can I be grateful to them for their kind intentions? Watching the two short figures and one tall one disappearing in the yard downstairs I didn't want to go back into my room. It was still full of his footsteps, his voice, and the crumbs of the biscuits he'd been eating. (p. 22)

Sophie's attraction to Ling Jishi provides us with the basic structure of her mental paralysis and sickness. If the sexual frustrations of the protagonist in Yü Dafu's "Sinking" cannot be separated from his sense of impotence as a Chinese man vis-à-vis the world, the sexual frustrations of Sophie cannot be separated from her social position as a Chinese woman who is bound by centuries of sexual etiquette. There is, unlike in "Sinking," no means for idealization in the form of a bigger, more important figure like "China" onto which Sophie can displace her frustrations, unless, as one can perhaps argue with regard to the later work of Ding Ling, she agrees to the desexualization of those frustrations by downplaying their traditionally and socially inscribed psychic premises. However, it is the refusal, or the inability, on Sophie's part to downplay such psychic premises that makes this story so interesting and disturbing. Heterosexual attraction for a man becomes the occasion for self-doubt, self-hatred, and self-repudiation:

> I want, I want to make myself happy. Day and night I'm always dreaming of things that would enable me to have no regrets when I die. . . .
> But can I tell what I really need? . . .
> I have to tell myself, "You're longing for that tall man." . . . Surely I shouldn't have to go to see him. If a woman's as reckless as that she's bound to come to a bad end. Besides, I still need people's respect. . . .
> Thinking it all over carefully now I'm worried that my impetuosity may have got me into an even worse mess. For the time being I'd better remain in this room heated by an iron stove. Do I have to admit that I've fallen in love with that overseas Chinese? I know nothing

about him at all. His mouth, his brows, his eyes, his fingertips . . . all
mean nothing. They aren't what one ought to need. If that's what I
think about I've been bewitched. I've made my mind up not to move,
but to concentrate all my efforts on recovering my health.

I've decided. I regret now the wrong things I did today, all the
things a lady should never do. (pp. 23, 24, 26)

Such contradictory feelings persist as she finally accomplishes her goal of receiving Ling Jishi's love. But as the two become intimately involved, Sophie
realizes that in spite of her physical infatuation with Ling Jishi, she feels dissatisfied with him in other respects:

I've found out from our latest conversations how pathetic his ideas are
and what he wants: money, a young wife who would know how to
entertain his business friends in the drawing room, and several fat, fair-
skinned and very well-dressed sons. What's his idea of love? Spending
his money in the whorehouse to buy a moment's physical pleasure, or
sitting on a well-upholstered settee with his arms round a scented body,
smoking a cigarette and joking with his friends, his left leg folded on
his right knee. If he wasn't feeling very cheerful he'd forget about it
and go back home to his wife. . . . I realized what a mean and low soul
there is in that noble and beautiful form I adore. . . . When I think of
how he kisses me on my hair I want to cry from shame. (pp. 43-44)

In spite of the appearance of an unabashed longing for sexual gratification
with a man, then, this longing is renegotiated, revised, and refuted in the course
of the narrative. The fact that Sophie's affair with Ling Jishi finally ends unhappily is thus predictable within the self-critical, self-tormenting trajectory that
her attraction to him follows.

As she writes of their good-bye in her last diary entry, this is the line with
which she concludes, in the form of a conversation she has with herself:

"Quietly go on living, and quietly die. I'm sorry for you, Sophie."
(p. 64)

We hear in this line once again the melancholic self-pity that characterizes
her entire narrative, but if our analysis were to end here, it would be complicitous with the kind of reading that sees Sophie as an example of an immature
woman who is yet "unable to move on to a broader vision of reality." Instead, I
would like to offer another reading by extending the space that is opened up
precisely by Sophie's switch into a dramatic dialogue with herself. There are several places in the narrative where this kind of switch can be seen, but the concluding line that I quoted suffices for the purposes of our analysis.

"I'm sorry for you, Sophie," of course, attests once again to the splitting of
the self between polarized feelings of longing and repudiation, between love and

hate; this is a process we have witnessed throughout the narrative. What it signals is the way the self is responding to itself as an other or from the position of
an other. However, the consciously conversational manner of this concluding
utterance alerts us to another meaning that is implied if not immediately evident
in this entire process. The dialogue "within" the self that is in turn presented as
dramatic dialogue points to another figure, a figure *in whose presence* Sophie is
talking with herself. In other words, the gesture of self-pity in the form of dialogue theatrically intensifies the process of subjectivity, by inscribing in it the
observation and understanding of an interlocutor, spectator, or reader.

Contrary to a reading that would, at this point, locate this other "figure" in
the actual reader, [37] I propose that we look, first of all, for that figure in the narrative. If we now reexamine the origins of Sophie's diary, we notice that she
started them for a special friend, Yun. On March 22, she writes:

> My mind's in turmoil, but I've forced myself to write this diary. I
> started it because Yun kept on asking me to in letters, over and over
> again. (p. 52)

Yun is the older woman friend who has told Sophie by letter earlier that "my
life and my love are useless to me now." We do not know exactly what Yun is
suffering from, since she would not tell Sophie, but there is the suggestion that
she is unhappily married because of "a lack of feeling" in the marriage that is
antipathetic to Yun's "highly strung and very passionate nature" (p. 33). Later
we hear Sophie lament this marriage in such a way as to reveal her deep attach-
ment to Yun, who is now dead:

> If she hadn't been tricked by God into loving that pasty-faced man
> she'd never have died so early and of course I'd never have drifted to
> Beijing by myself to struggle against disease without relatives or love.
> Although I've got several friends and they're very sorry for me, can my
> relationship with them be set on the scales against the love between me
> and Yun? *When I think of Yun I really ought to let go and weep aloud the
> way I used to when I was acting the spoiled child for her.* (p. 50; my
> emphasis)

The understanding from her older woman friend constitutes the fundamental
fantasy in Sophie's diary. That fantasy includes not only a "sickening" masochistic attitude toward suffering, but a masochistic introjection of the other's suffering into the self so that, in its own suffering, the self remembers and responds
to the other's. In this way, fantasy brings together "identification" and "desire"
in what becomes the deepest sense of *frustration* that underlies Sophie's narrative, the frustration that she is not understood by those around her. This frustration becomes most palpable and intolerable as she enters a heterosexual
involvement with Ling Jishi. In his essay "The Most Prevalent Form of

Degradation in Erotic Life," which I discussed earlier, Freud remarks as a kind of afterthought to this thesis on male subjectivity that "women show little need to degrade the sexual object" (p. 65). This statement is problematized by "Miss Sophie's Diary" in an illuminating way. For in the story, we see precisely Sophie's degradation of Ling Jishi, but instead of being a predetermining factor in her choice of a sex object, the degradation that Sophie feels toward him happens *after* they become lovers, when she discovers his "pathetic" ideas. This is a degradation that stems not from the need to separate the two strands of libidinal investment, affection and sensuality, as in the case of Freud's psychically impotent man, but rather from the disillusionment with a lack in the sexual partner—the lack, precisely, of a fusion between sensuality and affectionate understanding, between sexual love and sisterly or motherly love.

Thus, it is to the figure of a lover whom she *both* longs for and identifies with that the masochism of Sophie's diary is addressed. As masochism, Sophie's self-representation is inseparable from the fantasy for that which is impossible:

> If my dear Yun were still alive to read my diary I know she'd have embraced me, wept and said, "Sophie, my Sophie, why can't I be a bit greater so as to spare my Sophie all this grief?" But Yun is dead. If only I could weep bitterly with this diary in my hands. (p. 54)

Yet even though Yun cannot be present as an actual reader, she is present in Sophie's determination to continue to write:

> Although Yun has been dead for a long time now I couldn't bear to give up writing it. I suppose it must be that because of the very serious advice she gave me when she was alive I want to go on writing it for ever in her memory. So no matter how little I feel like writing I force myself to scribble half a page or so. I was already in bed, but *the sight of Yun's picture* on the wall was more than I could bear. I dragged myself out of bed and started writing this to spare myself the agony of yearning for her. (p. 53; my emphasis)

Instead of being frozen in time, then, the picture of the "mother" *moves* (verb transitive and intransitive): it touches Sophie the reader and it activates writing.

To return now to the phrase "not being able to move on": in their different ways Bing Xin and Ding Ling's stories are indeed about women's not being able to move on. Neither story offers a resolution to the difficulties faced by educated Chinese women coming to terms with their modern womanhood—a womanhood that gives them "choice" over their lives—but because of this they compel us to see the meanings of "sentimental feminine writings" in a much less "transparent" mode. In their different ways, too, the two stories clarify the implications of the negative Oedipus complex. What they offer is not simply the "woman's version" of the negative Oedipus complex, but also an alternative way of idealizing the mother.

The masculine scenarios of idealizing woman we read in Section 2 all partake of the mechanisms of dissociation, disavowal, and rejection, mechanisms that also structure identification against desire. In terms of the (positive) Oedipus complex, identification with the father means desire for the mother; subsequently, identification with the mother (in the form of familial affection) means desire for other women, and so forth. Desire is thus always construed in terms of what is different from the self and what, therefore, needs to be displaced, excluded, and debased (think of Freud's view of the women that can excite men's sexual passion). A woman whom a man reveres with affection poses special difficulties, in the sense that she is both what he identifies with *and* a woman (whose ontological status is "difference"). The way out is to exclude precisely that part of her that would otherwise make her at once too much like him (the ability to move psychically) and too different from him (the possession of her own physical desires)—what I have been calling "sexuality."

In Bing Xin and Ding Ling, desire and identification are no longer mutually exclusive for the women characters involved. This is possible because, instead of structural oppositions produced by the psychic mechanism of disavowal, we see a reversibility between the positions of the subjects and objects of love. Ying's identification with her mother and Sophie's identification with Yun are based not on a dissociation but rather a cotemporality with desire. Their identification is not accompanied by the psychic requirement that the other/mother remain "unmoving." On the contrary, it is precisely by not excluding the other/mother's psychic life—the narratives of her sorrows—that identification is possible. In turn, desire is no longer construed as difference or as a part of the self that needs to be discarded and debased in order to be exciting, but as an emotion that, in sympathy, fuses with the (m)other.

Furthermore, if identification and desire are now conjoined, it is not so much their conjunction per se as their conjunction in femininity—the locus of sacrifice—that brings forth the full intricacy of a new structure of fantasy. Hence "loving women": in this phrase we apprehend the complexities of identification and desire that center on the social demand for women's self-sacrifice; but also, the possibility for an alternative aesthetic that is based on a sympathetic feminine interlocutor/spectator/reader.

As we have seen in "Di yi ci yanhui" and "Miss Sophie's Diary," this sympathetic feminine position does not bring satisfactory endings but nonetheless undermines from within the stories' open invitations to strictly narratological, heterosexual readings. This position is produced, not simply by a lack (of sympathy) within the narrative, but through a reversible relay of understandings, all of which involve an apprehension of and negotiation with specific forms of lack that are essential to any subject's entry into cultural identity. This "relay of understandings" is one way of saying, with Silverman, that "what passes for 'femininity' is actually an inevitable part of all subjectivity" (Silverman, p. 149). Because of this, "what is needed . . . is not so much a 'masculinization' of the female subject as a 'feminization' of the male subject." The proposal for a sympathetic reader in the terms I argue above is thus a proposal for "a much more generalized acknowledgement . . . of the necessary terms of cultural identity" (Silverman, p. 149).

4

The point of this chapter has been to delineate a specific formalism in what otherwise appear to be "sentimental" habits of writing and reading in modern China. This formalism epitomizes, in part, the other readings of Chinese modernity I offer in this book. The obsession, constructed through global media, with being "Chinese"; the popularization and dispersal of traditional ideologies in accessible rather than arcane modes of writing; the attempts to construct, through narration, a new "national" self: all these concerns achieve an emotional intensity when a structure of masochism and fantasy is foregrounded as the general demand placed by modern Chinese literature upon its readers. The analytical prominence of "woman" is, throughout the course of my reading, never an accidental one. The structure of masochism and fantasy in which woman is idealized derives its cogency from the requirement of self-sacrifice that every Chinese woman experiences as the limit of her cultural existence. If feminine self-sacrifice was the major support of traditional Chinese culture, it is not surprising that, during a period of massive social transformations, the collapse of tradition would find its most *moving* representations in the figures of those who are traditionally the most oppressed, figures that become "stand-ins" for China's traumatized *self-consciousness* in every sense of the phrase. In this way, "woman" does not simply amount to a new type of literary content but, more so, to a new agency, a dialectic of resistance-in-givenness that is constitutive of modernity in a non-Western, but Westernized, context.

Notes

Notes

Preface

1. Abdul R. JanMohamed and David Lloyd, "Introduction: Minority Discourse—What Is to Be Done?" *Cultural Critique*, no. 7 (Fall 1987), p. 5.

2. Godzich, "Emergent Literature and the Field of Comparative Literature," in Clayton Koelb and Susan Noakes, eds., *The Comparative Perspective on Literature: Approaches to Theory and Practice* (Ithaca and London: Cornell University Press, 1988), p. 31.

3. Miyoshi, "Against the Native Grain," *South Atlantic Quarterly*, 87, no. 3 (Summer 1988), p. 531.

4. "On the Uses and Disadvantages of History for Life," in *Untimely Meditations*, trans. R. J. Hollingdale, intro. J. P. Stern (Cambridge: Cambridge University Press, 1983), p. 72.

Chapter 1. Seeing Modern China:
Toward a Theory of Ethnic Spectatorship

1. Brian Lambert, "Interview with Bernardo Bertolucci/The Last Emperor," *Twin Cities Reader*, Wednesday, December 9, 1987, p. 14; my emphases. Other remarks quoted from Bertolucci are taken from the same interview.

2. Trans. Anita Barrows (New York and London: Marion Boyars, 1977, 1986). Page references are given in parentheses in the text.

3. Kristeva, "Woman Can Never Be Defined," trans. Marilyn A. August, in Elaine Marks and Isabelle de Courtivron, eds., *New French Feminisms* (New York: Schocken Books, 1981), pp. 137–41.

4. Kristeva, "Women's Time," trans. Alice Jardine and Harry Blake, in *Signs: Journal of Women in Culture and Society*, 7, no. 1 (1981), p. 17.

5. "Women's Time," p. 17.

6. "Woman Can Never Be Defined," p. 137.

7. Kristeva takes this word from Plato, who speaks of "a chora . . ., receptacle . . ., unnamable, improbable, hybrid, anterior to naming, to the One, to the father, and consequently, maternally connoted." See "From One Identity to an Other," in her *Desire in Language: A Semiotic Approach to Literature and Art*, trans. Thomas Gora, Alice Jardine, and Leon S. Roudiez (New York: Columbia University Press, 1980), p. 133.

8. Spivak, "French Feminism in an International Frame," in her *In Other Worlds: Essays in Cultural Politics* (New York and London: Methuen, 1987), p. 146; emphases in the original. The attribution of a "before" to the "other" is not unique to Kristeva. On his visit to China, Roland Barthes observed this culture with the same kind of fascination. China becomes an object of his hallucination: "By gently hallucinating China as an object located *outside* any bright color or any strong flavor, any brutal meaning (all this not without a bearing on the relentless parade of the Phallus), I wanted to bring together in a single movement the infinite *feminine* (maternal?) of the object itself, that extraordinary way China, in my eyes, had of overflowing the boundaries of meaning, peacefully and powerfully, and the right to a special discourse, that of a slight deviation, or again a yearning, an appetite for silence—for "wisdom" perhaps. . . . This *negative* hallucination is not gratuitous: it is an attempt to respond to the way many Westerners have of hallucinating the People's Republic of China—in a dogmatic mode, violently affirmative/negative or falsely liberal." See "Well, And China?", trans. Lee Hildreth, in *Discourse*, 8 (Fall-Winter 1986–87), p. 120; my emphases. Those who are familiar with Barthes's work know that he "hallucinates" Japan in the same way in *Empire of Signs*, trans. Richard Howard (New York: Hill and Wang, 1982).

9. Silverman, *The Acoustic Mirror: The Female Voice in Psychoanalysis and Cinema* (Bloomington and Indianapolis: Indiana University Press, 1988), p. 112.

10. For a critique of the politics involved in Kristeva's conceptions of femininity, see Ann Rosalind Jones, "Julia Kristeva on Femininity: The Limits of a Semiotic Politic," *Feminist Review*, no. 18 (1984), pp. 56–73.

11. For a superb account of the ideologies accompanying the historical depictions of China in the past few hundred years in the West, see Raymond Dawson, *The Chinese Chameleon* (London: Oxford University Press, 1967); Dawson examines the notion of the Chinese as "a people of eternal standstill" thoroughly in chapter 4.

12. I borrow this term from Johannes Fabian, *Time and the Other: How Anthropology Makes Its Object* (New York: Columbia University Press, 1983), pp. 106–9. Fabian defines visualism as a deeply ingrained ideological tendency in anthropology, which relies for its scientific, "observational" objectivity on the use of maps, charts, tables, etc. The recommendations for such visual aids "rest on a corpuscular, atomic theory of knowledge and information. Such a theory in turn encourages quantification and diagrammatic representation so that the ability to 'visualize' a culture or society almost becomes synonymous for understanding it. I shall call this tendency visualism." Visualism "may take different directions—toward the mathematical-geometric or toward the pictorial-aesthetic." I return to Fabian's arguments later on in this chapter; references are indicated in parentheses by "Fabian" followed by page numbers.

13. Silverman, *The Subject of Semiotics* (New York: Oxford University Press, 1983), p. 225. A reprint of Mulvey's article, originally published in *Screen*, 16, no. 3 (Autumn 1975), can be found in *Movies and Methods*, vol. 2, ed. Bill Nichols (Berkeley and Los Angeles: University of California Press, 1985), pp. 303–15. Hereafter references to Silverman and Mulvey (in Nichols) are indicated in parentheses by their last names followed by page numbers.

14. Spivak, "Can the Subaltern Speak?", in Larry Grossberg and Cary Nelson, eds., *Marxist Interpretations of Literature and Culture: Limits, Frontiers, Boundaries* (Urbana: University of Illinois Press), pp. 296–97.

15. From the "Production Notes" attached to the film's compact disc soundtrack: "The logistics of the production were staggering. *The Last Emperor* brought together people from six nations. Actors came from America, Great Britain, China, Hong Kong and Japan to play the 60 main characters

in the story. 100 technicians from Italy, 20 from Britain and 150 Chinese worked for 6 months of shooting to put the film on the screen and 19,000 extras, including soldiers of the People's Liberation Army, appear altogether in the immense crowd scenes. Costume designer James Acheson gathered 9,000 costumers from all over the world."

16. *Video Review*, August 1988, p. 17.

17. Other feminist critics have produced readings of film that share this concern. See, for instance, Claire Johnston, *Notes on Women's Cinema* (London: Society for Education in Film and Television, 1973), pp. 2–4; Johnston, "Towards a Feminist Film Practice: Some Theses," in Nichols, ed., pp. 315–27; Mary Ann Doane, "Misrecognition and Identity," *Cine-Tracts*, 11 (Fall 1980), pp. 28–30; Doane, "Film and the Masquerade: Theorising the Female Spectator, " *Screen*, 23 (September-October 1982), pp. 74–87.

18. Mulvey, *Visual and Other Pleasures* (Bloomington and Indianapolis: Indiana University Press, 1989), pp. 159–76. (This essay was previously published in *Discourse* in 1985 and *History Workshop Journal* in 1987.) Hereafter references are indicated in parentheses by "Mulvey 2" followed by page numbers. Mulvey's revisions of her original argument can also be found in "Afterthoughts on 'Visual Pleasure and Narrative Cinema' inspired by *Duel in the Sun*," *Framework*, 6, nos. 15–17 (1981), rpt. in Constance Penley, ed., *Feminism and Film Theory* (New York: Routledge, Chapman and Hall, 1988), pp. 69–79.

19. For discussions of the term "suture" in cinema, see Stephen Heath, "Narrative Space," in *Screen*, 17, no. 3 (1976), pp. 66–112; "Notes on Suture," *Screen*, 18, no. 2 (1977/78), pp. 48–76; Jacques-Alain Miller, "Suture (Elements of the Logic of the Signifier)," *Screen*, 18, no. 4 (1977/78), pp. 24–34. Silverman's discussion in her book (pp. 194–236) demonstrates the theoretical connections between suture and discourse, subjectivity, cinema, ideology, and sexual difference.

20. To this end, the reader can turn to, for instance, John K. Fairbank, "Born Too Late," *New York Review of Books*, February 18, 1988.

21. (Bloomington: Indiana University Press, 1984). References to this book are indicated in parentheses by "de Lauretis" followed by page numbers.

22. *Dialectic of Enlightenment*, trans. John Cumming (New York: Continuum, 1987), pp. 120–67.

23. "Ideology and Ideological State Apparatuses (Notes towards an Investigation)," in his *Lenin and Philosophy and Other Essays*, trans. Ben Brewster (New York and London: Monthly Review Press, 1971). References to this essay are indicated in parentheses by "Althusser" followed by page numbers.

24. Hsia, "Obsession with China: The Moral Burden of Modern Chinese Fiction," in his *A History of Modern Chinese Fiction*, 2nd ed. (New Haven: Yale University Press, 1971), pp. 533–34.

25. Anderson, *Imagined Communities: Reflections on the Origin and Spread of Nationalism* (London: Verso and New Left Books, 1983).

26. Ibid., p. 68, note 6.

27. See the chapters "Tuché and Automaton" and "From Love to the Libido" in *The Four Fundamental Concepts of Psychoanalysis*, ed. Jacques-Alain Miller, trans. Alan Sheridan (New York and London: Norton, 1981), pp. 53–66; 187–202.

28. See "Fetishism" and "Splitting of the Ego in the Defensive Process," in his *Sexuality and the Psychology of Love*, ed. Philip Rieff (New York: Collier Books, 1963), pp. 214–19; 220–23. The two essays are also in Freud, *The Standard Edition of the Complete Psychological Works*, ed. James Strachey, trans. James Strachey et al. (London: Hogarth Press), vols. 21 and 23. See also the section "Unsuitable Substitutes for the Sexual Object—Fetishism," in *Three Essays on the Theory of Sexuality*, trans. James Strachey (New York: Basic Books, 1975), pp. 19–21; or Standard Edition, vol. 7.

29. Liu, *Chinese Theories of Literature* (Chicago and London: University of Chicago Press, 1975), p. 5.

30. Li, "Hermeneutics and Criticism," in *Chinese Culture Quarterly*, 1, no. 4 (1987), p. 65.

31. Martin and Mohanty, "Feminist Politics: What's Home Got to Do with It?", in Teresa de Lauretis, ed., *Feminist Studies/Critical Studies* (Bloomington: Indiana University Press, 1986), p. 196.

32. Spivak, "French Feminism," p. 138.

Chapter 2. Mandarin Ducks and Butterflies: An Exercise in Popular Readings

1. Portions of this chapter have been published, in modified form, in two articles: "Mandarin Ducks and Butterflies: Female Melancholy as Fiction and Commodity," *Western Conference of the Association for Asian Studies, Selected Papers in Asian Studies*, n.s., no. 21 (1986); "Rereading Mandarin Ducks and Butterflies: A Response to the 'Postmodern' Condition," *Cultural Critique*, no. 5 (Winter 1986–87), pp. 69–94.

2. For a comprehensive study of the movement, see Chow Tse-tsung, *The May 4th Movement: Intellectual Revolution in Modern China* (Cambridge, Mass.: Harvard University Press, 1960).

3. The Chinese vernacular had always been a part of traditional fiction and other colloquial literary genres, but its use was officially advocated for the first time under the new cultural conditions closely associated with the May Fourth movement. The two most quoted spokesmen for the use of the *baihua* were Hu Shi and Chen Duxiu, both of whom wrote for *Xin qingnian* [New youth], a magazine that began its publication in the 1910s and that was read mainly by Chinese students who had studied abroad and derived their ideas about revolution from an intellectual acquaintance with the West. See, for instance, Hu's "Wenxue gailiang chuyi" [Some suggestions for the reform of Chinese literature], *New Youth*, January 1917; and Chen's "Wenxue geming lun" [On literary revolution] in *New Youth*, February 1917. These two articles have been reprinted in Zhao Jiabi, ed., *Zhongguo xin wenxue daxi* [A comprehensive anthology of the new literature of China] (Hong Kong: Wenxue yanjiu she, 1962), vol. 1, pp. 62–71; 72–75. They have also been translated in part into English: see, for example, William T. de Bary et al., *Sources of Chinese Tradition* (New York: Columbia University Press, 1960), pp. 818–29; Chow Tse-tsung, *The May 4th Movement*, pp. 271–79.

4. Two short notes published by Mao Dun and Zheng Zhenduo under the title "My opinions of a Europeanized vernacular Chinese" in *Xiaoshuo yuebao* [*The Short Story Monthly*], 12, no. 6 (1921), read as follows. Mao Dun: "The two tasks that face those who are trying to write with the vernacular now are 1) to correct the general public's views about literature and 2) to improve the grammar that has been used habitually in China in the past few thousand years. Many have already come around to the necessity of the former task, but many are still doubtful about the latter. Hence some write in the vernacular by copying or translating Western doctrines, but meanwhile unconditionally object to the Europeanization of vernacular Chinese. Their reason is that a Europeanized Chinese would be incomprehensible to most people. True, this is the biggest reason, but not necessarily the most reasonable. We should first ask whether a Europeanized grammar is better than our old traditional grammar. If it is, we should try our best to spread its use, instead of giving up simply because it is, for the time being, beyond most people's comprehension." Zheng Zhenduo: "The traditional writing style of China is too old and becoming hackneyed and stereotyped. Many good thoughts and emotions, thus restricted, fail to be delicately expressed. This applies not only to classical but also vernacular Chinese. Hence, for the sake of improving literary art, I am all for Europeanizing the vernacular. Numerous examples of such a process can be found in different national literatures' transitional periods. But there is a limit to Europeanizing vernacular Chinese, which is that even though it does not resemble the vernacular that Chinese people write, it should still not be something that Chinese people cannot read."

5. The theme of "enlightenment" is the central argument in Vera Schwarcz's study of the intellectual impact this period had on subsequent decades in modern Chinese history. See *The Chinese Enlightenment: Intellectuals and the Legacy of the May Fourth Movement of 1919* (Berkeley, Los Angeles, London: University of California Press, 1986).

6. Hu Shi, *The Chinese Renaissance* (New York: Paragon, 1963); reprinted in *Republican China*, ed. Franz Schurmann and Orville Schell (New York: Vintage Books, 1967), p. 55.

7. I take this term from Raymond Williams's account of the "dominant," the "residual," and the "emergent" as ways of defining different moments in existing cultures. Williams, *Marxism and Literature* (Oxford: Oxford University Press, 1977), pp. 121–27.

8. See the account by Ping Jinya in Wei Shaochang, ed., *Yuanyang hudie pai yanjiu ziliao* [Research materials on the Mandarin Duck and Butterfly School] (Shanghai, 1962; rpt. Hong Kong: Sanlian shudian, 1980), pp. 127–29.

9. "When we speak of the early Republican vogue for Butterfly fiction in the narrow sense, we are strictly referring to the trio: Hsü Chen-ya [Xü Zhenya], Wu Shuang-je [Wu Shuangre], and Li Ting-yi [Li Dingyi]." C. T. Hsia, "Hsü Chen-ya's *Yü-li hun*: An Essay in Literary History and Criticism," *Renditions*, nos. 17 and 18 (1982), p. 216. Hereafter, all references to this essay will be indicated in parentheses by "Hsia" followed by page numbers.

10. E. Perry Link, Jr., *Mandarin Ducks and Butterflies: Popular Fiction in Early Twentieth-Century Chinese Cities* (Berkeley, Los Angeles, and London: University of California Press, 1981), p. 22. Hereafter, all references to this book will be indicated in parentheses by "Link" followed by page numbers.

11. For a brief synopsis of such "waves," see Link, "Traditional-Style Popular Urban Fiction in the Teens and Twenties," in Merle Goldman, ed., *Modern Chinese Literature in the May Fourth Era* (Cambridge, Mass., and London: Harvard University Press, 1977), pp. 332–33.

12. The Treaty of Nanking, signed in 1842 after China lost the Opium War (or the First Anglo-Chinese War), stipulated, among other things, the opening of five treaty ports for trade with Britain: Shanghai, Ningbo (Ningpo), Fuzhou (Foochow), Xiamen (Amoy), and Guangzhou (Canton).

13. Leo Ou-fan Lee, *The Romantic Generation of Modern Chinese Writers* (Cambridge, Mass.: Harvard University Press, 1973), p. 29.

14. Jacques Gernet, *A History of Chinese Civilization*, trans. J. R. Foster (Cambridge, New York, and Melbourne: Cambridge University Press, 1982), p. 611.

15. Ibid.

16. Ibid., pp. 611; 606–7; 607.

17. Rhoads Murphey, *Shanghai: Key to Modern China* (Cambridge, Mass.: Harvard University Press, 1953), p. 1.

18. For example, see Marie-Claire Bergère, " 'The Other China': Shanghai from 1919 to 1949," in Christopher Howe, ed., *Shanghai: Revolution and Development in an Asian Metropolis* (Cambridge: Cambridge University Press, 1981), p. 33.

19. John Pal, *Shanghai Saga* (London: Jarrolds, 1963), p. 14.

20. For a detailed discussion of the foreign settlements in Shanghai, see Murphey, *Shanghai*, Part 1.

21. Comparative ratios of prostitutes in other big cities in the same year were: London, one in 960; Berlin, one in 580; Paris, one in 481; Chicago, one in 430; Tokyo, one in 250. Murphey, ibid., p. 7.

22. Link, "Traditional-Style Popular Urban Fiction," p. 329.

23. Howe, ed., *Shanghai*, p. xv.

24. One of the most popular Butterfly periodicals, *Saturday* was published weekly for 100 weeks beginning in 1914, and then for another 100 weeks beginning in 1921. Allegedly, the editors took the name from Benjamin Franklin's *Saturday Evening Post*, intending for the Chinese magazine the same kind of popularity enjoyed by its American predecessor. See Zhou Shouzhuan, "Xianhua libailiu" [Leisure talk about *Saturday*], in Wei Shaochang, ed., *Yuanyang*, p. 130.

25. Wei Shaochang, ed., *Yuanyang*, pp. 277–79; 520–55. These figures are similar if not completely identical to those given in Fan Boqun et al., eds., *Yuanyang hudie pai wenxue ziliao* [Materials on Mandarin Duck and Butterfly literature] (Fuzhou: Fujian renmin chuban she, 1984), vol. 2, pp. 627–705.

26. Liang Qichao, Xin xiaoshuo [New fiction], no. 1; reprinted in Zhang Jinglu, Zhongguo chuban shiliao bupian [Supplement to historical materials on publishing in China] (Beijing: Zhonghua shuju, 1957), pp. 106–10.

27. Hu Shi, "Jianshe di wenxue geming lun" [On constructive literary revolution], New Youth, April 1918; rpt. in Zhongguo xin wenxue da xi, vol.1, pp. 155–68; also in Fan Boqun et al., eds., Yuanyang, vol. 2, pp. 711–13.

28. Zhou Zuoren, "Riben jin sanshi nian xiaoshuo zhi fada" [Prosperity of fiction in the recent thirty years in Japan], New Youth, July 1918; rpt. in Fan Boqun et al., eds., ibid., p. 714.

29. See Fan Boqun et al., eds., ibid., pp. 720, 734, 746.

30. Short Story Monthly, 13, no. 7 (1922); rpt. in Wei Shaochang, ed., Yuanyang, pp. 10–16. All translations are mine.

31. The phrase wen yi zai dao was derived from the historian Sima Qian's description, in Shi ji (Historical Record), of Confucius's alleged writing in the Annals. See Chow Tse-tsung, The May 4th Movement, p. 439, note 1. A moralistic interpretation of the phrase, whereby "dao" was given the definite meaning of "reason" or "lesson," and literature a subsidiary "carrier" status, dominated the literati for centuries.

32. Georg Lukács, Writer and Critic, ed. and trans. Arthur Kahn (London: Merlin Press, 1970), pp. 110–48.

33. In later years, Mao Dun clarified his position by no longer conflating realism and naturalism. In his well-known essay of 1928, "Cong guling dao dongjing," he associates naturalism with Zola and realism with Tolstoy, and indicates that his own principles of writing are realistic rather than naturalistic. See "From Guling to Tokyo," trans. Yu-shih Chen, in Bulletin of Concerned Asian Scholars, special issue, January-March 1976, pp. 38–44.

34. Wenxue xunkan [Ten-day periodical on literature], no. 38 (1922); rpt. in Fan Boqun et al., eds., Yuanyang, vol. 2, pp. 750–52. All translations are mine.

35. Xia Zhengnong, "Du Tixiao yinyuan" [Reading "Fate in tears and laughter"], in Wenxue wenda ji [Questions and answers about literature]; rpt. in Fan Boqun et al., eds., ibid., pp. 879–84.

36. As Joseph R. Levenson argues with regard to the Creation Society, a group of writers in the May Fourth period who were "imbued first with a western-tinged aestheticism," then turned toward Marxist commitment. Confucian China and Its Modern Fate, III (Berkeley and Los Angeles: University of California Press, 1965), III, p. 64.

37. This interpretation of the May Fourth literary revolution is given by Zhu Ziqing in his 1947 essay "Lun yansu" [On seriousness] in Zhongguo zuojia [Chinese writers], no. 1; rpt. in Fan Boqun et al., eds., Yuanyang, vol. 2, pp. 817–21.

38. Renditions, nos. 17 and 18 (1982). The entire issue and two additional essays were subsequently published as Chinese Middlebrow Fiction from the Ch'ing and Early Republican Eras, ed. Liu Ts'un-yan (Hong Kong: Chinese University Press, 1984).

39. Liu, ibid., p. 3.

40. Ibid., p. 23.

41. Ibid., pp. 39–40; my emphases.

42. George Kao, "Editor's Page," Renditions, nos. 17 and 18 (1982), unpaginated.

43. See Levenson's perceptive arguments on this in Part 2 of his Confucian China and Its Modern Fate, III. For a good example of the programmatic idealization of a "people's tradition" through culture, see Mao Zedong's "Talks at the Yenan Forum on Literature and Art," in Mao Tse-tung on Literature and Art (Beijing: Foreign Language Press, 1960), pp. 1–43.

44. Wei Shaochang, ed.,Yuanyang, p. 1.

45. Fan Boqun et al., eds., Yuanyang, vol. 1, p. 1.

46. Link, "Traditional-Style Popular Urban Fiction," p. 338.

47. Ibid., p. 340.

48. Ibid., p. 341.

49. John Berninghausen and Ted Huters, "Introductory Essay," *Bulletin of Concerned Asian Scholars*, 8, no. 1 (1976), p. 2.

50. Link, "Introduction to Zhou Shou-juan's 'We Shall Meet Again' and Two Denunciations of This Type of Story," *Bulletin of Concerned Asian Scholars*, 8, no. 1 (1976), p. 14.

51. Joan W. Scott, "Gender: A Useful Category of Historical Analysis," *American Historical Review*, 91, no. 5 (December 1986), p. 1067.

52. Pierre Macherey, *A Theory of Literary Production*, trans. Geoffrey Wall (London and Boston: Routledge & Kegan Paul, 1978), p. 6. Hereafter references to this book are indicated in parentheses by "Macherey" followed by page numbers.

53. See "A Letter on Art in Reply to André Daspre" and "Cremonini, Painter of the Abstract," in *Lenin and Philosophy*, trans. Ben Brewster (New York and London: New Left Books, 1971), pp. 221–28; 229–42. See also "The 'Piccolo Teatro': Bertolazzi and Brecht," in *For Marx*, trans. Ben Brewster (London: New Left Books, 1977), pp. 129–52. For a relatively recent, lucid discussion of Althusser's writings on art, see Michael Sprinker, *Imaginary Relations* (London: Verso, 1987).

54. The work is cited as the precursor of Butterfly love novels (*xie qing xiao-shuo*) in Wei Shaochang, ed., *Yuanyang*, p. 108; and in A Ying, *Wan qing xiaoshuo shi* [The history of late Qing fiction] (Shanghai: Commercial Press Limited, 1937), pp. 72, 264. The Chinese terms for the novel of "love" or "sentiment" are varied, but they all use the character *qing*: *xieqing xiaoshuo* (sentiment-describing fiction), *aiqing xiaoshuo* (sorrowful-sentiment fiction), *yanqing xiaoshuo* (sentiment-narrating fiction), *kuqing xiaoshuo* (suffering-sentiment fiction), *canqing xiaoshuo* (catastrophic-sentiment fiction), etc. Unless specifically stated, the first publication dates and places of Butterfly stories in book form are unverifiable. The most popular of these stories were usually serialized in literary magazines and subsequently published and reprinted several times, often by different publishers. The publication information that I am providing is often what is given in various published accounts of modern Chinese literary history; otherwise it depends entirely on the copy of a story I happen to have been able to obtain. A brief description of Wu Woyao's life and works is found in *Henhai, Qingbian* [Two novels by Wu] (Tianjin: Guji chuban she, 1987), pp. 1–5.

55. In his study of Wu Woyao's novel, Michael Egan correctly identifies this asymmetrical narrative structure when he points out the much richer psychological depiction of Dihua, without whose reactions the tale of her beloved's degeneration would be meaningless. Egan, "Characterization in *Sea of Woe*," in Milena Doleželová-Velingerová, ed., *The Chinese Novel at the Turn of the Century* (Toronto, Buffalo, London: University of Toronto Press, 1980), pp. 165–76.

56. The Chinese idiom for entering the monastery or nunnery is *chu jia*, which means, literally, going out of the family.

57. A brief biography of Li Dingyi is found in Wei Shaochang, ed., *Yuanyang*, pp. 510–11, which indicates him to be a frank, talented scholar who had great success in writing but who was eventually driven out of the Shanghai area during Yuan Shikai's rise to power in the early 1910s.

58. The date for the book's first appearance is uncertain. Some historians claim it to be around 29 B.C., while others date it to within the first century A.D. See, for example, Esther S. Lee Yao, *Chinese Women: Past and Present* (Mesquite, Tex.: Ide House, 1983), p. 10; Elisabeth Croll, *Feminism and Socialism in China* (London: Routledge & Kegan Paul, 1978), p. 14. Liu Xiang, a historian of the former Han dynasty (202 B.C.-A.D. 24), is generally acknowledged to be the author-compiler.

59. For a discussion of the *lie nü* tradition, see Marina H. Sung, "The Chinese Lieh-nü Tradition," in Richard W. Guisso and Stanley Johannesen, eds., *Women in China: Current Directions in Historical Scholarship* (Youngstown, N. Y.: Philo Press, 1981), pp. 63–74. The article points out how, as the desirable character traits possessed by "virtuous" women in earlier times gradually developed into powerful social and legal restrictions on women's behavior, "chastity" increasingly became the most important attribute of the virtuous woman.

60. The book lists about 125 biographies of women, from legendary times to the Han dynasty. Liu Xiang classified them according to seven categories: (1) *mu yi* (exemplary mothers), (2) *xian*

ming (virtuous and wise women), (3) *ren zhi* (benevolent and intelligent women), (4) *zhen shun* (chaste and obedient women), (5) *jie yi* (chaste and righteous women), (6) *bian tong* (reasoning women), and (7) *nie bi* (pernicious courtesans).

61. "Preface" (*mu lu xü*) to the *Lie nü zhuan*.

62. Not being a historian myself, I am grateful to Dorothy Ko for pointing out to me the existence of this invaluable source of research material, and also for Susan Mann's "Suicide and Chastity: Visible Themes in the History of Chinese Women," a paper delivered at the Sixth Berkshire Conference on the History of Women, June 1-3, 1984, Smith College, Northampton, Mass. Mann's brilliantly written piece has given me many insights into the problems I was dealing with in rather inadequately informed ways.

The "local gazetteers" were semiofficial histories of counties throughout the Chinese Empire. With occasional exceptions, most counties had around four to six gazetteers, published between the sixteenth and the early twentieth centuries. Written by classically trained Confucian scholars, these gazetteers included information on a wide variety of topics, usually beginning with geography and climate, moving on to population, tax records, local customs and establishments such as schools, monuments, temples, markets, official bureaus, and finally focusing on the unique traditions that made a particular county worthy of special recognition. Among the distinguishing features of a county were its proud records of heroic individuals, male and female. But while the males were often "heroic" because of their various honorable deeds in the public world (e.g., building bridges, passing examinations with flying colors, or visiting the emperor), the women were consistently presented as martyrs in the domestic realm.

Addressing the women anonymously as *lie nü* (virtuous woman), *lie fu* (virtuous married woman), or *zhen fu* (chaste married woman) after their fathers' or husbands' surnames, these records of famous women in the counties told of virgins resisting molestation, widows refusing remarriage from their late teens until the time they died, widows serving their in-laws faithfully, and widows who successfully brought up their children alone. The "life" stories always concluded with a description of the women's "ends," which varied from the most mundane natural deaths (of illness or sorrow) to the most horrifying suicides imaginable: women swallowed metals, cut their necks, stabbed their thighs, starved themselves, hanged themselves, froze themselves in cold water, hurled themselves into wells, and smashed their heads against walls or against their husbands' coffins. Widows were also considered heroic if they deliberately disfigured themselves to make themselves "unmarriable" and thus chaste forever.

63. This statement is made, curiously enough, by a legendary woman-goddess called Su Nü (the Plain Girl) in her conversation with Emperor Huang Di (one of the earliest culture heroes who were supposed to have lived between 2852 and 2357 B.C.) in *Su nü jing* [The Plain Girl's book]. A treatise of sex based on the idea of a greater sexual proficiency in the female, it can be found in the collection of sexual handbooks and other writings published by Ye Dehui under the title *Shuangmei jingan congshu* (Changsha, Hunan, 1907). For a reference to the Plain Girl's origins in Chinese literature, see R. H. Van Gulik, *Sexual Life in Ancient China* (1961; rpt. Leiden: Brill, 1974), p. 74.

64. "Nei xun" [Teachings for the inside], twenty chapters, written by Queen of the Emperor Renxiao of the Ming dynasty, *Mo-hai chin-hu* (Taipei, 1969), 22:13, 247-13, 301; quoted in Marina H. Sung, "The Chinese Lieh-nü Tradition," p. 71.

65. "Pen-ming Chieh," *K'ung-tzu chia-yü* (Taipei, 1962), p. 63; quoted in Sung, "The Chinese Lieh-nü Tradition," p. 66.

66. *Li Chi* (*Book of Rites*), trans. James Legge, ed. C. C. Chai and W. Chai, 2nd ed. (New York, 1967), vol. 1, 479; quoted in Richard W. Guisso, "Thunder over the Lake: The Five Classics and the Perception of Woman in Early China," in Guisso and Johannesen, eds., *Women in China*, p. 58.

67. *Li Chi*, vol. 1, pp. 77–78; quoted in Guisso and Johannesen, eds., *Women in China*, p. 58.

68. Ban Zhao (A.D. ?–116), woman author of "Nü jie" [Lessons for women]; quoted in Sung, "The Chinese Lieh-nü Tradition," p. 71.

69. Cheng Yi (1033–1107), a neo-Confucian scholar of the Song dynasty (A.D. 960–1127); quoted in Sung, ibid., p. 72. Some historians attribute the saying to Zhu Xi, another neo-Confucianist who lived several generations later.

70. My favorite example is "popo mama," an idiom made up of "grandmother" and "mother," meaning "wishy-washy" or "sentimental."

71. Guisso dates the origins of women's subordination to *before* the *I Ching* (*The Book of Changes*), supposedly the most ancient book of the *Five Classics*, the earliest corpus of extant literature: "It seems clear . . . that there existed an order of cosmological precedence even before the *I Ching*. . . . the *Five Classics* did not initiate female subordination but justified it." Guisso and Johannesen, eds., *Women in China*, p. 50.

72. The most striking feature about Chinese suicide is its relation to gender. Whereas in other countries the male suicide rates often exceeded the female by three or four times, in China women were as likely as men to kill themselves and in some periods more likely. For a detailed discussion, see Margery Wolf, "Women and Suicide in China," in *Women in Chinese Society*, ed. Margery Wolf and Roxane Witke (Stanford: Stanford University Press, 1975), pp. 111–42.

73. Some fairly recent statistics show a steady increase in both the numbers of suicides and disfigurement cases among Chinese women from 1100 B.C. to A.D. 1725. See Tung Chia-tsun, "The Statistics of Sacrificed Women," *Contemporary History*, 3, no. 2 (1937), pp. 1–5; quoted in Esther S. Lee Yao, *Chinese Women*, pp. 78–82. Although the collected data are only available up to 1725 (early Qing), Tung believes that the trend of women killing themselves continued to increase and reached a peak in the Qing.

74. An explicit and extensive account of allegory is offered by Benjamin in *The Origin of German Tragic Drama*, trans. John Osborne (London: New Left Books, 1977). Benjamin's understanding of allegory is, to my mind, more accessible through some of his other works, notably his studies of Baudelaire and Brecht. I discuss Benjamin's work in greater detail in "Mandarin Ducks and Butterflies: Toward a Rewriting of Modern Chinese Literary History" (Ph.D. dissertation, Stanford University, 1986).

75. More details of Xü's life and works can be found in the sections devoted to him in Link, *Mandarin Ducks and Butterflies*; Hsia, "Hsü Chen-ya's *Yü-li hun*"; Wei Shaochang, ed., *Yuanyang*, pp. 461–62; Liu Yangti, ed., *Yuanyang hudie pai zuopin xuanping* [Criticisms of selected works of the Mandarin Duck and Butterfly School] (Chengdu: Sichuan wenyi chuban she, 1987), pp. 621–66.

76. See note 69, this chapter.

77. The *Wenshi muxun* [Maternal instructions of Madam Wen], cited by Ann Waltner, "Widows and Remarriage in Ming and Early Qing China," in Guisso and Johannesen, eds., *Women in China*, pp. 140–41. In China, families used to have their own sets of laws and instructions that were recorded and passed on from generation to generation. Normally "circulated" only among family members, the laws and instructions of some outstanding families in some parts of the country have been publicly preserved and are thus available for historical study.

78. Waltner, "Widows and Remarriage," p. 146.

79. In China, where the "left" has always had connotations of the depraved, the treacherous, and the heretical, a woman "married to the left" is a remarried widow. See Waltner, ibid., p. 131. Sociologically, this bias against the left is also a well-known fact in the traditional Chinese instructions for costumes. In the Zhou dynasty, men and women wore a jacket "closed in front by putting the right-hand lapel over the left," a custom considered by the Chinese as one of the features that distinguished them from the barbarians. In the nineteenth century, when anti-Western currents in Japan and China were very strong, buttoning coats left over right was referred to as one of the signs of Western inferiority. See Van Gulik, *Sexual Life in Ancient China*, p. 11. Esther Yao goes back even further in *Chinese Women* (p. 58), stating that, as clothing became more complicated and extravagant with the availability of linen and silk by the time of the emperor Huang Di, *yi* (the Chinese word for

outer clothes) was to have an opening on the right-hand side because "an opening on the left was only found among barbarians."

80. See the analysis of this in Lee, *Romantic Generation*.

81. For an extensive discussion of Lin Shu's life and works, see the section devoted to him in Lee, *Romantic Generation*.

82. A Ying, *Wan qing xiaoshuo shi*, p. 274. The subject of early Chinese translations of foreign texts is one that deserves a full-length study. For our purposes here, I should mention that Lin Shu's translations set the stylistic standards for the translation of fiction until the May Fourth Movement. Yan Fu, another important late Qing translator who also wrote in classical Chinese, was famous for his translations of nonfictional texts such as the works of Darwin and Huxley on evolution. Other translation methods of the time included using Japanese translations of Western texts for retranslation into Chinese, and direct translation into Chinese by writers who read the original language.

83. My comparisons are based on *La Dame aux Camélias*, preface by André Maurois (Paris: Gallimard, 1974); *Camille*, trans. Edmund Gosse (New York: Modern Library, n. d.); and *Cha hua nü yi shi*, trans. Lin Shu (Leng Hong Sheng) (Shanghai: Commercial Press Limited, 1939). Page references are indicated in parentheses.

84. Typically, Marguerite is transformed from her Western self into her Chinese self in the following manner.

French: "Il y avait dans cette femme quelque chose comme de la candeur.

"On voyait qu'elle en était encore à la virginité du vice. Sa marche assurée, sa taille souple, ses narines roses et ouvertes, ses grands yeux légèrement cerclés de bleu, dénotaient une de ces natures ardentes qui répandent autour d'elles un parfum de volupté, comme ces flacons d'Orient qui, si bien fermés qu'ils soient, laissent échapper le parfum de la liqueur qu'ils renferment.

"Enfin, soit nature, soit conséquence de son état maladif, il passait de temps en temps dans les yeux de cette femme des éclairs de désirs dont l'expansion eût été une révélation du Ciel pour celui qu'elle eût aimé. . . .

"Bref, on reconnaissait dans cette fille la vierge qu'un rien avait faite courtisane, et la courtisane dont un rien eût fait la vierge la plus amoureuse et la plus pure. Il y avait encore chez Marguerite de la fierté et de l'indépendance: deux sentiments qui, blessés, sont capables de faire ce que fait la pudeur"(*La Dame*, pp. 101–2).

English: "There was a kind of candour in this woman. You could see she was still in the virginity of vice. Her firm walk, her supple figure, her rosy, open nostrils, her large eyes, slightly tinged with blue, indicated one of those ardent natures which shed around them a sort of voluptuous perfume, like Eastern vials, which, close them as tightly as you will, still let some of their perfume escape. Finally, whether it was simple nature or a breath of fever, there passes from time to time in the eyes of this woman a glimmer of desire, giving promise of a very heaven for one whom she should love. . . .

"In this girl there was at once the virgin whom a mere nothing had turned into a courtesan, and the courtesan whom a mere nothing would have turned into the most loving and purest of virgins. Marguerite had still pride and independence, two sentiments which, if they are wounded, can be the equivalent of a sense of shame" (*Camille*, p. 79).

Chinese:

此女高操凌雲・不污塵穢・

凡人之親馬克・及馬克之加禮於人・

均不為知支・意者須有精頴

敦摯之人・始足以匹之・
馬克接人・恆傲狷落落・
不甚為禮・余固知馬克之貞・
非可以鄙陋干也

(*Cha hua nü*, p. 22). For those who do not know Chinese, a rough translation from the above classical Chinese passage back into English would go something as follows: "This woman is of high chastity. No dust or dirt can spoil her. Most people do not understand this. It takes a really fine and honest person to match her. In all her dealings with others, she shows a certain arrogance and a lack of *li* [propriety]. I therefore know that her chastity (or integrity) cannot be seen in vulgar or common terms."

85. *French*: "Et puis des filles comme moi, une de plus ou de moins, qu'est-ce que cela fait?" (*La Dame*, p. 110).

English: "And then, girls like me, what does it matter, one more or less?" (*Camille*, p. 87).

Chinese:

然女子之身薄命若我者・
生死亦何足數

(*Cha hua nü*, p. 25). In English from the Chinese: "But girls with my kind of meager fate, what does it matter, life or death?"

86. For example, the French "On se gêne toujours avec une femme" (*La Dame*, p. 111), translated into English as "One must always be particular with a woman" (*Camille*, p. 89), becomes

吾一生見婦人・
恆以禮自律

(*Cha hua nü*, p. 25), which would be translated back into English as "I always discipline myself with *li* when I see women in my life." The French "Je ne vous connais que d'aujourd'hui et ne vous dois pas compte de mes actions" (*La Dame*, pp. 116–17), translated into English as "I didn't know you till today, and I am not responsible to you for my actions" (*Camille*, p. 94), becomes

君 今 日 方 邂 逅 我 · 我 何 能

於 未 識 君 前 · 為 君 守 貞

(*Cha hua nü*, p. 27), which would be translated back into English as "You only met me today. How could I have kept my chastity for you before I knew you?"

87. Compare *La Dame*, p. 117, *Camille*, p. 94, and *Cha hua nü*, p. 27.

88. Compare, for instance, *La Dame*, p. 117, *Camille*, p. 95, and *Cha hua nü*, p. 28; *La Dame*, p. 114, *Camille*, p. 91, and *Cha hua nü*, p. 28.

89. *La Dame*, pp. 139–42; *Camille*, pp. 115–17; *Cha hua nü*, p. 34.

90. In Chinese love stories, the male is often shown to possess feminine qualities, and to base his poetic feelings consciously on Lin Daiyü, the virgin girl lover in *The Dream of the Red Chamber*. At the beginning of *Yü li hun*, for example, Mengxia buries the fallen flowers in emulation of Daiyü's act in the famous episode in *The Dream*.

91. Zhang Henshui was perhaps the most prolific writer of Butterfly fiction. Details of his life and works can be found in the sections devoted to him in Link, *Mandarin Ducks and Butterflies*; Wei Shaochang, ed., *Yuanyang*, pp. 515–16; Sally Borthwick, "Translator's Preface" to "Chang Henshui: Fate in Tears and Laughter," *Renditions*, nos. 17 and 18 (1982), pp. 255–61; Zhang Mingming, *Huiyi wo di fuqin Zhang Henshui* [In reminiscence of my father Zhang Henshui] (Hong Kong: Wide Angle Lens Press, 1979); Zhang Zhanguo and Wei Shouzhong, eds., *Zhang Henshui yanjiu ziliao* [Research materials on Zhang Henshui] (Tianjin: Tianjin renmin chuban she, 1986); Liu Yangti, ed., *Yuanyang hudie pai zuopin xuanping*, pp. 91–96. I discuss his significance as a popular writer more extensively in chapter 3 of my Ph.D. dissertation, mentioned in note 74, this chapter. Quotations from *Ping-hu tongche* are taken from an edition of the text published in Shanghai in 1941, and are indicated in parentheses by *PHT* followed by page numbers. All translations are mine.

92. Benjamin, *Illuminations*, ed. Hannah Arendt, trans. Harry Zohn (New York: Schocken Books, 1969), pp. 217–51.

93. Benjamin, "On Some Motifs in Baudelaire," in *Illuminations*, p. 186.

94. Benjamin, "Baudelaire," p. 188.

95. To quote Benjamin in full: "If the distinctive feature of the images that rise from the *mémoire involontaire* is seen in their aura, then photography is decisively implicated in the phenomenon of the 'decline of the aura.' What was inevitably felt to be inhuman, one might even say deadly, in daguerreotypy was the (prolonged) looking into the camera, since the camera records our likeness without returning our gaze. But looking at someone carries the implicit expectation that our look will be returned by the object of our gaze. Where this expectation is met (which, in the case of thought processes, can apply equally to the look of the eye of the mind and to a glance pure and simple), there is an experience of the aura to the fullest extent. 'Perceptibility,' as Novalis puts it, 'is a kind of attentiveness.' The perceptibility he has in mind is none other than that of the aura. Experience of the aura thus rests on the transposition of a response common in human relationships to the relationship between the inanimate or natural object and man. The person we look at, or who feels he is being looked at, looks at us in turn. To perceive the aura of an object we look at means to invest it with the ability to look at us in return" ("Baudelaire," pp. 187–88).

96. Lee, *Romantic Generation*, p. 32.

97. Joseph T. Chen, *The May Fourth Movement in Shanghai* (Leiden: Brill, 1971), p. 2.

98. See Schivelbusch, *The Railway Journey: The Industrialization of Time and Space in the 19th Century* (New York: Berg, 1986).

99. Benjamin, "The Storyteller," in *Illuminations*, p. 86.

Chapter 3. Modernity and Narration—in Feminine Detail

1. A version of this chapter was delivered at the Conference on Modernism and Contemporary Chinese Literature in Hong Kong, December 1987. A modified version of the section dealing with Lu Xun has been published in an article called " 'It's you, and not me': Domination and 'Othering' in Theorizing the Third World," in Elizabeth Weed, ed., *Coming To Terms: Feminism/Theory/Politics* (New York: Routledge, Chapman and Hall, 1989), pp. 152–61.

2. Chang, "Chinese Life and Fashions," reprinted in *Lianhe wenxue (Unitas)*, 3, no. 5 (1987) (Special Issue on Eileen Chang), p. 67.

3. I am referring to the opening passages of Foucault's preface to *The Order of Things* (London: Tavistock, 1970), in which the classification method of "a certain Chinese encyclopedia" cited by Borges is identified as what "transgresses the boundaries of all imagination, of all possible thought" (p. xvi).

4. Chang, "Chinese Life and Fashions," p. 71.

5. Naomi Schor, *Reading in Detail: Aesthetics and the Feminine* (New York and London: Methuen, 1987), chapters 2 and 5.

6. Ibid., p. 97.

7. De Man, *Blindness and Insight: Essays in the Rhetoric of Contemporary Criticism* (Minneapolis: University of Minnesota Press, 1983), p. 148.

8. See Hu Shi's "Jianshe di wenxue geming lun" [On constructive revolution in Chinese literature], *New Youth*, April 1918; rpt. in Zhao Jiabi, ed., *Zhongguo xin wenxue da xi* [A comprehensive anthology of the new literature of China] (Hong Kong: Wenxue yanjiu she, 1962), vol. 1, pp. 155–68; also in Fan Boqun et al., eds., *Yuanyang hudie pai wenxue ziliao* [Materials on Mandarin Duck and Butterfly literature] (Fuzhou: Fujian renmin chuban she, 1984), vol. 2, pp. 711–13.

9. Quoted in Chow Tse-tsung, *The May 4th Movement* (Cambridge, Mass.: Harvard University Press, 1960), pp. 273–74.

10. Hu Shi, "Jianshe di wenxue geming lun," in *Zhongguo xin wenxue da xi*, vol. 1, pp. 166–67.

11. Zhou Zuoren, "Ren di wenxue" [Human literature], in *Zhongguo xin wenxue da xi*, vol. 1, pp. 219–25.

12. Fu Sinian, in *Zhongguo xin wenxue da xi*, vol. 1, p. 243.

13. Ibid., p. 247.

14. Joseph R. Levenson, *Confucian China and Its Modern Fate*, I (Berkeley and Los Angeles: University of California Press, 1965), p. 127.

15. Ibid.

16. Zheng Zhenduo, "Xin wenxue guan di jianshe" [The construction of a new concept of literature], *Wenxue xunkan* [Ten-day periodical on literature], no. 38 (1922); rpt. in Fan Boqun et al., eds., *Yuanyang*, vol. 2, p. 751.

17. Michael Nerlich, "On the Unknown History of Our Modernity," Occasional Paper No. 3 (Center for Humanistic Studies, University of Minnesota, Minneapolis), p. 13.

18. Cf. Hu Shi's arguments in the essay referred to in note 8. Lu Xun's *Zhongguo xiaoshuo shi lüe* (*A Brief History of Chinese Fiction*) can be seen in the same light.

19. Laclau, "Towards a Theory of Populism," in *Politics and Ideology in Marxist Theory: Capitalism-Fascism-Populism* (London: New Left Books, 1977), p. 196.

20. All references to Průšek in this chapter are taken from his *The Lyrical and the Epic: Studies of Modern Chinese Literature*, ed. Leo Ou-fan Lee (Bloomington: Indiana University Press, 1980), and indicated in parentheses by "Průšek" followed by page numbers.

21. Guo Moruo, *Revolution and Literature*, p. 6; quoted in Marián Gálik, *The Genesis of Modern Chinese Literary Criticism* (London: Curzon Press; Bratislava: Veda, 1980), p. 58.

22. Liu Shousong, *Zhongguo xinwenxue shi chugao* (1957), vol., 2, p. 248; quoted in Yi-tsi Mei Feuerwerker, *Ding Ling's Fiction: Ideology and Narrative in Modern Chinese Literature* (Cambridge, Mass.: Harvard University Press, 1982), p. 143.

23. Andrew H. Plaks, "Towards a Critical Theory of Chinese Narrative," in Plaks, ed., *Chinese Narrative: Critical and Theoretical Essays* (Princeton: Princeton University Press, 1977), pp. 309–52. References are indicated in parentheses by "Plaks" followed by page numbers.

24. Quotations from Ba Jin's novel are either taken from Sidney Shapiro's abridged translation, *The Family* (Beijing: Foreign Languages Press, 1964), or are my own translations. In the former case they are indicated in the text by *Family*; in the latter, by the Chinese title *Jia* (Hong Kong: Tiandi tushu youxian gongsi, 1985). All references are given in parentheses with page numbers.

25. This first appears in Ba Jin's preface to the tenth printing of *Jia* in 1937, then in the epilogue to the edition published by Renmin chuban she in 1953, and also in an essay called "He duzhe tan jia" [Discussing *Jia* with my readers], which was rewritten from the epilogue to the novel's English translation of 1956 and published in 1957. These three pieces are appendixed in the edition of *Jia* mentioned in the preceding note.

26. See Olga Lang, *Pa Chin and His Writings* (Cambridge, Mass.: Harvard University Press, 1967), p. vii.

27. Interestingly, this passage is abridged in Shapiro's English translation.

28. Ba Jin, *Chuang wai* [Outside the window] (Hong Kong: Nan hua shudian), p. 135. All translations from this text are mine.

29. Ba Jin, *Chuang wai*, pp. 232–33.

30. Ba Jin, "Wo yao fen bi xie xia qü" [I must continue writing boldly]; quoted in Wang Yingguo, "Ba Jin: Heart Is Kept Burning," in Zeng Xiaoyi, ed., *Zou xiang shijie wenxue, zhongguo xiandai zuojia yü waiguo wenxue* [To world literature: The influence of foreign literature upon modern Chinese writers] (Changsha: Human renmin chuban she, 1985), p. 259.

31. Quotations from *Hong* are taken from the 1983 edition published by Renmin chuban she. All translations are mine.

32. See John D. Berninghausen, "The Central Contradiction in Mao Dun's Earliest Fiction," in *Modern Chinese Literature in the May Fourth Era*, ed. Merle Goldman (Cambridge, Mass.: Harvard University Press, 1977), pp. 233–59; M. A. Abbas and Tak-wai Wong, "Mao Dun's 'Spring Silkworms': Rhetoric and Ideology" (Center of Asian Studies, University of Hong Kong: Contemporary Chinese Studies Seminar Programme Working Paper No. CC 20); Yu-shih Chen, *Realism and Allegory in Mao Dun's Early Fiction* (Bloomington: Indiana University Press, 1987).

33. Examples of descriptions of female intimacy can be found on pp. 40, 43, 44, and 127–28 in Mao Dun's text.

34. Quotations from Lu Xun's story are taken from *The Complete Stories of Lu Xun*, trans. Yang Xianyi and Gladys Yang (Bloomington: Indiana University Press, and Beijing: Foreign Languages Press, 1981), and indicated in parentheses by *Complete Stories* followed by page numbers.

35. Marston Anderson, "The Morality of Form: Lu Xun and the Modern Chinese Short Story," in *Lu Xun and His Legacy*, ed. Leo Ou-fan Lee (Berkeley, Los Angeles, and London: University of California Press, 1985), pp. 34 and following.

36. Patrick Hanan, "The Technique of Lu Hsün's Fiction," *Harvard Journal of Asiatic Studies*, no. 34 (1974), p. 95, J. Průšek, "Lu Hsün's Huai Chiu: A Precursor of Modern Chinese Literature," *Harvard Journal of Asiatic Studies*, no. 29 (1969), pp. 169–76. Both references are quoted in Anderson, ibid., p. 32.

37. See Anderson's succinct argument on p. 44 of his article.

38. "Tong yan wu ji" [The guileless words of a child], in *Liu yan* [Gossip] (Taipei: Huangguan chuban she, 1968), p. 18. I take the English translation from Edward M. Gunn, Jr., *Unwelcome Muse: Chinese Literature in Shanghai and Peking 1937–1945* (New York: Columbia University Press, 1980), p. 203.

39. "Zhongguo di ri ye" [China's day and night], in *Zhang Ailing duanpian xiaoshuo ji* [Collected short stories by Eileen Chang] (Taipei: Huangguan chuban she, 1968), p. 502. Hereafter the collection is referred to as *Duanpian*.

40. "Ziji di wenzhang" [My own writing], in *Liu yan*, p. 26.

41. "Jin suo ji" ("The Golden Cangue"), in *Duanpian*, p. 183. Chang's own translation of this passage is as follows: "Your new sister-in-law's thick lips, chop them up and they will make a heaping dish." See "The Golden Cangue," in Joseph Lau et al., eds., *Modern Chinese Stories and Novellas 1919–1949* (New York: Columbia University Press, 1981), p. 548. Quotations from this story are taken from this translation; page numbers are given in parentheses.

42. "Jin yü lu" [Embers], in *Liu yan*, p. 48.

43. Ibid., p. 51.

44. Preface to the second printing of *Chuan qi* [Romances]; rpt. in *Duanpian*, p. 3.

45. *Bansheng yuan* (Taipei: Huangguan chuban she, 1969), p. 13.

46. *Duanpian*, p. 128.

47. See Ke Ling, "Yao ji Zhang Ailing" [To Eileen Chang from faraway], *Lianhe wenxue*, 3, no. 5 (1987), p. 91.

48. That Chang's writings testify to the presence of a "humane tradition" is C. T. Hsia's observation in *A History of Modern Chinese Fiction*, 2nd ed. (New Haven: Yale University Press, 1971), p. 426. In this and another book, *Aiqing, xiaoshuo, shehui* [Love, fiction, society] (Taipei: Chun wenxue chuban she, 1970), Hsia names Chang as the best and most important Chinese writer today (*History*, p. 389; *Aiqing*, p. 32). For many, Hsia's opinion is what accounts for the wide popularity that Chang's writings now enjoy. Opposing Hsia's interpretation at the other extreme is the work of Tang Wenbiao, for whom Chang's world is a dead one because it lingers on characters of the Shanghai of the foreign concession period. See Tang's *Zhang Ailing za sui* [Eileen Chang chop suey] (Taipei: Lianjing chuban shiye gongsi, 1976); see also *Zhang Ailing juan* [Collected writings on Eileen Chang] (Hong Kong: Yiwen tushu gongsi, 1982), which he edited. Chen Bingliang's *Zhang Ailing duan pian lun ji* [Collected critical essays on Eileen Chang's fiction] (Taipei: Yuanjing shiye gongsi, 1983) focuses on Chang's techniques, themes, and characters in detail; it includes a bibliography and summary of the existing scholarship on Chang that I find useful. *Lianhe wenxue*'s special issue on Chang, already mentioned in the preceding notes, also shows some of the familiar methods with which Chang's work is often approached.

Chapter 4. Loving Women:
Masochism, Fantasy, and the Idealization of the Mother

1. Small portions of this chapter were presented at the Midwestern Conference on Asian Affairs (University of Wisconsin-Madison) and the New England Association for Asian Studies Annual Conference (Wesleyan University) in 1988. The discussion of Ling Shuhua forms part of a published essay, "Virtuous Transactions: A Reading of Three Stories by Ling Shuhua," *Modern Chinese Literature*, vol. 4 (1988), pp. 1–16.

2. Tso Shun-sheng, *Chung-kuo hsien-tai ming-jen i-shih* (Hong Kong, 1951), p. 12; quoted in Leo Ou-fan Lee, *The Romantic Generation of Modern Chinese Writers* (Cambridge, Mass.: Harvard University Press, 1973), pp. 44–45. In an interesting account of Lin Shu's life and works, Lee interprets Lin Shu's inclination toward dramatic emotional expressivity as an attempt to put "sentiment" on a par with "morality": "Lin Shu, as a moralistic Confucianist, attempted to bridge the gap between morality and sentiment by imbuing sentiment with the same degree of seriousness that he had accorded moral behavior. To him, sentiment (*ch'ing*) is more than the 'inner' reflection of propriety (*li*) as prescribed in the *Analects*; sentiment *is* morality" (p. 46). As is evident from this chapter, I am interested in Lin Shu's sentimentalism primarily as a way to understand the formalism of "sympathetic" response in modern Chinese stories.

3. Denis Diderot, "On Dramatic Poetry," in Barrett H. Clark, ed., *European Theories of the Drama* (Crown Press, 1965), p. 238; quoted in Steve Neale, "Melodrama and Tears," *Screen*, 27, no. 6 (1986), p. 6.

4. *Diderot's Selected Writings*, selected and edited, with an introduction and notes by Lester G. Crocker (London: Collier-Macmillan, 1966), p. 110. I am indebted to Jay Caplan's *Framed Narratives: Diderot's Genealogy of the Beholder* (Minneapolis: University of Minnesota Press, 1985) for my knowledge of Diderot's definition of virtue.

5. This is Caplan's argument in his book. Caplan offers the reading that Diderot's plays are structured around what might be called a *tableau* whose content is familial in nature. When a member of the family, often the father, is missing, this creates a "lack" in the *tableau*. This lack, which causes the characters in the play to suffer, is then filled by the audience or the "beholder," whose sympathy compensates for the sacrifice of the missing family member. The beholder thus completes the *tableau* through active participation in a work of art. My understanding of a sympathetic spectator-reader position in modern Chinese literature differs from Caplan's model by an emphasis on the psychoanalytic and gendered specificities inscribed in such a position, specificities that by necessity overturn the stability of the *tableau*-versus-beholder construction.

6. Laplanche, *Life and Death in Psychoanalysis*, trans. and intro. Jeffrey Mehlman (Baltimore and London: Johns Hopkins University Press, 1976), p. 29.

7. *The Standard Edition of the Complete Psychological Works* (hereafter *SE*), trans. James Strachey (London: Hogarth Press, 1953), vol. 14; *A General Selection from the Works of Sigmund Freud*, ed. John Rickman, M.D. with appendix by Charles Brenner, M.D. (New York: Doubleday Anchor Books, 1957), pp. 70–86. References to this essay are taken from the latter source and are indicated in parentheses by "Instincts" followed by page numbers. Freud's theory of masochism can also be found in "The Economic Problem of Masochism," in *SE*, vol. 19, pp. 159–70.

8. See the chapter called "Aggressiveness and Sadomasochism," in *Life and Death*, pp. 85–102.

9. Laplanche, *Life and Death*, p. 102.

10. *Sacher-Masoch: An Interpretation*, trans. Jean McNeil (together with the entire text of *Venus in Furs* from a French rendering by Aude Willm) (London: Faber and Faber, 1971). Hereafter references are indicated in parentheses by "Deleuze" followed by page numbers.

11. The connections between masochism and the role played by the mother in the so-called preoedipal phase of sexual development have been widely explored. A small list of the works on this topic includes the following: Theodore Reik, *Masochism in Modern Man*, trans. M. H. Beigel and G. M. Kruth (New York: Farrar, Straus, 1941); Bernhard Berliner, "On Some Psychodynamics of Masochism," *Psychoanalytic Quarterly*, no. 16 (1947), pp. 459–71; E. Bergler, *The Basic Neurosis* (New York: Grune and Stratton, 1949); Victor Smirnoff, "The Masochistic Contract," *International Journal of Psycho-Analysis*, no. 50 (1969), pp. 666–71; Gustav Bychowski, "Some Aspects of Masochistic Involvement," *Journal of the American Psychoanalytic Association*, no. 7 (April 1959), pp. 248–73; Kaja Silverman, "Masochism and Subjectivity," *Framework*, no. 12 (1980), pp. 2–9.

12. "Masochism and the Perverse Pleasures of the Cinema," in Bill Nichols, ed., *Movies and Methods*, vol. 2 (Berkeley and Los Angeles: University of California Press, 1985), p. 610.

13. Neale, "Melodrama and Tears," p. 22.

14. Ibid., pp. 21–22.

15. Xiao Hong, "Yongjiu di chongjing he zhuiqiu" [A permanent fantasy and pursuit], in *Xiao Hong (Zhongguo xiandai zuojia xuanji congshu)* [Modern Chinese writers selections series] (Hong Kong: Sanlian shudian, Renmin wenxue chuban she, 1982, 1987), p. 2.

16. Trans. Howard Goldblatt, in Joseph S. M. Lau, S. T. Hsia, and Leo Ou-fan Lee, eds., *Modern Chinese Stories and Novellas 1919–1949* (hereafter *MCSN*) (New York: Columbia University Press, 1981), pp. 456–64. Hereafter page references are indicated in parentheses in the text. For the historical details about Xiao Hong's life and works, see Goldblatt's *Hsiao Hung* (Boston: Twayne, 1976). Goldblatt also gives an informative analysis of Xiao Hong's use of autobiography in her work

Shangshijie (*Market Street*) in "Life as Art: Xiao Hong and Autobiography," in Anna Gerstlacher, Ruth Keen, Wolfgang Kubin, Margit Miosga, and Jenny Schon, eds., *Women and Literature in China* (Bochum: Studienverlag Brockmeyer, 1985), pp. 345–63.

17. Trans. Jane Parish Yang, in *MCSN*, pp. 197–99. Page references are indicated in parentheses in the text. A brief introduction to Ling Shuhua's life and works can be found on the pages of *MCSN* immediately preceding her story. For other biographical details, the reader may consult the appendixes to *Ling Shuhua xiaoshuo ji*, vols. 1 and 2 (Taipei: Hongfan shudian, 1984, 1986), and Ling's *Ancient Melodies*, intro. V. Sackville-West (London: Hogarth Press, 1969). See also Clara Yü Cuadrado's argument for deep philosophical and artistic meanings in Ling's portraits of women, "Portraits of a Lady: The Fictional World of Ling Shuhua," in Angela Jung Palandri, ed., *Women Writers of 20th-Century China* (Eugene: The Asian Studies Program at the University of Oregon, 1982), pp. 41–62; and Don Holoch's argument that women's experiences presented by Ling expose the terror of the Chinese patriarchal order, in "Everyday Feudalism: The Subversive Stories of Ling Shuhua," in Anna Gerstlacher et al., eds., *Women and Literature in China*, pp. 379–93.

18. *Sexuality and the Psychology of Love*, ed. Philip Rieff, pp. 58–70; also in *SE*, vol. 11, under the title "On the Universal Tendency to Debasement in the Sphere of Love." References to this essay are taken from the former source and indicated in parentheses by "Erotic Life" followed by page numbers.

19. Hsia, *A History of Modern Chinese Fiction 1917–1957*, 2nd ed. (New Haven: Yale University Press, 1971), p. 109.

20. Trans. Joseph S. M. Lau and C. T. Hsia, in *MCSN*, pp. 125–41. Hereafter page references are given in parentheses in the text. Biographical details about Yü Dafu, as well as analyses of his works, can be found in the pages of *MCSN* immediately preceding his story; in Hsia, *A History*; and in Leo Ou-fan Lee, *Romantic Generation*. Anna Doležalová offers an account of Yü Dafu's concept of literature in "Two Novels of Yü Ta-fu—Two Approaches to Literary Creation," *Asian and African Studies* (1968), no. 4, pp. 17–29. Zhang Xiuya discusses how one of Yü Dafu's later works, "Chi gui hua" [Late-blooming osmanthus], differs from the "decadence" of his early ones such as "Sinking"; see "Guanyü Yü Dafu" [On Yü Dafu], in Su Xuelin, Zhang Xiuya, and Lin Haiyin, eds., *Jindai zhongguo zuojia yü zuopin*, vol. 1 (Taipei: Chun wenxue yuekan she, 1967), pp. 74–94. In *The Genesis of Modern Chinese Literary Criticism (1917–1930)* (London: Curzon Press; Bratislava: Veda, 1980), Marián Gálik discusses the relations between Yü Dafu's work and the literature of decadence in late nineteenth-century Europe in a chapter called "Yü Ta-fu and his Panaesthetic Criticism," pp. 104–28.

21. See the respective accounts by Hsia and Lee in their works referred to in the preceding note. See also Michael Egan's interesting argument in "Yu Dafu and the Transition to Modern Chinese Literature," in Merle Goldman, ed., *Modern Chinese Literature in the May Fourth Era* (Cambridge, Mass., and London: Harvard University Press, 1977), pp. 309–24. In an account that rightly emphasizes the significance of irony in Yü Dafu's story, Egan points out that it is not sex per se, but its connection with the protagonist's psychology that defines the modernity of "Sinking": " 'Sinking' is neither particularly daring nor explicit when compared to previous works in Chinese fiction. What makes the story modern is not its erotic dimension but the fact that sexual acts are important not as plot or actions in themselves, as had been the case in the past, but for their effect on the psychology of the hero. The protagonist's mental response to his sexual activities is the true subject of the narrative" (p. 316). However, I cannot agree with Egan's conclusion that the plot of "Sinking" is "essentially apolitical and individualistic, as opposed to social and ideological" (p. 321).

22. *Chanyü ji* (Shanghai, 1933), p. 5; translated and quoted by Gálik, *Genesis*, p. 104; my emphasis.

23. Trans. Sidney Shapiro, in *Stories from the Thirties* (Beijing: Panda Books, 1982), vol. 1, pp. 111–41. Details about Xü Dishan's life and works can be found in *MCSN*, pp. 39–40; *Xü Dishan xuanji* (Taipei: Li ming wenhua shiye gufen youxian gongsi, 1975, 1976), pp. 1–10; *Xü Dishan*

(*Zhongguo xiandai zuojia xuanji congshu*) [Modern Chinese writers selections series] (Hong Kong: Sanlian shudian, Renmin wenxue chuban she, 1982), pp. 233–56.

24. *Ba Jin wenji* (Hong Kong: Nanguo shuban she, 1970), vol. 10, pp. 10–46. The part about Nanny Yang exists, in a more elaborate manner, as an independent story; it is translated as "Nanny Yang" by Perry Link in *MCSN*, pp. 293–304. References to the Nanny Yang episode are taken from Link's translation and indicated in parentheses by "Link" followed by page numbers. All other translations, with page references from the *Wenji*, are mine. Two detailed studies of Ba Jin's life and works are Olga Lang, *Pa Chin and His Writings: Chinese Youth Between the Two Revolutions* (Cambridge, Mass.: Harvard University Press, 1967), and Nathan K. Mao, *Pa Chin* (Boston: Twayne, 1978).

25. See the chapter "Below Stairs: The Maid and the Family Romance" in Peter Stallybrass and Allon White, *The Politics and Poetics of Transgression* (Ithaca: Cornell University Press, 1986), pp. 149–70.

26. Silverman, *The Acoustic Mirror* (Bloomington: Indiana University Press, 1988). References to this work are indicated in parentheses by "Silverman" followed by page numbers. In different ways from Silverman's, Nancy Chodorow's theory about mothering in Western culture also offers a critique of Freud's oedipal story through extensive discussions of women's libidinal development. However, I find her reliance on object-relations psychoanalysis limiting and unuseful for my purposes. See *The Reproduction of Mothering: Psychoanalysis and the Sociology of Gender* (Berkeley, Los Angeles, London: University of California Press, 1978).

27. *The Ego and the Id*, trans. Joan Riviere and James Strachey (New York: Norton, 1962), p. 23; the essay can be found in *SE*, vol. 19.

28. *Bing Xin xiaoshuo ji* (Shanghai: Kaiming shudian, 1943), pp. 257–68. All translations from this story are mine. Bing Xin's life and work are discussed briefly in Yi-tsi Feuerwerker, "Women as Writers in the 1920's and 1930's," in Margery Wolf and Roxane Witke, eds., *Women in Chinese Society* (Stanford: Stanford University Press, 1975), pp. 143–68. See also Gloria Bien, "Images of Women in Bing Xin's Fiction," in Palandri, ed., *Women Writers of 20th Century China*, pp. 19–33.

29. "Ji xiao duzhe si ban zixù" [Preface to the 4th edition], *Ji xiao duzhe* [To young readers] (Shanghai: Kaiming shudian, 1933, 1949), p. 1.

30. Feuerwerker, "Women as Writers," p. 145.

31. Ibid., p. 168.

32. Afterword to Caplan, *Framed Narratives*, p. 100. The emphasis on "common" is mine.

33. In this respect, see, for instance, Silverman's critique of Kristeva's work in chapters 2 and 3 of *The Acoustic Mirror*.

34. In *Miss Sophie's Diary and Other Stories*, trans. W. J. F. Jenner (Beijing: Panda Books, 1985), pp. 13–64. Two elaborate accounts of Ding Ling's life and work are Chang Hun-mei, *Ting Ling: Her Life and Work* (Taipei: Institute of International Relations, 1978), and Yi-tsi Feuerwerker, *Ding Ling's Fiction: Ideology and Narrative in Modern Chinese Literature* (Cambridge, Mass.: Harvard University Press, 1982). Feuerwerker's investigations are also published in the following articles: "Ting Ling's 'When I Was in Sha Chuan (Cloud Village),' Archives," *Signs: Journal of Women in Culture and Society*, 2, no. 1 (1976), pp. 255–79; "The Changing Relationship between Literature and Life: Aspects of the Writer's Role in Ding Ling," in Goldman, ed., *Modern Chinese Literature*, pp. 281–308.

35. See, for instance, Ding Yi (Ting Yi), *Zhongguo xiandai wenxue shi lüe* (Beijing: Zuojia chuban she, 1955; Hong Kong: Wenhua ziliao gongying she, 1978), pp. 306–7; this work is available in English as *A Short History of Modern Chinese Literature* (Port Washington, N.Y.: Kennikat Press, 1970). See also *Zhongguo xiandai wenxue shi* [Modern Chinese literary history] (Jiangsu renmin chuban she, 1979), pp. 474–75.

36. *Modern Chinese Literature*, 2, no. 2 (1986), p. 134. See also her "Feminism and Literary Technique in Ting Ling's Early Short Stories," in Palandri, ed., *Women Writers of 20th-Century China*, pp. 63–110.

37. Cf. note 5,

Index

Index

Compiled by Robin Jackson

Theory and History of Literature

Rey Chow grew up in Hong Kong and received her Ph.D. in Modern Thought and Literature from Stanford University. She is an assistant professor of comparative literature at the University of Minnesota, where she is affiliated with the Departments of East Asian Studies and Women's Studies. She has contributed articles to *Cultural Critique, New German Critique, Radical America, Modern Chinese Literature, Dialectical Anthropology, Discourse, Camera Obscura,* and *Differences.*